POLITICS, TECHNOLOGY AND DEVELOPMENT

Politics, Technology and Development

Decision-Making in the Turkish Iron
and Steel Industry

Joseph S. Szyliowicz

Foreword by Frances Stewart

St. Martin's Press   New York

First published in the United States of America in 1991

Printed in Hong Kong

ISBN 0–312–05335–5

Library of Congress Catologing-in-Publication Data
Szyliowicz, Joseph S.
Politics, technology, and development: decision-making in the
Turkish iron and steel industry / Joseph S. Szyliowicz: foreword by
Frances Stewart.
p.   cm.
Includes bibliographical references and index.
ISBN 0–312–05335–5
1. Steel industry and trade—Turkey.   2. Iron industry and trade
—Turkey.   I. Title.
HD9526.T92S97   1991
338. 4'7669142'09561—dc20   91–43365
                                                                  CIP

To Irene, Michael and Dara

Contents

List of Illustrations   x

List of Tables   xi

List of Abbreviations   xii

Foreword by Frances Stewart   xv

Preface   xix

Rational Decision-Making, Washington Style   xxii

1   Technological Decision-Making and National Development
    *Why Do So Many Technology Transfer Projects
    Encounter Serious Difficulties?*   1

    Introduction
    The technological project
    The technology transfer process
    The nature of technological mastery
    Politics, policy and decision-making
    Technological decisions and project analysis
    The project cycle and technological decision-making
    Technological decision-making, technology transfer and the
        project cycle

2   Iron and Steel and Development in Turkey
    Turkey Implements a Development Strategy   39

    Introduction
    Strategies of development
    Role of the iron and steel sector
    The global scene
    Ataturk's development strategy
    The Karabük plant
    The emergence of a multi-party system

The arrival of national planning
Turkey's development strategy and its consequences
Conclusion

3 The Decision to Build ERDEMIR
 AID Agrees to Build a Steel Mill 76

The negotiations
The design issues
The impact issues
The management issues
The implementation
Conclusion

4 Salvaging the Project
 All It Takes Is Money . . . 106

Introduction
Turkish perspectives
The AID response
The new studies
The new loan
The sinter plant decision
Conclusion

5 The Expansion of ERDEMIR
 Enter the World Bank 126

Introduction
Project approval
The impact issues
The design issues
The management issues
The implementation
The Stage II expansion – the decision process
The design of the expansion
The implementation
Conclusion

6 ISDEMIR, SIDEMIR, Karabük: Projects and
Comparative Perspectives
 Steel, More Steel, Ever More Steel . . . 156

Introduction
The ISDEMIR project
The design issues
The impact issues
The management issues
Implementation and operation
The SIDEMIR project
The Karabük expansion
Comparative perspectives
Conclusion

7 Projects and Politics
   Towards Rational Decision-Making   189

   Introduction
   The quality of the technological decisions
   Politics and technology transfer
   The nature of technological decision-making
   The emergence of a new perspective
   Conclusions

Notes   230

Bibliography   251

Index   263

List of Illustrations

1.1 Basic analytical framework 12
1.2 Analytical framework including degree of technological transfer 15
1.3 Analytical framework incorporating political variables 23
1.4 Analytical framework incorporating further aspects of the decision-making process 31
1.5 Final analytical framework for the technology transfer process 37
2.1 Turkey: location of steel mills, iron ore deposits and coal mines 47
3.1 Location of Ereğli 84

List of Tables

2.1	World iron and steel production (millions of tons)	46
2.2	Production of the Karabük plant (tons)	59
2.3	Production of the Karabük plant 1940–70 (000 tons)	64
2.4	Development and projected growth of the Turkish iron and steel sector	71
2.5	Iron and steel production and consumption in Turkey 1930–83 (millions of tons)	72
3.1	Profit and loss statement for ERDEMIR (US$000)	94
3.2	Stock ownership of ERDEMIR (end 1963)	101
4.1	Demand projections for ERDEMIR (000 tons)	116
5.1	Production (000 tons) and financial data 1966–70	127
5.2	Available market and output projections for the ERDEMIR expansion project (000 tons)	138
5.3	Growth of ERDEMIR workforce 1972–78	152
6.1	Cost escalation of ISDEMIR	158
6.2	Estimated manufacturing cost for various sites (TL000)	158
6.3	Estimated manufacturing costs, SIDEMIR	169
6.4	Karabük capacity and production	172
6.5	Capacity utilization of Turkish plants	180
6.6	Coke oven productivity of Turkish plants (1980–81)	181
6.7	Blast furnace productivity of Turkish plants (1980–81)	183
6.8	Steel shop productivity of Turkish plants (1980–81)	184
6.9	Rolling mills productivity of Turkish plants (1980–81)	185
6.10	Profitability of Turkish plants (TL million)	188

List of Abbreviations

AID	Agency for International Development (*see* USAID)
AFL/CIO	American Federation of Labor/Congress of Industrial Organizations
BOF	Basic Oxygen Furnace
CHP	Republican People's Party (Cumhuriyet Halk Partisi)
CPM	Critical Path Method
DFL	Development Loan Fund
DISK	Confederation of Revolutionary Trade Unions (Devrimci Isci Sendikalari Konfederasyonu)
DP	Democratic Party
EEC	European Economic Community
ERDEMIR	Eregli Iron and Steel Works
HAK-IS	Confederation of Islamic Workers Trade Unions
IDRC	International Development Research Council
IBRD	International Bank for Reconstruction and Development (later, the World Bank)
ICSI	International Consulting Services, Inc.
IMF	International Monetary Fund
ISDEMIR	Iskenderun Iron and Steel Works
JP	Justice Party
LDC	Less Developed Countries
LD Converter	Linz-Donawitz Converter
MISK	Confederation of Nationalist Workers Trade Unions (Milliyetci Isci Sendikalar Konfederasyonu)
MNC	Multi-National Corporation
MTHM	Million of Thermal Units
OECD	Organization for Economic Cooperation and Development
OEEC	Organization for European Economic Cooperation (later OECD)
OTA	Office of Technology Assessment
PERT	Project Evaluation and Review Technique

SIDEMIR	Sivas Iron and Steel Works
SPO	State Planning Organization
TDCI	Turkey Iron and Steel Works (Turkiye Demir Celik Isletmeleri)
TL	Turkish Lira
TURK-IS	Confederation of Turkish Workers' Trade Unions
UNIDO	United Nations Industrial Development Organization
USAID	US Agency for International Development (*see* AID)
UNPAD	United Nations Public Administration Division
UNCTAD	United Nations Conference on Trade and Development
UNDP	United Nations Development Program
UEC	US Steel Engineers and Consultants, Inc.

Foreword

This book describes the development of the Turkish iron and steel industry. It documents in detail how and why decisions were made in relation to each of the major integrated plants, both from the perspective of the Turkish government and the aid-donors, who were heavily involved in financing and management.

By providing a detailed history of these projects, especially of Ereğli, from its conception in the late 1950s, through its construction, early operation and subsequent expansion, the study greatly illuminates important aspects of project choice and development, in particular the role of cost-benefit analysis and project appraisal; the issue of technology transfer; and motivations and decision-making among aid-agencies and governments. In each area it challenges the simple-minded conceptions that lie behind much text-book analysis of these issues, and, more significantly, behind the policy advice proffered by many economists, and included in World Bank programmes.

Cost-benefit analysis has formed the central plank of economists' advice on project selection, particularly since Little and Mirrlees, Das Gupta, Marglin and Sen, and Squire and van der Tak published their guidelines. These works develop a quite elaborate methodology for selecting projects according to their costs and benefits, so that those projects will be selected that maximise net social benefits and social welfare.

This study shows the irrelevance in practice of much of this methodology. In the first place, the decision to go ahead with the steel project at Ereğli was made, in principle, *before* any detailed evaluation took place, and no comparisons were made at any time between the proposed project and any alternatives. Secondly, the numerous evaluations undertaken later – after the first decision had been made – revealed basic deficiencies. Almost invariably the assumptions which formed the basis of the calculations proved wrong – for example with respect to demand, to the availability, quality and price of raw materials and energy and to operating efficiency. As a consequence the high profitability predicted initially for the plant never materialised, and successive investments were necessary to make it conceivable that the initial funds would ever be repaid. The mistakes made in the evaluations were not, it appears, just unlucky developments associated with this particular project, but intrinsic to project choice in developing countries in an uncertain world. They thus throw real doubt on the methodology typically advocated, especially, as the author underlines, to its focus on the evaluation stage, rather than project identification and development, project management and operational efficiency. Thirdly, there was very little serious attempt to incorporate social as opposed to private costs and benefits into the evaluations beyond a very rough and ready look at international competitiveness, an (unjustified) allusion to benefits to regional development to justify what would otherwise appear as rather ill-judged decisions, and later reference to environmental considerations to secure some restraints on the heavy environmental pollution caused.

On technology transfer, this study provides an important addition to the accumulating evidence that technology transfer is not a simple matter of taking a technology developed in one place and installing it elsewhere, where operations and productivity will be duplicated. In fact – as this case powerfully shows – considerable adaptation to the initial technology is almost invariably needed, often requiring research, investment and training, to make the technology transferred work. Building the plant was a very complex task. 'Though all the engineering and scheduling details were worked out in Pittsburgh in advance numerous changes and much engineering had to be carried out at the site because of unforeseen eventualities' (p.96). Infrastructure – especially transport – was lacking, the raw materials turned out to be of inferior quality, and considerable training was needed of both workers and management. The latter created particular problems for high-level management efficiency, especially because of political interventions in the 1970s, but interestingly for lower levels of management, training and upgrading workers proved most effective. All in all, the result was much lower capacity utilization and productivity than anticipated on the basis of US operations. When it first operated the Turkish plant needed 40 man-hours per ton, compared with eight in the US.

While the experience thus sheds important light on the complexity of the technology transfer process and on the need for considerable local resources to make it efficient, as also demonstrated by recent work of Katz in Latin America and of Lall in India, in addition it shows that learning occurs as time proceeds, raising productivity over time. By the end of the 1970s, the hours required at Ereğli per ton had fallen to 20, despite considerable political and economic problems. It seems likely that with further experience and expansion, productivity will rise further and costs fall, so that the plant may well become competitive internationally. If this occurs, then, despite the weakness of evaluation procedures and the non-economic approach to decisions, the initial intuition of the Turkish government to undertake the project as a contribution to development may well prove correct. The process of improved performance over time – starting with very high costs – also challenges the view that import protection should be minimal and projects undertaken only if they can be competitive in a very short time. With such a perspective, there is no question but that a proper evaluation would have rejected this project, and thus prevented a learning process which may soon pay off.

Another area in which this book greatly increases our understanding is that of motivation of both the government and aid agencies. The Turkish government was concerned, as Professor Szyliowicz notes, with 'maximizing investments rather than careful planning'. Iron and steel, in particular, represented for the Turkish state like many others, a central aspect of industrialization and modernization. The motivations of aid-donors consisted in a mixture of political-cum-philosophical and bureaucratic: development, as most of us understand it, was just a byproduct. The US loan agreed in 1960 was the largest USAID had ever made; yet, as noted, prior evaluation was minimal. The main motivation at that stage was to support the Turkish private sector, since it was intended that the plant should be privately owned and operated (even here expectations proved incorrect, since the Turkish private sector was more far-seeing than the aid agency and refused to take up shares in any quantity, recognising that the project was unlikely to be profitable). The motivation for subsequent aid finance was mainly bureaucratic – primarily to rescue and thereby justify the initial decision. When the World Bank came on the scene in the 1970s, its motivation was also political and philosophical – to support Turkish private sector development and to reward Turkey for following approved macro-policies. With this in mind, the Bank turned a blind eye to the fact that 'even with all the [optimistic] assumptions . . . the new expansion could be justified only with difficulty and, if more stringent standards were applied, the project could hardly be defended at all' (p. 142).

While Professor Szyliowicz criticizes the simple view of the left in Turkey that the project was just an exemplification of dependency, the project's history refutes any naive view that aid-agencies are

motivated solely, or even primarily, by developmental considerations. Yet, at the end of the day, as noted earlier, the experience of
the steel plant at Ereğli may well prove positive for Turkish development, in terms of its impact on technological and economic capacity,
although probably not with respect to social goals of development.
Still, unnecessarily high costs were incurred and different policies
could have enhanced its contribution to Turkey's development.

This is the story of some 'typical development projects, each of
which encountered numerous obstacles which were not foreseen by
their architects' despite many studies. As such, this study has
relevance far beyond the confines of the steel industry or Turkish
development and deserves a very wide readership among those
seriously concerned to understand the process of development.

FRANCES STEWART
International Development Centre,
Oxford

References

Dasgupta, P., S. Marglin and A. K. Sen, 1972, *Guidelines for Project
Evaluation*, New York: United Nations.
Katz, J., 1982, 'A list of "main" issues from recent research on science
and technology in the framework of the IDB/ECLA/UNDP/IDRC
program', mimeo, Buenos Aires.
Lall, S., 1987, *Learning to Industrialise,* London: Macmillan.
Little, I.M.D. and J. A. Mirrlees, 1974, *Project Appraisal and Planning
for The Developing Countries*, London: Heinemann.
Squire, L., and H. G. van der Tak, 1975, *Economic Analysis of Projects*,
Washington, DC: World Bank.

Preface

This book is testimony, if more were needed, to the role of chance in human affairs. Several years ago, having co-authored a study of the Aswan Dam for the Rand Graduate Institute which was developing materials for courses in technology and public policy, I began to think about studying another large project to determine whether the pattern of decision–making in the Aswan Dam case was idiosyncratic or whether it was commonplace. That pattern had led to significant problems and, though one could not easily assess whether the dam's benefits exceeded its costs, there was no doubt that the costs that were incurred, social, economic, cultural and environmental, were much higher than they needed to be.

At this moment, the College of Business Administration of the University of Denver invited Mr Fletcher Byrom, Chairman of the Board of Koppers Corporation, to spend a few days on campus. I had the good fortune to meet him and, in the cause of our talk, mentioned that I was thinking of studying a major project in the Middle East, preferably in Turkey, where I had carried out extensive field research. He said that he knew the perfect project. His company had recently built an integrated iron and steel plant at Ereğli, on the Black Sea coast, and had successfully brought it into operation within 36 months. He kindly offered to provide me with access to the relevant documents.

Accordingly, I submitted a proposal to the Rand Graduate Institute for a study of this plant. The work was designed to supplement the earlier case study by focusing more explicitly upon technology transfer issues. The proposal was accepted and the study was published as *Designing, Managing and Implementing Technological Projects: The Case of the Ereğli Iron and Steel Works* (Boston, Mass.: Intercollegiate Case Clearing House, 1982).[1]

While carrying out this project, I became interested in the overall condition of Turkey's iron and steel sector and began to explore the possibility of expanding the work that I had done and placing it within a larger context, both theoretical and empirical. A Fulbright Senior Research Fellowship in the summer of 1983 enabled me to carry out the necessary research and a sabbatical year in 1984–5 at St Antony's College, Oxford, gave me the opportunity to write a first draft.

There were obviously many persons and organizations to whom I am indebted. Mr Byrom more than fulfilled his promise to cooperate in the study. He and his associates at Koppers introduced me to the romance of iron and steel and were unfailingly helpful. I am particularly indebted to Mr Lawrence C. Smith who had served as the project manager at Ereğli and his associates, Mr William Kahl and Mr Jim Van Ackeren, who spent many hours answering my numerous questions with patience and understanding. Through them I came to meet Mr Suphi Yavazca, head of the ERDEMIR purchasing mission in Pittsburgh who also provided me with much helpful information. They also led me to Mr John Rankin, of United States Steel Engineers and Consultants, who had been actively involved in the plant's expansion. He not only gave freely of his knowledge of iron and steel in general, and the plant in particular, but made available the extensive studies that his company had carried out for the expansion.

Since the project was originally funded by AID, I also met and interviewed several present and former employees who had been involved with ERDEMIR, including Mr Steve Lintner, Mr Ted Lustig, Mr Peter Benedict, and Mr Rodney Young. They provided me with much valuable, first-hand information and also permitted me to consult AID's extensive documentation. The World Bank too was involved in the project and several members of its staff were especially helpful, particularly Mr William P. O'Neill and Mr Bertil Walstedt.

Many Turkish scholars and officials also cooperated in this study. I was kindly received at ERDEMIR and Karabük and learnt much from seeing the plants at first hand. Professor Osman Okyar, a valued colleague, was very supportive and, since he served a term as Chairman of ERDEMIR's board, his cooperation was particularly significant. In addition, several present and former members of the State Planning Office and the National Productivity Center provided me with valuable data, shared their extensive knowledge with me, and helped me in numerous other ways. Specifically I must thank Mr Isin Çelebi, Mr Serdar Tan, Mr Attilla Terzeien, Mr Ibrahim Yurt and, especially Mr Engin Oruç.

Several of my colleagues at the Graduate School of International Studies (GSIS) commented on an early draft and advanced numerous ideas on how to improve it. I am especially indebted to Barry

Hughes, Don Parker, Haidar Khan and Arthur Gilbert. I am also grateful to Robert Hazan and David Mazzarella who were valuable research assistants, to Eduardo Saxe-Fernandez who, though formally a graduate student, contributed like a colleague, to Asma Barlas who prepared the charts, to my daughter Dara who spent a considerable part of a summer serving as my secretary, and to Carolyn Bolden and Carol Taylor of the Faculty Computing Laboratory of the University of Denver who spent many hours trying to make UNIX files print out properly on newly installed laser printers. Mr T. M. Farmiloe of Macmillan was a patient and understanding editor, Mrs Rosemary Thorp of St Antony's College an encouraging and helpful one. Ms Anne Rafique and Ms Clare Wace ably supervised the transition from manuscript to published book.

It is obvious that I was offered much good advice and many valuable suggestions; if I had been more receptive, perhaps the result would have been better, but I alone am responsible for what follows.

JOSEPH S. SZYLIOWICZ
Greenwood Village, Colorado

Rational Decision-Making, Washington Style

Ah, the Woodrow Wilson Bridge. Oh, that bridge. We're coming upon it now, still moving okay. Maybe this is the day to make it across (maybe this is the day to hit the lottery, too) . . . hold it . . . here come all the brake lights . . .

Yes. Stopped on the Beltway. Stuck waiting to get onto the Wilson Bridge . . . Welcome to the Woodrow Wilson Wait.

Who among us has not run into this? It's a rite of initiation for newcomers. From the Virginia and Maryland banks of the Potomac, four lanes approaching the bridge merge into three narrow ones across the river, We get the hourglass effect, plus we get a drawbridge, the only one left on the 42,500-mile interstate highway system. It gets raised about 25 times a month.

The facts are that the Wilson Bridge is no bigger or better today than it was when it was finished in 1961, and even then (my emphasis) highway engineers didn't like it. It was designed to carry a peak load of 75,000 vehicles a day. 'In a real bind we knew we could push it to 100,000 but that was not satisfactory,' said Francis C. Turner, the former chief engineer who built it. Well it hit 100,000 a decade ago and the most recent average count was 137,530 vehicles a day . . .

People are beginning to get just a tad irritated . . .

How did we get into such a mess? The bridge builders weren't happy in the first place. 'We didn't build the structure we would have built if we'd had our druthers,' recalled Turner . . . When Congress authorized money for the bridge in 1956, 'they limited it, I believe, to $14 million,' Turner said, 'We built it for that but we cut corners to do it. There were no sidewalks, no median lane dividers, no shoulders.'

There had been some discussion of building more lanes, or an arching span that would clear boat masts, 'but we dismissed that because the difference in costs made it impossible.' Turner said. 'We didn't want to build that drawbridge,' he said, but had to because of federal laws giving ships priority on navigable waterways . . .

Ron Shaffer, 'The whys, wherefores and runaround on the Woodrow Wilson Bridge', The Washington Post, 2 September 1988, pp. E1–2. © 1988, *The Washington Post*, reprinted with permission.

1 Technological Decision-Making and National Development

Why Do So Many Technology Transfer Projects Encounter Serious Difficulties?

INTRODUCTION

Only a short time ago technology was widely hailed as the means by which mankind could achieve a new level of well-being. Through its application, advanced countries would become post-industrial societies characterized by harmony and the rational management of problems; the Third World would achieve self-sustaining economic growth and modernize rapidly. Today such views are held by a minority and are generally regarded as reflecting a naive optimism. To apply modern technologies, let alone to master them, has proven to be a complex and expensive proposition. Often the results have been disappointing and the costs, direct and indirect, extremely high.

Yet elites everywhere strive continuously to take advantage of modern technology because they recognize that, whatever their goals, only by harnessing its awesome potential can they improve the quality of life of their citizens and enhance the power and prestige of their state. In much of the world, leaders focus upon industrial technologies because they believe that every state needs an industrial base. And, ever since the Industrial Revolution, the iron and steel sector has generally been considered as the critical sector, as the sector that will serve as the forge of development. The roar of the blast furnace has become a potent symbol of power and modernity.

Nowhere is this more true than in Turkey where development, since the founding of the Turkish Republic, has been equated with heavy industrialization. Turkish governments of every ideological persuasion have emphasized iron and steel and have striven, through what is now called 'technology transfer', to build a powerful capability in this sector. Today, after over forty years of effort, Turkey

1

possesses three large integrated iron and steel works with a capacity of over four million tons. Yet, each project has encountered difficulties of various kinds, the sector as a whole has not served as the forge for development that Turkish policy-makers since the days of Ataturk had expected, and many experts believe that difficult challenges may well lie ahead.

This history is by no means unique. On the contrary, it is quite commonplace. Few states have successfully developed the structural and cultural system required for the effective utilization of modern technology. Most have been unable to operate technologies transferred from abroad at international levels of productivity, to maintain and adapt them to fit particular local conditions, or to develop new technologies to meet specific needs. They have failed to master the technologies with which they hope to modernize and achieve national power. One result is evident everywhere: the world is littered with projects that have failed to achieve their objectives and act as a drain on limited resources.[1]

Whether a country seeks to develop an iron and steel capability or whether it emphasizes some other sector in its drive to industrialize, technology transfer projects of one sort or another are always involved. Projects are the carriers of technology, they are the means by which states and organizations can acquire and master the technologies which they need to modernize. If they fail to do so, the projects inevitably become burdens rather than assets to countries seeking to overcome the affliction of underdevelopment. Such burdens can be alleviated only if the decisions that are made facilitate the acquisition of technological knowledge and improve the process of project design and implementation. The challenge that confronts Third World states is obvious – if they are to develop, they must design and implement successful projects. The extent to which they can do so will shape national economies and societies for decades, will determine whether dreams of development, of an improved quality of life, of national power, will be realized.

In this work I plan to analyze why failure is so commonplace in technology transfer projects, why they so often achieve sub-optimal outcomes. I shall do so by focusing on two fundamental aspects of this problem: (1) project design and implementation and, (2) technological mastery. For a project to be successful its conception must be sound, its implementation effective and the recipient must achieve a complete understanding of its technologies. Poor design can doom any project but good design does not ensure success. A project can be well sized, in a good location, enjoy high quality inputs and meet a market need but, if the technologies are not mastered, difficulties will inevitably arise. Decisions at several levels and by many actors control the extent to which a project is soundly conceived and carried out and the amount of technological learning that takes place. These are part of a larger policy framework whose dynamics shape the decision process, its content and the outcomes.

Accordingly, I shall carry out an analysis of both politics and decisions in the Turkish iron and steel industry. Since no work in English treats this vital sector, I shall give some detailed information of the historical and technical aspects of various plants but my primary concern is with the nature of technological decision-making in regard to project design and implementation and the achievement of technological mastery. I shall focus particularly upon the history of one plant (ERDEMIR) in order to gain a detailed understanding of the decision-making process but I shall also analyze the other major projects and carry out a comparative evaluation of the extent to which different plants have achieved technological mastery. I selected the iron and steel industry because it represents a highly strategic sector that has been accorded a high priority in many countries; the Turkish experience is by no means unique.[2]

In this way I plan to blend a detailed case study into a larger context. Though the case study method can be, and often has been, applied in such a manner that it provides a detailed understanding of a unique event without permitting generalizations to be drawn from the study, it can make important theoretical as well as empirical contributions if the linkages between the case and theoretical perspectives are defined clearly.[3] Accordingly, I now turn to an elaboration of the conceptual and theoretical issues and of the analytical framework that inform the study.

THE TECHNOLOGICAL PROJECT

Projects come in many sizes and shapes – they can be, *inter alia,* large or small, agricultural and industrial, experimental and demonstrational, capital intensive or labor intensive, designed to increase output or develop new capabilities. However, despite their variety, they all share some common characteristics: '. . . purposefulness, some minimum size, a specific location, the introduction of something qualitatively new, and the expectation that a sequence of further development moves will be set in motion.'[4]

My concern is with a specific kind of development project – the large technology transfer project, the type which requires major investments, the participation of foreign and domestic actors, a complex infrastructure, a long time-frame from inception to completion, and which, inexorably (because of the opportunity costs involved) determines the course of development for many years to come.

This kind of project almost always encounters unexpected difficulties. Over twenty years ago, a noted economist, Albert Hirschman, seeking to explain why so many World Bank sponsored projects failed to achieve their objectives, concluded that:[5]

If the project planners (and this usually includes the World Bank officials involved in financing the project) had known in advance all the difficulties and troubles that were lying in store for the project, they probably would have never touched it . . .

But policy-makers should not be discouraged by this state of affairs because in all the projects he studied:

. . . advance knowledge of these difficulties would . . . have been unfortunate, for the difficulties and the ensuing search for solutions set in motion a train of events that not only rescued the project, but often made it particularly valuable.

Whether this optimistic view is justified or polyanish, whether the 'hiding hand' actually transforms bad projects in this manner, whether they do in fact become 'particularly valuable', is one of the issues that will be clarified by this study but our experience with large projects, which have become increasingly common since World War II, does suggest that such optimism is not always warranted. While some have been successful (the Polaris, the Manhattan Project), others have been 'disasters', being either abandoned completely after vast infusions of time, money and skills (the nuclear airplane), or, more commonly, have come on stream much later and at much higher costs than originally anticipated (the Concorde).

As they have proliferated, large technological projects (which were originally designed to produce new technologies) have received increasing scholarly attention. One author has suggested that size is the critical variable, that any large-scale program will probably encounter difficulties because it tends to be inflexible, non-incremental, rigidly focused, and does not fit harmoniously into a pluralist political system.[6] Other factors are also involved, however. Large projects have been known to fail in non-pluralist societies. Moreover, as Gerald Steinberg has noted, it is necessary to distinguish between social programs and technological innovation projects and even among projects. Some, like the moon landing, needed only incremental changes in known technologies, others required major breakthroughs; some possessed fixed goals, others were dependent upon an opponent's capabilities which were themselves changing. Successful projects tended to possess fixed goals and require only minor changes in existing technologies.[7]

The importance of these factors is reaffirmed by the work of another scholar, Peter Hall, who studied the fate of several 'great planning disasters', some of which, including the San Francisco BART system and the Concorde, were technological projects.[8] He identified three types of uncertainties that create pitfalls for any project, two of which are similar to those discussed above. The first, based on the system that is being developed, subsumes goal and technology considerations. The second, decisions by external actors, often create totally unexpected difficulties for any project. The rise in oil prices, for example, had a disastrous impact upon projects everywhere. To these he adds a third: unexpected changes in the values of key elites and other significant publics. New consumption patterns, for example, will affect the demand for the output of particular projects.[9] To minimize the risks posed by these factors, Hall suggests that decision-makers use a cautious approach, that every project be subjected to a two-stage risk-adverse decision process. First should come a rigorous commercial evaluation, then a broader analysis that incorporates externalities such as distributional issues.[10]

Although Hall believes that such an approach 'would have avoided most of the planning disasters' that he studied, and many others as well,[11] it is not at all clear that this prescription would actually produce improved outcomes, especially in the case of large technology transfer projects. A study of such projects (none of which required any development of new technology at all) revealed that, even though all were subjected to detailed analyses, they cost, on average, between 100 and 150 per cent more than had been estimated and came on stream at least one or two years behind schedule.[12]

Projects of this kind have proliferated rapidly. In the seventies their number increased thirtyfold; over 1,600, costing more than $100 million each, were planned during the decade. Their total value climbed from $15.3 billion in 1970 to $1,010 billion by 1979. Although the largesse that flowed to the oil producing countries shaped this phenomenon (the largest and most expensive projects being located in the OPEC countries), macroprojects are scattered throughout the world. Ninety of the 120 developing nations embarked upon at least one. Saudi Arabia ranked first in terms of total investment in such projects ($150 billion), followed by Iran, Brazil, Egypt, Algeria and Australia. Turkey ranked eleventh on the list, investing $26.2 billion in thirty-seven projects.[13]

Some of the reasons why problems occurred so frequently can be related to factors identified by other scholars. The first of these is size – the larger the project, the greater the costs and the delays.[14] A second is the complexity of the system for projects in certain industries ran into more difficulties than others. Those in aluminium, copper, nickel and oil and gas encountered cost escalations of at least 100 per cent, construction delays averaging two years, and were postponed or suspended 20 per cent of the time. Steel, on the other hand, falls into a middle category.[15] Along with other metals, paper and fertilizer, such projects had cost overruns of between 30 and 100 per cent and construction delays but were seldom postponed or cancelled. Projects involving manufacturing and cement production almost always were trouble free.[16]

The environment, local and global, also affected project outcomes. It did so in two ways. First, it created uncertainties which the author considers to be 'beyond management's control' – changes in inflation and exchange rates and, especially, in market conditions. Secondly, the very nature of the new environment posed difficulties which were not adequately anticipated or planned for. These which are labelled as being 'within management's control' are the kinds of variables that are integral to any transfer for they include local climatic, economic and social conditions. Murphy considers the failure to understand and deal with these 'the greatest single error' in project management,[17] but she fails to explore the fundamental issue of why experienced and skilled personnel should have made such elementary errors, let alone why they should so often have been caught by surprise by economic developments.

Similar findings emerge from an important empirical study that sought to identify the factors that are responsible for the widespread failure of major projects throughout the world and which, after carefully analyzing every available study and tracing the fate of eight important European projects, develops a model that incorporates the factors that emerge as prerequisites for project success. Most significantly, Morris and Hough conclude that project failure is seldom due to managerial incompetence, rather 'many projects overrun because of circumstances "external" to the project – whether price escalation, government action, strikes, corporate decisions, or acts of God . . .' and suggest that improved project management requires that 'we must learn to manage these . . . factors more effectively.'[18]

All these studies, then, identify certain important factors that make for project failure – size, technological complexity, uncertainties and a lack of appreciation of the local environment. What remains vague is why these factors should be so prevalent, why decision-makers in the private and the public sector should be so fallible, why they are so seldom prepared to deal with 'external factors', why their planning is so weak, why they fail to make accurate projections, and why projects are so frequently poorly managed and implemented.

One scholar, E. J. Feldman, does seek to answer these questions, but only for democratic industrial societies. He discusses several explanations, two of which have already been considered – inherent difficulties in forecasting because of methodological and other problems and the inability to anticipate changes in economic conditions or technology. The others are (1) the inability of bureaucracies to cope with a high degree of project complexity (especially when the private sector is involved), and (2) the role of citizen protest, a widespread phenomenon, especially in the USA. He emphasizes, however, that these factors do not suffice to explain the phenomenon, that the focus must be upon 'political structure and choice'. Accordingly, he suggests that the fate of megaprojects is determined by three variables: (1) adequate financing, (2) management by an agency with adequate power, and (3) the nature of citizen access to the political system. Each of these is inherently political because: 'The availability of adequate financing depends upon the capacity of the government to make and sustain commitments; the concentration of authority varies according to the degrees of fragmentation in the structures of power; accessibility . . . depends upon the range of institutionalized mechanisms.'[19]

Though Feldman explicitly accords political variables the attention that they deserve, his generalizations are not necessarily applicable to many large technology transfer projects for these usually enjoy strong state support, are often the responsiblity of a powerful agency, and citizen protest is rarely, if ever, an issue. Nevertheless, his analysis does highlight variables that must be considered if one is to explore the nature of the choices that are made and the factors that influence these choices. In the sections that follow I shall attempt to build upon these and other findings in order to develop a model that identifies the key variables and their interrelationships.

THE TECHNOLOGY TRANSFER PROCESS

One fundamental reason why decision-makers commit the errors that they do is that they often fail to conceptualize the nature of technology accurately. It has been argued, for example, that industrial projects are more likely to fail than agricultural ones because the technologies involved appear, at first glance, to be easily transferable from one culture to another whereas those involving agriculture are more obviously site specific.[20] In reality, of course, industrial projects are equally subject to environmental constraints but many policy-makers still regard technology in a narrow, deterministic way, as consisting merely of machines that can be transferred easily. Such a perception can and often does contribute significantly to project failure, for those holding it tend to underrate the significance of the environment (thus committing 'the greatest single error') as well as the complexities inherent in any transfer.

Technology encompasses much more than machines and software; it also includes bodies of skills and knowledge that, though often unwritten, are essential to ensure the effective and efficient use of the machine.[21] It can best be conceptualized as a system with particular characteristics.[22] When viewed in this way, the inputs include knowledge, raw materials, parts of all types, the throughput, the manufacturing process, its organization and control, the output, the finished product. Each of these elements interacts with other systems in the environment that are themselves complex but whose effective functioning is essential if the technology is to operate as intended. The attributes of a technological system have been specified as follows: it is inexhaustible, practically self-reproducing and, above all, dynamic, diffusable and adaptable. From the point of view of technology transfer, the conception of a technological system possesses an important implication: the entire system can never be transferred, only certain of its elements.[23] For a transfer to be successful, for these elements to be productive, the entire system must be understood.

This circumstance further complicates what is already a process that is far more complex than is often believed to be the case. The nomenclature obfuscates the essential nature of the phenomenon; the term 'technology transfer' is a misnomer because it implies that the activity occurs naturally, that it is relatively easy and cost free, and that it is neutral, distributing its costs and benefits equitably. In reality, it is, of course, none of these; it is an expensive, difficult, conflictual process involving many interactive dimensions – actors, mode (joint venture, licensing, etc.), content (the technology itself), channel (manpower training, plant construction, etc.), and impact.[24] Moreover, it is a dynamic process that moves through various stages, at each of which problems can emerge that often lead to failure and frustration rather than goal achievement.[25] Yet, if some or all of the major actors do not perceive the process in this manner, they are likely to make poor decisions, at some point or other, that will negatively affect the outcome. If a transfer is to succeed, both sender and receiver, each of whom seeks to achieve different objectives, must expend large amounts of time, money and effort.

Often such investments are not made in the required amounts or in the proper sequence. Receiving organizations take many forms (state enterprise, MNC (multinational corporation) affiliate, independent firm, joint venture) and vary widely in their goals, cultures, resources and strategies. A detailed study of technology transfer in Turkey, for example, categorized receivers into three types, 'commercial', 'assembly', and 'industrial', on the basis of their goals and orientations. The 'commercial' receivers chose a partner rather than a technology, the 'assembly' receivers were influenced by technical and financial criteria; only the 'industrial' group made its decisions on the basis of technological criteria.[26]

In Turkey, as in many other countries, few receivers fall into the last category. Most do not possess any detailed knowledge of the costs and characteristics of available technologies and have a limited absorptive capacity. Such a capability, which is vital to a successful transfer, is determined by several factors, an obvious one being the degree to which the firm has already assimilated the same or similar technologies. Most Third World transfers do not involve such a recipient; they usually take the form of a 'greenfield transfer' in which a new plant has to be built, a managerial team and labour force recruited and trained, and the necessary infrastructure created. This sort of transfer is the most difficult of all to carry out successfully for it requires a considerable amount of learning by the recipient and considerable effort by the supplier as well. Moreover, one may anticipate that numerous problems will arise in attempting to relate the elements being transferred to newly created and existing systems. When Turkey first decided to buld an iron and steel sector, it had to engage in this kind of transfer. Successive transfers should proceed ever more smoothly.

The importance of organizational level variables deserves to be emphasized because they determine the choices that are made and the manner in which the technologies are utilized. The same technology can be deployed very differently within as well as between sectors. In any given sector, for example, one can find firms that employ essentially the same technology yet achieve dramatically different levels of productivity and efficiency.[27]

Several scholars have sought to identify why this should be the case. They have found that resources and goals are important dimensions, that some organizations were committed to and able to acquire the knowledge embodied in the transfer. They were then able to implement changes in the imported technologies that extended capacity, changed the mix of the goods produced, and even permitted the use of different raw materials. Some engaged in this behaviour as a deliberate strategy, in order to achieve international competitiveness. Others did so as a defensive strategy in order to deal with unexpected problems. Still others have not attempted to make any changes in the technologies, regardless of the efficiency and productivity that was attained.[28] Structure and culture also play an important role. Organizations differed in their ability to master a technology because of the degree of centralization, hierarchy and patterns of interaction. The ability to solve problems requires an understanding of the technology by persons within different units, but not all organizations operate in a way that facilitates the diffusion of knowledge.[29] A comparison of the Indian and Japanese cotton textile industries demonstrated clearly that such variables as the quality of management, the incentive structures for innovation and career mobility, and the nature of the mechanisms which diffused technical information to managers, were far more influential than prices and tariff policies.[30]

Still, one cannot overlook the role of external factors. The behavior of firms is influenced not only by their internal characteristics, but by the nature of their environments as well. An extensive study of technology transfer to Turkey, for example, revealed that difficulties in obtaining foreign exchange to purchase inputs and spare parts, the operation of a protectionist economic system and, above all, the nature of public policies greatly influenced the decisions that firms made.[31] I shall return to the role of the state when I discuss strategies and policies in detail below.

The behaviour of the supplier firm provides another set of variables. Though it wishes to increase its profits, it usually also seeks to retain control over its technology. Owners have traditionally attempted to implement rigid rules for the acquisition and use of their technologies (e.g. tied purchases and export prohibitions) and to obtain as high a price as possible. Increasingly, their efforts have been limited by the policies of the host governments who have passed legislation forbidding such restrictions and specifying the terms under which technologies may be imported into their societies, not always with positive results. The sender government is usually less influential but its concerns, which may involve its balance of payments, its relationships with allies and adversaries, or its power and prestige, are also reflected in its policies. Often international actors (each of whom has particular motivations and goals) also play a significant role. They seek to influence development strategies and policies in various ways. The World Bank, for example, has for many years been urging countries to place a greater emphasis upon markets and exports, and Unido has consistently advocated a strategy of heavy industrialization.

The technology transfer process is, therefore, one which involves several actors and which is profoundly influenced by the interactions between them. The nature, content and outcomes of these interactions is determined by the goals and resources of individual actors and the policies that they adopt and, since states and governments are major actors, politics is an inherent part of the process.[32] I shall return to these issues when I discuss policy and decision-making below. The structures and relationships that I have been discussing are depicted schematically in Figure 1.1.

THE NATURE OF TECHNOLOGICAL MASTERY

Implicit in the earlier discussion of the nature of technology and of the role that technological variables play in project outcomes is the concept of 'mastery'. Only if the receiving organization learns to

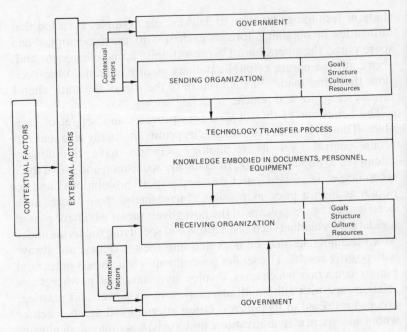

Figure 1.1 Basic analytical framework.

manipulate the technology can any transfer be considered a success, otherwise only 'technology trade' has taken place.[33]

The importance of achieving this capability within organizations and of diffusing it widely has by now become almost universally recognized. Only by doing so can the bonds of technological dependency ever be broken, control over important sectors of the national economy exercised, and wise bargains reached with multinational corporations and other suppliers of technology.[34] In the absence of mastery, states and organizations are unable to utilize foreign technologies efficiently and effectively since, any imported technology probably (and some scholars have argued inevitably) requires some modification. Even if it does not, problems will inevitably arise and without mastery the 'solutions' that are devised may further complicate matters. And, if a state wishes to develop 'appropriate' technologies or to build a base for the creation of a comparative advantage in other sectors, it must acquire a deep understanding of technological systems. In sum, technology mastery is the key not only to the efficient and effective use of the technology which has been transferred, but the knowledge thus attained has important spill over effects for other related technological activities. As Dahlman and Westphal point out:

> The increased mastery that results from experience with previously established technologies contributes to an economy's capacity to undertake independent technological factors including replication or adaptation of foreign technologies as well as the creation of new technology.[35]

To determine when a firm has mastered a technology is no easy matter. Scholars have suggested that the ability to perform various tasks of differing complexity can be identified and that these provide criteria for evaluation. On the basis of the rise of the electronics industry in South Korea, for example, L. Kim identified three separate stages. The first, 'implantation', is marked by foreign personnel in key positions, production for the local market, low levels of productivity and high costs. At the second stage, 'assimilation', local personnel take over, local inputs are utilized, costs decline, production becomes diversified. At the third stage, 'improvement', the firm engages in research and development, adapts foreign technology, and becomes internationally competitive.[36] Although, as Atamer points out, the utility of this model is limited (not all firms seek to penetrate the international market),[37] some of its criteria are useful and can be combined with those developed by other scholars. R. Dore, for instance, has suggested that technological mastery should be disaggregated into two conceptually distinct dimensions. The first, the learning capacity, essentially involves the ability to assimilate, to understand a technology. The second, the creation capacity, is subdivided into the ability to modify and adapt imported technologies and the ability to create a new technology.[38] This distinction between two general categories of tasks – the ability to absorb and utilize the technology productively and to modify existing technologies and create new ones – has also been made by Fransman and King who include, in the first group, searching for technological alternatives, making optimal choices, successfully operating, adapting and modifying the technology, and in the second, carrying out R&D activities and even basic research.[39] If I am to assess the degree of mastery that is achieved in various transfers, I must develop explicit criteria that will permit me to do so. Accordingly, I integrate these activities into the following levels. The first, the 'implantation' stage, involves the ability to operate the technology at low levels of productivity and quality. The second, the 'assimilation' stage, is characterized by decreasing costs, increasing quality and the ability to maintain the technology. The third, the 'competitive' stage, is reached when the firm can compete internationally and when it can make minor modifications to its technologies. The fourth stage, 'modification', is marked by the firm's ability to make significant technological innovations and to manage its own expansion. The final stage, 'autonomy', is reached when the firm carries out extensive R&D and is able to meet its needs by developing new technologies and combining them with existing technologies in novel ways.

How the incorporation of these factors expands the analytical framework is depicted in Figure 1.2.

POLITICS, POLICY AND DECISION-MAKING

Some scholars and practitioners have argued that most countries must inevitably fail in their attempts to master technology. In their view the international economic order is so structured that the core nations have preserved neocolonial patterns of dominance by controlling the production and dissemination of technology. Developing countries who seek to modernize must turn to the core countries for the technologies they need. Yet, because modern technology has been developed to meet the needs and conditions of the developed societies and are controlled by them, its nature and transfer benefits the core countries and prevents, or at least does not facilitate, genuine development. It is usually inappropriate and produces destructive impacts including aggravated unemployment, excessive urbanization, growing social inequalities and other socio-cultural pathologies. Nor is this destructiveness acquired cheaply. Because of differences in power, information and resources between buyers and sellers, developing countries incur heavy financial costs when they purchase these technologies. And, the functioning of this system prevents peripheral countries from developing their own technological capabilities because local elites benefit from a tacit alliance with the foreign technology producers and desire the same goods that are available internationally. As a result, local firms have no incentive to engage in research and development, scientific and technological activities are considered of marginal significance and dedicated scientists and technologists choose to emigrate rather than struggle in

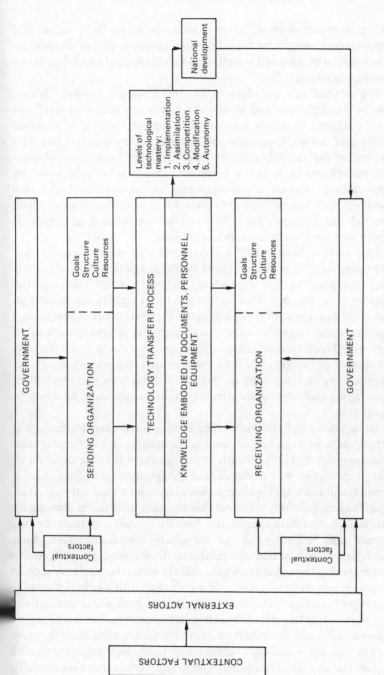

Figure 1.2 Analytical framework incorporating output variable.

an environment that is, at best, indifferent to their needs and importance. Under these conditions one cannot expect more than the development of a limited scientific and technological capability in any developing country.[40]

The dependency paradigm (often misleadingly labeled 'theory' despite its numerous and sometimes conflicting elaborations)[41] has been criticized by many scholars who accept the role of external forces and actors, especially multinational corporations, but who emphasize the centrality of the state. In their view, technological underdevelopment is not a condition that has been imposed by manipulative external actors operating in the core, rather it is a condition that has evolved over time for a variety of reasons, both internal and external, but which can be corrected if governments design and implement appropriate policies.

This view is buttressed by recent research which suggests that technological change in the Third World is not occurring along the lines predicted by the dependency school; on the contrary, the transfer of technology from the core to the periphery has benefitted industrial development there and many of these countries are making significant and successful efforts to advance the technological level of various industrial sectors and to produce sophisticated goods not only for their own markets but for export as well.[42] Some scholars have analyzed the development of the ERDEMIR iron and steel plant from a dependency perspective: I shall discuss their analyses in Chapter 4.

To acknowledge the importance of overcoming technological dependency, of achieving technological mastery, is far simpler than to accomplish it. Until recently it was assumed that the creation of such a capability was a simple and straightforward matter, that it would result from appropriate policies based on a national plan. But, it has become painfully apparent that the costs involved in drawing up national plans often exceed the benefits[43] and that planning for science and technology is an extremely complicated task. One important reason is that the relationships involved are still poorly understood, although certain generalizations can be made. A second is that, as emphasized above, we are dealing with a complex system that is profoundly affected by external forces, both within and outside the state. Accordingly, although most countries, for a variety of reasons, including the values of international organizations, do draw up national plans and have science and technology organizations of one sort or another, few of these (including Turkey) have successfully devised and implemented policies that have promoted the achievement of technological mastery.

The difficulty in doing so becomes apparent when we consider that policies in many areas involving numerous actors are involved. Attention must be paid to such topics as the development of a domestic scientific and technological capacity, the diffusion of technological innovations, the assessment and control of technologies that are transferred from abroad and the linking of the technological system with the educational system and with the productive sectors. In the case of iron and steel, for example, planners should consider the extent to which the sector has achieved technological mastery and identify its existing and future needs. Then appropriate research and development activities must be promoted, academic and in-house training programs for workers, engineeers and managers inaugurated or improved, imports made of foreign technologies related to the domestic infrastructure, international developments monitored, foreign technologies screened, and the domestic capability to meet increasing portions of the sector's technological requirements enhanced.

Moreover, even carefully designed policies may prove ineffective unless they are implemented in an appropriate environment. A major international research project has demonstrated the extent to which 'explicit' policies, that is those that are oriented specifically towards technology, seldom produce hoped for results. 'Implicit policies', designed to accomplish other goals (protecting domestic industry through tariffs, raising revenue through a particular tax, and so on), often have a much greater impact on the functioning of the technological infrastructure in general and upon technological decisions in particular than do the policies which governments hope will enhance technological capabilities.[44] These findings are reaffirmed by a recent study which found that parastatals (state economic enterprises) in Tanzania were making decisions that ran counter to national policy because of the impact of other policies, the nature of their environments, their relationship to other institutions, and the kinds of problems that they had to face.[45] Accordingly, a strategy designed to achieve technological mastery in the iron and steel industry must also be sensitive to and coordinated with policies in many areas. We shall see below the extent to which Turkey has developed such an appropriate web of policies.

The development and implementation of such policies are clearly complex and difficult tasks and not all states are capable of, or interested in, such an undertaking. States have made very different choices in regards to development in general and technology in particular. Some have been content to purchase foreign technologies and to create a modern enclave that is operated and maintained largely by foreigners, to operate at the 'implantation' stage of technological mastery. Saudi Arabia and other Persian Gulf states where, for social and cultural reasons, modern industries are almost totally dependent for their functioning upon expatriates and foreign workers fall into this category.[46] At the other extreme are such countries as Taiwan, South Korea and Japan which have deliberately implemented a strategy designed to indigenize foreign technologies. The well-known slogan 'take it apart and improve it' reflects the commitment of the Japanese to the mastery of technology, to become so knowledgeable about its functioning that their experts could create a superior product. Hence the specific strategy that a state adopts must be included in the analysis for it guides the working of the policy process and thus significantly affects (as I have already pointed out) the behavior of the receiving organization. It also influences, as I shall demonstrate in Chapter 2, patterns of national development and international economic relations.

Choosing a strategy is a political event. It requires specific political decisions with significant costs and benefits that are differentially distributed among individuals, groups and classes within any society. Not all governments, because of the nature of their support, their values, the strength of their position, are willing to promote the kinds of policies that are required to achieve technological mastery. Others may be committed to the concept but the balance of societal forces and interests may inhibit any meaningful movement. One expert, for example, has emphasized the extent to which scientists, who tend to enjoy greater power and prestige than technologists and, believing that investments in science inevitably lead to the development of technology, often successfully limit planning to the allocation of resources to specific research projects.[47] In still others the context and the possibility exists but the government may lack the necessary skills, determination or understanding to exploit the opportunity. F. Sagasti has emphasized the significance of one of these variables, though from a technocratic perspective:

> In the last analysis only the political will of government . . . will legitimize science and technology planning. The test for this is whether, in the face of resource constraints and adverse political pressures, science and technology planners are given enough

political support and resources to manoeuvre the development of science and technology along the directions *they* [my emphasis] establish.[48]

Although the personality, attitudes and other characteristics of political leaders are important elements that must be considered when analyzing decisions and policies, other factors must also be taken into account for decision-makers do not operate in a vacuum. In particular one must consider the nature of the policy process and the character of the political system in which it is embedded. Otherwise one cannot explain why changes in governments do not always lead to changes in policies, why some states, such as Japan and South Korea, have adopted and implemented policies that have enabled them to master modern technologies while others, such as Saudi Arabia, have not yet done so. To understand such differences it is essential to consider the ways in which power is distributed and decisions made.

Numerous typologies have been advanced by scholars seeking to capture the essential elements of political systems and various efforts have been made to identify their relationship to policy outputs. The research results to date are inconclusive, perhaps because of the difficulties of appropriately differentiating among systems that fall into the same general category.[49] Accordingly, I shall categorize the regimes that have enjoyed power since the establishment of the Turkish Republic in 1924 on the basis of two criteria that seem particularly relevant in terms of policy. The first of these is the degree to which power is centralized or decentralized, to which the system is 'pluralistic' or 'authoritarian'. The second is the degree to which the 'social core group' (the power holders at the center of the state) are in conflict over goals and values.[50] Minimally, these can be combined to produce four different regime types, each of which should produce different types of policies. In a centralized system with a low degree of conflict, for example, policy should be consistent over time, integrated across issue areas and oriented towards the achievement of long-term goals, whereas in a decentralized, conflictual system, policy should be fragmented, *ad hoc* and short term in orientation.[51]

If one analyzes Turkish political history from this perspective, one can identify several distinct regime types. The first, the Ataturk period, was characterized by a cohesive, centralized system. This was followed, in 1950, by a pluralist system in which a dominant government ruled until it was overthrown by the military in 1960.

Military sponsored governments ruled until 1965 when civilian authority was restored and one party came to power. The new pluralist system was marked by increasing intra- and inter-elite conflict and, following another military intervention in 1970 and rule by 'technocratic' governments supported by the military, new elections in 1973 created a situation wherein no single party enjoyed a majority. The resulting governments were weak coalitions that proved unable to deal with many of the country's problems, including a high level of political violence. In 1980 the military took over and, determined to establish a stable democratic order, ruled with a strong hand until 1983 when a new, popularly elected government came to power. In subsequent chapters I shall identify more precisely the nature of these regimes, their development strategies and the particular policies that they adopted towards the iron and steel sector.

Whatever the regime type, government leaders always confront systemic problems concerning which decisions of some kind have to be reached. Several basic models have been advanced to explain just how and why leaders make the choices that they do. The first and best known of these, the rational actor model, is the classical one which assumes that it is possible to delineate precisely the boundaries of the system, identify a set of preferences and all the alternatives, and gather the necessary information to achieve an optimal result. In addition, it assumes that bargaining and negotiations are not an integral part of a decision process.[52] Increasingly, these assumptions were questioned by critics such as Herbert Simon who argued that collective decisions were not made on the basis of such rigorous requirements. He developed an alternative 'bounded rationality' model with 'satisficing' rather than 'optimizing' as the central concept; in other words decision-makers tend to select the alternative which is 'good enough'.[53] He also focused upon the psychological aspects of decision-making, on individual and group perceptions of risks and opportunities and, in subsequent work, he and other members of the 'Carnegie School' emphasized the manner in which human beings filter information for decisions and how organizations resolve conflicts through uncertainty-avoidance and problemistic search tendencies.[54] Charles Lindblom also rejected the rational approach. He suggested that decision-makers, constrained by time, cost, lack of information and imprecise policy goals, act incrementally, making small moves on particular problems and that they coordinate decisions on the basis of 'partisan mutual adjustment'. This approach has been criticized for its emphasis upon existing and past practice and its tendency to frame options so as to eliminate those that might entail dramatic change.[55] Since each of these models contains weaknesses, some scholars, such as A. Etzioni, have attempted to develop models that combine the positive aspects of each. His 'mixed scanning' model is designed to permit the decision-maker to make synoptic choices at the strategic level and incremental ones at the tactical level.[56]

Although the satisficing and incremental approaches offer quite distinct views of decision-making, they are often incorporated within a 'bureaucratic politics' category. This model was first developed by Graham Allison who sought to identify the extent to which the behavior of US policy-makers dealing with the Cuban missile crisis conformed to the rational actor model and analyzed their decisions in terms of a bureaucratic politics and an organizational process model as well. He concluded that policy emerged as a political 'resultant of various bargaining games among players'.[57] The distinction between the organization process model, whereby decisions stem from organizational patterns and incremental change, and the bureaucratic politics model wherein outcomes are determined by the power and skill of the actors rather than the routines of their organizations was not precisely defined and, in subsequent work, these two were merged.[58] The resulting model has gained widespread attention and has also been criticized on several grounds – its failure to consider the decisive role of the President, the exclusion of non-bureaucratic actors, and the belief that the key players are least likely to consider the interests of their organizations.[59]

Another line of attack upon the rational actor model came from scholars who were concerned with the 'images', 'attitudinal prisms', or 'belief systems' of the decision-makers. Among the most influential are M. Brecher who analyzed several foreign policy decisions, and J. Steinbrunner who utilized three models to analyze a single decision.[60] These were the rational, the cybernetic which incorporates feedback within a satisficing framework (variety is reduced and uncertainty limited by the responses that we have established), and the cognitive which focuses on the mind's belief structure, upon the ways in which this influences choice. Stein and Tanter have attempted to build on this literature by applying these concepts to different stages of the decision process, thus creating seven models, three 'pure' (the rational, cybernetic and cognitive), and four 'mixed'.[61]

Of all these general models, the rational one is widely considered to be the most relevant for science and technology which is usually regarded as the policy arena wherein 'scientific procedures' can best be applied.[62] Yet, it has become quite obvious that policy-making in this area is also a political event, that it cannot be isolated from politics. The nature of the relationship, however, remains unclear. One scholar has argued that science and technology policy is usually neither 'political' nor 'scientific' but contains aspects of each.[63] Others have concluded that politics establish the 'ground rules' within which rational analysis can be carried out:

> An important distinction should be made . . . between technical and political decisions . . . . A purely technical decision cannot be made until someone or some group has made a political decision as to the ground rules by which technical decisions will be made.[64]

The extent to which either of these characterizations adequately describes the relationship between political variables and technological decisions is one of the topics to be explored in detail. The political variables that I have been discussing can be incorporated into the analytical framework as shown in Figure 1.3.

TECHNOLOGICAL DECISIONS AND PROJECT ANALYSIS

That numerous factors are intertwined in any technological issue has recently been emphasized by Harold Linstone. After carefully reviewing many of the extant decision-making models, he concluded that, since every technological problem contains technical, organizational and individual dimensions, none of the major models (the rational, the cognitive, the cybernetic) permit us deal adequately with every dimension. He advocates the use of 'multiple perspectives', analyzing each dimension from a technical (rational), organizational (the viewpoint of the affected and affecting organizations) and personal perspective (how individual goals, self-interest and belief systems affect and are affected by the issue). Though the technical perspective is most useful in analyzing the technical dimension and so on, each approach is expected to contribute useful insights into each dimension.[65]

Although one can readily accept the utility of a broad perspective, it is not at all obvious that Linstone's approach, which raises significant difficulties of its own, especially in terms of trade-offs and costs, would lead to more enlightened outcomes. Nevertheless, his central points – that single models are inadequate, that rational

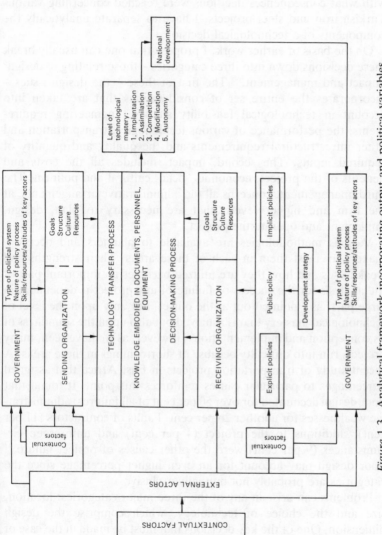

Figure 1.3 Analytical framework incorporating output and political variables.

analysis does not suffice even for the 'technical' elements, and that any technological issue must be disaggregated – are well taken. Accordingly, if I am to gain an understanding of how and why, and with what consequences decisions were reached concerning various Turkish iron and steel projects, I have to separate analytically the components of a technological decision.

On the basis of earlier work, I propose that one can usually break these decisions down into three categories – those relating to design, impact and management.[66] The first of these – the design issues – incorporates the entire set of considerations that are taken into account in technological feasibility studies, engineering requirements, the performance of various technologies, transportation and other infrastructural requirements and the quality and quantity of required inputs. The second, impact, includes all the costs and benefits of the project, economic, social, cultural and political. The third, management, concerns all the administrative arrangements, at the firm and higher levels, that are necessary to plan, design, implement and operate the project.

Various methodologies are available to planners and decision-makers to assist them in each of these areas. Their strengths and weaknesses and how they are utilized becomes an important part of the analysis for the success or failure of any project is dependent in large part, as I pointed out at the outset, not only upon the level of technological mastery that is achieved but also upon the soundness of its conception and implementation. However, as we have seen, many projects run into difficulty because of shortcomings in these areas. A recent study of transportation projects in East Africa that assigned percentages to particular causes reinforces this point. It found that poor design accounted for over 50 per cent of all failures, administrative weaknesses for another 26 per cent. Faults of contractors (11 per cent), additions to the project (4 per cent) and unforeseen circumstances (9 per cent) were the other causes of project failure.[67] Poor design may account for an even higher percentage since the categories are probably not mutually exclusive.

Problems can arise in any of the three major categories: location, size and the choice of technology, which comprise the design dimension. One of the key decisions that must be made in the case of an iron and steel plant – or any other project for that matter – is its location. Obviously, different sites possess different advantages in terms of transportation, accessibility to markets, availability of inputs and so forth, and careful analyses must be made of their respective costs and benefits. A poor choice can doom a project to high production costs which make its products non-competitive.

This is obviously true of iron and steel plants. Because of important technological innovations in ocean transportation, these are no longer located near the source of raw materials as was the case when US and European plants were being built. Now the preferred site is on a sea coast with a good harbour because of the changing patterns of raw material acquisition. Trade in iron ore has grown very rapidly in recent years, both in terms of quantity and the distance that the material is shipped, because of technological improvements in iron-ore carriers. Today vessels that carry half a million tons are quite common and efficient new methods of handling and storing these huge quantities have been installed in many ports. Great decreases in the cost of imported raw materials have been accompanied by sharp increases in demand, developments which have favoured the exploitation of large, high-quality deposits in Brazil, Australia, Peru and elsewhere. The trend is towards long-term contracts and captive mines, a trend which, by making possible long-term planning, has important implications for the future of the industry. Similar developments have affected coal, the other critical raw material.

The second category is size. In many industries, including iron and steel, size is directly related to the cost of production; large integrated plants benefit from significant economies of scale. Such plants, however, are extremely expensive. Sometimes the available funding may not permit the construction of an optimally sized plant; sometimes the projected market demand may not justify such an investment.[68]

The third category covers the specific technologies to be employed. In any sector, numerous options are usually available but research has revealed that, in many cases, what economists would consider the 'optimal' choice is not made. An important body of research seeks to explain this phenomenon.[69] One fundamental factor is the extent to which alternatives are available in any sector. Considerable variations exist, but even in the case of iron and steel, which is characterized by relatively low levels of substitutability,[70] numerous choices always have to be made. In the case of the ERDEMIR plant, for example, the planners had to decide whether to use the established open hearth furnace or the newer basic oxygen furnace method to produce steel, whether to build a sinter plant, and what kind of rolling mill equipment to select. Other important factors include the objectives of the firm, the values of the decision-makers (they often possess a passion for sophisticated technologies and believe that 'appropriate technology' is second rate), the amount of information, the strength of the bargaining position and the degree of competition.[71]

The second dimension, impact, can be disaggregated into economic and non-economic aspects. The former incorporate all the elements that are usually considered in any cost–benefit analysis. The latter, which has attracted increasing attention in recent years, includes the ecological consequences and the ways in which the project impacts on social and political organizations of all types.

Determining the value of any project is no easy matter. Earlier I pointed out that one scholar, after analyzing several 'great planning disasters', concluded that all projects should be subject first to a rigorous commercial analysis and then to a broader one that considers the national costs and benefits. This, in fact, is the accepted practice – both of these separate though related criteria are usually employed. Commercial profitability is the one emphasized by private entrepreneurs who seek a return of at least 20 per cent after taxes on their investment. The rate of return is calculated on the basis of estimates of such variables as capital costs, production costs and income from sales. Well-known techniques are used to arrive at these estimates but the possibility of significant errors plagues any analyst. Especially critical is the capital cost of the project for, if this is not established correctly, practically all of the financial projections will be erroneous and the viability of the project may well be endangered.[72]

A second area of concern is the amount of 'working capital' (the difference between current assets and current liabilities) that is available. In the USA a 2 : 1 ratio of current assets to current liabilities is the rule; in most developing countries this usually falls to 1.5 : 1, sometimes more. The smaller the amount of working capital, the greater the debt burden that the project must carry, and the greater the danger that the project will fail.[73]

A third important aspect involves the estimation of potential sales revenues. This is perhaps the single most important element in determining the feasibility of any project. An appropriate level of demand for the product must exist if the project is to be successful. Hence three basic questions have to be answered: (1) what is the size of the existing market? (2) How is it likely to grow in the future? and (3) How much of this market can the project capture?[74] The importance of answering these questions accurately can not be overemphasized. The projected market determines the production plans and thus 'sizes' the major facilities involved. In the case of iron and steel works, these facilities involve the expenditure of millions of dollars and can be altered to any significant degree only if very large additional expenditures are made. Various techniques are used to determine market size but, whatever the method, 'The essential point is that the assumed growth in . . . demand should be conservative . . .'[75]

If a market exists, the project must usually be able to produce at a cost that will enable it to compete successfully with other producers at home and abroad. If it is not competitive, the costs will be passed on to the citizenry through tariffs or subsidies. Hence comparative production costs represent the second major dimension of any feasibility analysis: 'One of the most important facts that can and must be known about an industrial project is its probable unit cost of production . . . A project which lacks a production cost advantage will always be a problem.'[76] Often these are estimated quite optimistically and the project finds itself facing serious cash-flow problems. One expert cautions: '. . . if a pioneer plant in a non-industrial country achieves half of capacity output in its first operating year, three-quarters in the second, and reaches 90 per cent in the third year, it is doing well – probably better than most. To count on more may be unrealistic.'[77] As we shall see, realism is not always a hallmark of project designers and planners.

Forecasts of operating costs are also frequently wrong. These are particularly difficult to estimate due to a lack of reliable data in many key areas. For example, one must calculate the raw material costs, the labor costs (an especially troublesome area, because of the assumptions that have to be made concerning the number of workers, the salary levels, and so on), maintenance costs, management costs and depreciation. Usually, the estimates turn out to be unrealistically low.[78]

After the commercial profitability of a project has been established, planners must still determine its contribution to national development. To do so other criteria have to be introduced into the analysis but, frequently, the only one that is utilized is the degree to which the project will save foreign exchange. Most developing countries suffer from chronic foreign exchange difficulties and projects are often justified on the ground that they will save that precious resource. As we shall see, this was certainly the case for the Turkish decisions to build and expand its iron and steel industry. A project that ranks high on this dimension, however, may still yield a low rate of return for the country's economy when all its costs and benefits are calculated.

To arrive at the 'real' national costs and benefits is no simple matter because of such conceptual and practical difficulties as: (1) incorporating all the economic costs and benefits of a project; (2) obtaining accurate data – regulations and restrictions of various kinds, tariffs, fixed exchange rates, unrealistic interest rates and artificially high wages all distort the actual situation; (3) assigning monetary values to the costs and benefits; and (4) making accurate calculations.[79] Not only are these computations easily subject to error but a project's potential contribution should not be measured in economic terms alone; environment and equity and other considerations which are extremely difficult to deal with should also be factored in.

Sophisticated techniques – methods of calculating discount rates, of assigning shadow prices and the like – have been developed in recent years. They have gained widespread currency, largely as a result of efforts by donor agencies, seeking to improve and rationalize what has always been and clearly continues to be a difficult and troublesome process. Many have published their own manuals,[80] promoted research to improve available methodologies, and sponsored training programs for administrators and planners. Their efforts have not yielded very exciting results and even formerly enthusiastic proponents have lowered their expectations. The OECD has published a book by an experienced Swedish official that is highly critical of existing practice,[81] and at a meeting sponsored by another agency to discuss the problem, no consensus emerged as to whether its use would lead to the selection of 'first-best' projects; it was agreed, however, that poor projects would be rejected.[82]

Even this modest conclusion would be questioned by some for two reasons.[83] First, most practitioners would agree that project analysis remains an art form and that the passion for precision should not override the canons of common sense, that quantification should be limited to those variables for which such calculations are appropriate, and that other variables should be neither slighted nor neglected totally.[84] Sophisticated techniques are, frequently, 'far too complicated, time consuming, and expensive',[85] and this deters planners and consultants so that studies of limited utility whose costs often outweigh their benefits continue to proliferate.

Second, as I have argued above, the traditional perspective that considers the rational actor model the most applicable to technological decisions must be questioned; one simply cannot overlook the role of political factors in the process. At a minimum these determine the 'ground rules' within which technical analyses will be carried out. Frequently, however, political factors play a more direct role, determining the conclusions that will be reached for technical analyses can be utilized to justify or destroy any project and the studies that are produced are frequently designed to do just that.[86] As one expert has noted: 'As a rule planners approve or reject projects on the basis of tacit or explicit dictates by those in power, and the quantification of costs and benefits is the "professional way of doing it." '[87] Political considerations influence the process in another way. There is now a tendency to advance only certain kinds of projects for support, projects that may not be the most desirable in terms of a country's needs. And, whatever the project, most governments regard the studies as formalities to be dispensed with as quickly and painlessly as possible; many rely on foreign experts who churn out the required analyses on demand.[88] In such circumstances problems are practically guaranteed to arise once the desired funds have been secured and implementation begins.

Even when careful, detailed studies are almost always made of the design and the economic and financial aspects of the impact dimensions, much less attention is usually paid to the third dimension, management, even though it plays an important role at each stage of the project cycle and is widely recognized to be a major bottleneck. Many LDCs lack the high level and technical personnel required to operate and maintain projects or the environment in which they can operate effectively.[89] Yet most studies slight the issue of administrative feasibility, largely ignoring such managerial aspects as organizational arrangements, their type, location and relation to other inputs in the private and public sector, recruitment and training programs, administrative and control procedures, and so on. Why this should be the case is not clear though some have suggested that lending agencies tend to focus upon the design rather than the implementation of development projects. Their emphasis on cost–benefit analysis may also play a role; planners trained in these techniques are predisposed to consider finance rather than administrative capacity as the major bottleneck to development.[90] Whatever the cause, the tendency is widespread. The World Bank has been criticized for neglecting managerial issues and, when AID conducted an internal review, it found that key managerial concepts, though incorporated in manuals, were applied haphazardly. A later report concluded that 'the project management function . . . never has been thoroughly studied and established as part of a systematic, overall analysis of Agency organization and procedures.'[91]

All the projects that I shall discuss were the subject of numerous studies by highly qualified organizations and consultants. Yet they all achieved outcomes that were less successful than anticipated. Why and how this occurred and the extent to which the generalizations presented above are relevant are topics that I will expect to clarify as I analyze the studies that were carried out. The considerations that I have discussed can be integrated into the analytical framework as shown in Figure 1.4.

THE PROJECT CYCLE AND TECHNOLOGICAL DECISION-MAKING

The analysis of any decision involving a technical project is complicated not only by the fact that, even from a technological perspective, numerous dimensions and sub-dimensions are involved, but further by the fact that a project is not a static phenomenon involving a single decision. Rather it passes through different stages, in the course of which new decisions have to be made. Moreover, the nature and the characteristics of the decisions vary across the lifespan of a project. Accordingly it is necessary to consider the different stages and their characteristics, a task which is not facilitated by the lack of a consensus on the number and type of stages that are involved.[92] For the sake of simplicity, I shall, in the following discussion, collapse them into five: initiation, appraisal, approval, implementation and completion.

Project initiation

Ideally, projects should be identified on the basis of national plans, sectoral analyses and the like. Projects should be integrated and geared to achieve particular objectives but, in actuality, they seldom arise as a result of such careful planning and analysis. Rather, major projects in developing countries are conceived by officials reacting to various pressures and needs including maintaining or extending support, legitimizing their commitment to national development (airports, steel mills and dams are particularly attractive because of their great symbolic value),[93] salvaging an existing project or elimi-

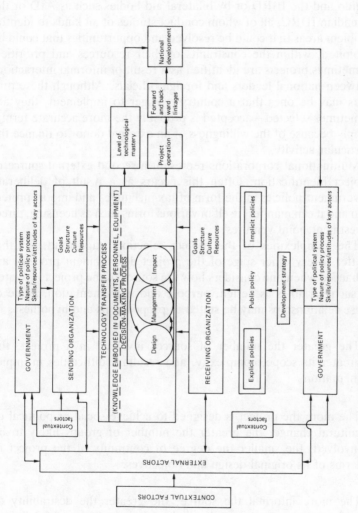

Figure 1.4 Analytical framework incorporating project decision variables.

identification.'[94] The surprising result, given the pressing needs of LDCs in so many sectors, is a shortage of good ideas that deserve further analysis.

Many projects, therefore, are identified by external actors such as Unido and the IBRD or by bilateral aid bodies such as AID or the Canadian IDRC, all of whom conduct studies of all kinds to identify problem areas that could be resolved and opportunities that could be exploited, within the constraints of their resources and priorities. Sometimes projects are identified as a result of informal interactions between national leaders and foreign officials. Although these projects may be ones that a country is eager to implement, they are sometimes selected – accepted is probably the more accurate term – simply because of the willingness of an external donor to finance the particular activity.

Multinational corporations represent a second external source of project identification. Often this occurs as a result of deliberate government policies in the form of tax incentives and import protection and it can manifest itself in various forms such as licensing, direct investment, joint ventures.

The complexities of the project selection stage (and, for that matter, every other stage of the project development process) are enhanced when one considers how the source of the project is related to such variables as design, purpose and implementation. Some of these relationships may be stated as propositions and hypotheses:[95]

The greater the number of sources involved in a project, the greater its scope, complexity, and resultant difficulties in implementation.

The more the project is designed to achieve social or political or cultural change, the greater the number of groups likely to be involved, the smaller the degree of continuity of the project in terms of its original design and objectives.

The more informal the source, the greater the desirability of subjecting the project to detailed analysis in terms of feasibility, desirability, relation to national goals and the like. Conversely, the more formal the source, the smaller the desirability of detailed analysis and the greater the likelihood that the project will receive the required levels of support, both internally and externally.

Whatever the source, any project will be redefined in terms of purposes, content, size and components as it moves through the project cycle.

The source often determines the organizational form of the project to suit its own preferences, needs, and priorities. International agencies prefer new autonomous organizations, ministries, their own administrative structures.

Project appraisal

Following the identification of a particular idea, it is necessary to translate it into a specific project. Now all the issues that were discussed above as part of the design, impact and management dimensions should be addressed in detail, yet most studies are marked by all the deficiencies considered earlier. As a result, this stage is often characterized by (1) the inadequate involvement (sometimes the overinvolvement) of host governments, (2) unrealistic expectations in terms of the available and needed time and resources, (3) inadequate specification of evaluative criteria and output targets, (4) poor analyses of input requirements, market demands and maintenance needs, (5) inadequate concern with and preparation for unanticipated events, and (6) a neglect of local cultural and social conditions.

Project approval

All studies are usually designed to persuade bilateral and multilateral aid donors that a project is desirable, that it can compete successfully with alternative investment possibilities, and that it represents a wise use of limited resources. Above all, the merits of any project should be determined on the basis of comparison with alternative investment possibilities. As one expert has noted: 'The acid test that the candidate project has to meet is that it must emerge from the process of choice among alternatives as offering the best claim upon scarce resources.'[96] Yet this is seldom the case: 'In the prevailing system, little attention is paid to alternatives . . . Once a project has been selected for consideration it generally ends up being implemented.'[97]

Approval usually involves an agreement among various actors – foreign donors, national governments and other concerned parties – over such aspects as the terms of the loans, the conditions of participation, and so on. This phase often involves extensive negotiations because each participant has its own interests and the process of reconciling those interests is a political one involving the basic issue of the distribution of power, access to decision-makers and control over resources. Since donors have their own priorities, projects often have to be presented in the form that renders them most attractive to the potential supplier of foreign aid.

Project implementation

Following agreement on the details, the project has to be organized and implemented but, often, there is only a limited resemblance between what has been so painstakingly studied and the actual shape that the project takes. As one expert has noted:

> . . . the project gathers its own momentum, bureaucratic and political, and later inputs of qualitative or quantitative considerations become mere 'cosmetics' unrelated to the basic 'reality' of the project and designed to mislead the decision-makers . . . This is one of the reasons for the commonly observed characteristics, namely the differences between real and formal project preparation.[98]

In any case, the project has to be implemented in some form or other and various administrative arrangements are possible, each with its own set of advantages and disadvantages. Whatever the form, personnel must be recruited, construction schedules arranged, and supplies and equipment procured. Problems frequently encountered here center around obtaining the requisite resources, the inability or unwillingness of governments to carry out their commitments, inadequate coordination, conflict between indigenous staff and foreign experts, and bureaucratic difficulties such as corruption and the autonomy of various units (customs officials have been known to delay the import of materials for months despite the pleas of other administrators). Hence it is not surprising that this is the stage where most projects exceed their costs or time schedules[99] or that a UN study has remarked: 'In the course of implementation of development projects, the frequency of unpredicted delays and bottlenecks is a significant part of the reality to be reckoned with.'[100]

Ultimately, the extent to which such difficulties can be overcome and a project successfully implemented depends on the quality of the management, particularly of the project manager. His role is so fundamental that UNDP studies have concluded that his attributes will determine whether a project is completed on schedule or not.[101] To recruit a well-qualified project manager is no simple matter for such persons are rare. One report noted:

> At present, the common manager with a purely technical background often lacks the administrative and managerial capacity to run a project smoothly. Even one with an administrative background may not have the training and aptitude to implement a project speedily and effectively.[102]

Essentially, the project manager has to perform two basic functions: build a management team, and develop and implement a detailed plan to cover such aspects as budgeting, scheduling and reporting. Often these functions are not performed adequately even though here too sophisticated techniques such as the critical path method (CPM), project evaluation and review techniques (PERT), and network analysis have been developed and widely disseminated. Effective project implementation also requires the development of a system of reporting and feedback in order to ensure appropriate monitoring.

Project completion

As a project proceeds through these stages it may become clear that the project should not be continued because of the costs that would be incurred by its completion and operation. Seldom, however, is a defective project terminated promptly; on the contrary, anyone promoting a particular project will usually make some investment as rapidly as possible in order to guarantee that it be completed. Many factors, including a fear of losing the investments already made, the political repercussions of confessing failure, of resistance by potential beneficiaries, or simply the decision-makers' lack of knowledge of the actual situation due to faulty administrative arrangements can all, and many times do, work in favor of continuation.

Even successful projects encounter problems at this stage. These usually take one of two forms: outputs are not diffused to as wide a range of recipients as had been anticipated or they are not utilized as planned. These problems are so common that many experts have sought to explain why there are so many discrepancies between the original designs and the actual result. Such work takes into account the kinds of issues discussed above but emphasizes the importance of socio-political factors as well. One study, for example, suggests that two sets of variables are relevant, the first of which includes the project characteristics (its resources, design and goals) and its environment. Varying benefits accrue to different groups, and such factors as the degree of change required, the amount of resources provided, the characteristics of the bureaucrats involved, and so on, are all relevant. The second, and at least equally significant, set involves the character of the political system in which the project is designed and implemented.[103]

Once a project has been completed, regardless of the degree to which it meets its original goals, responsibility for operation and maintenance of the new facility is turned over to a different organization. This changeover necessarily involves a transition period because people with new skills will be required to operate, manage and maintain the new facility, and because linkages with other units must be established in order to ensure a constant and adequate supply of inputs and the effective utilization of outputs. Once again, the quality of management is a decisive factor in ensuring a successful transition and effective operation of the project.

All experts agree on the importance of thorough project evaluation because the information that such an effort yields is extremely valuable. It can identify problems whose resolution can improve the performance of the project and additional areas of investment that can further enhance its value. Moreover, evaluation helps build a 'learning curve' and can develop a group within the country that recognizes and knows how to deal with the problems and difficulties in project development and implementation and can thus contribute greatly to improved investment decisions in the future.[104]

Each of these stages involves decisions that can be analyzed in terms of how the three dimensions discussed above – design, impact, and management – were handled. Although each of these is not equally salient at each stage, some invariably arise, but to analyze each of these dimensions for each stage of any project would be a terribly complex and difficult task because any project possesses a long and involved history with many major decision points. In the case of ERDEMIR, for example, these include (1) the original decision, (2) the 'interim expansion', (3) the Stage I expansion, and (4) the Stage II expansion. Each of these can be considered as representing a separate project and could, therefore, be analyzed in

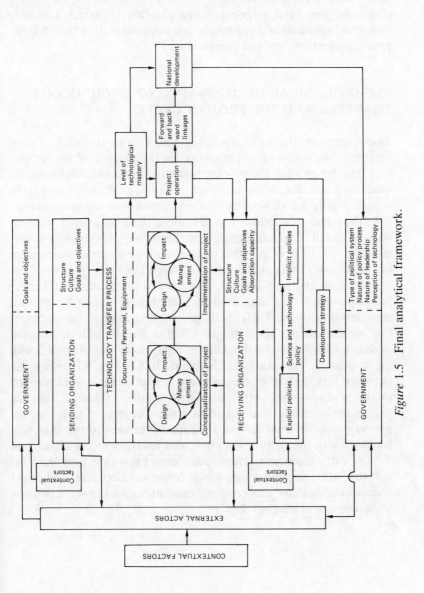

Figure 1.5 Final analytical framework.

terms of the project cycle discussed above. The purposes of this study, however, can be adequately served by condensing the project cycle into two basic stages: conceptualization (in which I include initiation, appraisal and approval), and implementation (which comprises implementation and completion).

TECHNOLOGICAL DECISION-MAKING, TECHNOLOGY TRANSFER AND THE PROJECT CYCLE

These, then, are the major conceptual referents for this study. Taken together they represent a framework for the analysis of the technology transfer process, the political and other factors that influence its outcome, and the ways in which technological decision-making occurs. Figure 1.5 shows how all these dimensions are interrelated.

In the pages that follow, I shall explore these topics and relationships in detail. Chapter 2 considers alternative development strategies, the role of iron and steel therein, and the major characteristics of the industry in its global setting. It then traces the growth of the Turkish iron and steel industry and assesses the results that Turkey has achieved by pursuing its particular strategy. Then I turn to a consideration of the ERDEMIR project and analyze the decisions that were made at various stages. Chapter 3 deals with the original decision, Chapter 4 with the 'interim expansion', and Chapter 5 with the two major expansions of the plant. In Chapter 6 I discuss the decisions relating to the other iron and steel plants that were planned in the seventies and carry out a comparative evaluation of each plant's performance in order to assess the degree of technological mastery that has been achieved. Chapter 7 returns to the analytical framework in the light of the study and analyzes recent changes in Turkey's development strategy, their impact upon the iron and steel industry, and the implications for its future development, and draws general conclusions concerning the relationship between politics, technology, and development.

2 Iron and Steel and Development in Turkey

Turkey Implements a Development Strategy

INTRODUCTION

Just as our understanding of technology and its potential have been oversimplified for decades, so have the difficulties that are inherent in the struggle to achieve modernity, a struggle that continues to be waged daily throughout the globe. At first, especially in the decades following World War II, it was naively expected that infusions of capital and technology would achieve the same results in what were then termed the 'underdeveloped countries' as the Marshall Plan had for Europe. That illusion was quickly dispelled as it became clear that Europe's infrastructures of skills, technology, values and social systems were unique.

Since then, numerous theories and paradigms have been advanced that seek to explain how and why development can be achieved. These include, *inter alia,* a linear view of development, balanced vs. unbalanced growth, the importance of capital, human resources, values, and the role of the international economic order. And, over time, the meaning of development has altered so that it is now widely accepted that the process involves more than increases in GNP. Qualitative changes in social, technological and cultural structures are also required.

STRATEGIES OF DEVELOPMENT

Many models are available. One can follow, among others, the Russian example of heavy forced industrialization, the Maoist model of social mobilization and simultaneous development of industry and agriculture, or the Japanese emphasis upon technological innovation and an export orientation. Essentially, any country confronts several choices: to emphasize agriculture or industry, capital or labor inten-

39

sive technologies, an import substitution or an export orientation, light or heavy industry, and the private or the public sector.

All these choices – and more can be identified – are interrelated but a recent study combined them into three fundamental strategies. A country can specialize in primary products or pursue an import substitution orientation (a variation of this involves a balanced production and trade strategy) or specialize in a specific industrial sector geared to the international market.[1] The first strategy has traditionally been adopted by countries possessing certain kinds of natural resources such as oil, tin and copper, though some (Malaysia and the Ivory Coast) have done so on the basis of agricultural products. Primary exports represent their major source of foreign revenues. Often, this strategy leads to industrialization when income levels and investment have reached a certain level as occurred in Denmark and Canada. This strategy, however, suffers from three major weaknesses. First, it is no easy matter to make the transition to a more balanced form of development that includes the export of manufactured items. Second, growth is highly concentrated sectorally, and third, the country remains dependent upon foreign capital.

The second strategy, wherein countries seek to emphasize both agriculture and industry is the most common. Here one can differentiate between those who have attempted to add manufactured goods to their exports of traditional primary goods and those who have been more inward oriented. The difference between these two groups is one of degree for both protect their infant industries, but there is a distinct tendency by the former group towards shorter periods of protection and a consistently greater concern with export promotion.

Most countries, including Turkey, have followed the latter course. They have emphasized industrialization through import substitution and were never interested in exporting manufactured goods at all. This strategy, though widely practiced, has been severely criticized by economists because a considerable body of research has demonstrated that it leads to slower development than would be the case if a more aggressive export policy had been pursued, resources are channeled away from agriculture, the domestic demand is ultimately met, and the industrial sector, which prospered behind tariff walls, proves incapable of competing in the international market. And the claims by its proponents that it insulates a country against external forces and a debt crisis and that authoritarian politics are required to pursue successfully an export promotion strategy have not been validated.[2] These findings and the activities of the World Bank have persuaded policy-makers in many countries (including Turkey since 1979) to turn their economies outwards by taking steps to make their industries more competitive and export oriented, but some countries remain committed, for ideological and political reasons, to what is now generally considered to be an obsolete orthodoxy. I will discuss the Turkish experience in detail below and in Chapter 7.

The third strategy, promotion of industrial exports, has been followed by such 'newly industrialized countries' as Taiwan, Hong Kong, Singapore and South Korea, who have achieved a superior growth rate, greater increases in manufacturing output (their share of world industrial output grew from 5.4 per cent in 1963 to 9.7 per cent in 1977, of world manufacturing exports from 2.5 per cent to 7.9 per cent)[3] and an increasing ability to rely on domestic as opposed to foreign capital. This success is due, to a significant degree, to the explicit attention that these countries have accorded to achieving international competitiveness in specific sectors by mastering key technologies; the importance of doing so, regardless of the strategy that is followed, should be obvious from the discussion in Chapter 1.

THE ROLE OF THE IRON AND STEEL SECTOR

These technologies almost always include industrial ones because industrialization, in some form or other, has played and continues to play an important role in the economy of practically every country. Heavy industry is widely considered the key ingredient in modernization, the means of forging static, traditional societies into dynamic modern ones enjoying high per capita incomes and rapid economic growth. Through industrialization, the problems of poverty, ignorance, and overpopulation are to be overcome. As J. Nehru once put it: 'Real progress must ultimately depend on industrialization.'[4]

This faith in industrialization stems from the obvious fact that almost all of the developed, prosperous societies are industrialized nations (Switzerland, New Zealand, Norway and Denmark being the notable exceptions), that developing countries have to import manufactured goods of practically every sort, that their exports of primary products are often subject to adverse price fluctuations, and that these products are often processed abroad then imported by the original country at high cost. Nor should one overlook the significance of national prestige and national security considerations for ruling elites.

Such factors are particularly applicable to decisions involving the iron and steel sector because it possesses a very high symbolic attraction and is widely regarded as representing an important indication of the level of economic progress that has been achieved. In addition, iron and steel are basic requirements for a domestic armaments industry. Not surprisingly, therefore, the desire for iron and steel mills has been so widespread that one former practitioner has noted: 'It has been the experience of almost every official in the administration of economic assistance to developing countries to be asked eventually for funds for technical assistance for the construction of a steel mill.'[5]

In justifying their desire for an iron and steel capability, countries present four major arguments: (1) steel is an important input into every aspect of a developing economy; (2) because of its fundamental importance, steel is a commodity in which countries have to be self sufficient; (3) a supply of steel, at a stable price, is a requisite for national independence and security; (4) local production will permit large savings in scarce foreign exchange.

An emphasis upon iron and steel can also be justified on narrow economic development grounds because this industry ranks extremely high in terms of its catalytic effects on economic activities in other sectors. Its forward and backward linkages are among the highest of any sector.[6] And one noted economist, A. Hirschman, has advanced a striking argument for the establishment of an iron and steel plant in a developing country, an argument that any decision-maker probably finds irresistible. He suggests that even if the plant is not a sound economic project, it may well serve the cause of development anyway:

> The government promotes industrialization by setting up an iron and steel industry . . . power and transportation shortages appear and inadequacies in education become far more apparent than before, so the government is impelled to improve its performance in these fields . . . the construction and operation of the plant and its contribution to industrialization may build up the kind of pressure that will help the government correctly to discharge its 'proper functions' thanks to having first undertaken an improper one.'[7]

Whether the 'hiding hand' can rescue defective projects and also spur governments to adopt sensible priorities will be illuminated by the Turkish case. These are, of course, numerous examples of iron and steel plants that continue to act as a drain upon national economies and which have not served as catalysts for beneficial changes in other sectors.

Finally, one should note that some Third World countries may have been influenced in their decision to develop an iron and steel capability by the attitudes of international organizations. Many agencies of the UN, especially Unido, have actively promoted iron and steel manufacturing. In 1977, to use a recent example, one of its studies argued: 'Efforts to expand the iron and steel sector assume great importance owing to its leading role in the development process.'[8]

The development of the non-western steel industry has also been attributed to a different set of considerations than the ones that emphasize the factors that push LDC elites into developing this sector. This paradigm, discussed in Chapter 1, focuses on the structure of the international economic order and attributes the shift in the global iron and steel industry to the emergence of a new international division of labor, to the attractiveness of low wage rates for international capital. Capital and technology flow to those countries which promise the highest returns to foreign investors, many of whom are US banks. The production of steel in a developing country, in this view, holds major advantages in terms of profitability because of low labor costs, ready access to raw materials, modern plants and a lack of concern with environmental quality. In other words:

> The internationalization of capital – the spread of the multinational corporation, the remarkable upsurge in foreign lending by banks, the creation of unregulated, 'off-shore' money markets – reflects and bolsters a shift in manufacturing in general from the advanced to the underdeveloped capitalist countries; from countries where unions are relatively well developed and wages and conditions relatively high, to countries where unions are outlawed, weak or co-opted, and wages are dismally low.[9]

Whether the development of the Turkish iron and steel industry can be attributed to these factors will become evident as we discuss its growth and the decisions that were made in individual projects.

THE GLOBAL SCENE

Whatever the reasons, recent decades have witnessed a remarkable change in the international structure of the iron and steel industry. At the time of World War II, thirty-two countries produced steel; today the number is over seventy. Seven countries – the US, Great Britain, France, West Germany, Italy, Belgium and Luxembourg – accounted for about 70 per cent of the world's steel output; by the mid seventies, their share had dropped to about 35 per cent. Japan and the Soviet Union had become major producers as had many Third World countries.[10] Today about fifty LDCs possess some kind of iron and steel capability.

This change in global production patterns, to which the rapid emergence of new technologies has contributed greatly, has had important consequences for the USA and other established steel producers. They found themselves forced to compete with new and modern producers in many countries, notably Japan, while their own plants, for a variety of reasons including heavy sunk costs and technological inertia, remained saddled with obsolete equipment. While new facilities producing 10 million tons of steel were built in the USA in the sixties and seventies, for example, Japan built integrated plants with a capacity of 100 million tons. Hence the USA was still producing large quantities of steel with technologies that were obsolete whereas its competitors were using such technologies as the basic oxygen furnace and continuous casting.[11] Accordingly, productivity in US plants was one-third less than in Japan[12] and the US share of steel production has declined markedly from 47 per cent of world production in 1947 to 16 per cent in the mid seventies to 10 per cent in 1986. The Western European countries also suffered, though to a lesser degree; their share declined from 26 per cent in 1950 to 16 per cent in 1986.[13]

Nevertheless, the US iron and steel industry, in the mid eighties, was characterized by two quite distinct trends. On the one hand, part of it is depressed; once proud giant corporations such as Bethlehem Steel now face grave financial difficulties, many plants have closed, thousands of workers laid off, and numerous formerly thriving communities have been devastated. On the other hand, many new steel-making companies which utilize the new electric furnace technology to make steel from scrap metal are thriving; these mini mills are expected to occupy 40 per cent of the American market by the year 2000.[14] A similar trend is not observable in Western Europe, probably because of different industrial policies. There, governments have attempted to rationalize the industry, closing down older integrated plants and guaranteeing the others a specific share of the market which is thus effectively closed to new entrants.[15]

Only a few of the newcomers, about twenty, are major producers; they account for 90 per cent of Third World production which rose from around 4 million metric tonnes in 1950 to 27 million tonnes in 1965 and 92 million tons in 1981.[16] Turkey's contribution to this increase was significant; its industry grew to include private and public enterprises, large integrated plants and small mini mills, the number of which rose from 18 with a total production capacity of over 900,000 tons in 1977 to 20 with a capacity of over 1,300,000 tons by 1983.[17] Overall, Turkey's capacity rose from 300,000 tons in 1960 to 5 million tons in 1985; as a result it became the twenty-fifth largest producer in the world, producing more steel than Sweden and Austria and almost as much as Taiwan. The location of its integrated plants and its raw material deposits is shown in Figure 2.1. Where Turkey stands in comparison to other iron and steel producers is presented in Table 2.1 which is arranged by the country's 1985 rank.

Steel production, however is no longer expanding at the same rate as it has in recent decades because many countries face growing financial constraints, costs have escalated (from about $360 per ton in the sixties to about $650 in the 1970s to well over $1,000 per ton), and external lending agencies are reluctant to support the construction of new plants at a time of world steel surpluses. Hence, steel-making capacity in the LDCs reached about 110 million tons by 1985, a figure that was still nearly double that of 1977 but significantly below Unido projections of 175 million tons by 1985, later reduced to 140 million tons.[18] Unido, however, continues to believe that heavy industrialization is the only viable strategy for development and argues that the developing countries will again soon be assigning a high priority to building iron and steel complexes.[19]

In short, a new international division of labor in steel-making has taken place in recent years.[20] As new producers have emerged throughout the globe and established producers have been forced to accommodate by cutting back, the advantages of the new producers – easy access to raw materials, late entry, cheap labor, regulation free environment, the active backing of the state and, for energy rich countries, favorable energy costs – have been discussed at length, as have the consequences of their emergence. What has not been emphasized adequately, however, is the degree to which only a small

Table 2.1 World iron and steel production (millions of tons)

		1950	1965	1985
1.	USSR	27.3	91.0	154.5
2.	Japan	4.8	41.2	105.3
3.	USA	87.8	119.0	80.4
4.	China	0.7	10.3	46.5
5.	West Germany	12.1	36.8	40.5
6.	Italy	2.4	12.9	23.8
7.	Brazil	0.8	3.0	20.5
8.	France	10.6	19.6	18.8
9.	Poland	2.5	9.1	16.1
10.	United Kingdom	16.6	26.7	15.8
11.	Czechoslovakia	3.2	8.6	15.2
12.	Canada	3.1	9.1	14.7
13.	Belgium-Luxembourg	6.2	13.7	14.6
14.	Romania	0.6	3.4	14.4
15.	Spain	0.8	3.5	14.2
16.	South Korea	—	1.2	13.5
17.	India	1.5	6.4 (ingots)	11.1
18.	South Africa	0.8	3.2	8.6
19.	North Korea	—	1.2	8.4
20.	East Germnay	1.3	4.4	7.9
21.	Mexico	0.4	2.5	7.3
22.	Australia	1.3	5.5	6.4
23.	The Netherlands	2.4	3.1	5.5
24.	Taiwan	—	—	5.1
25.	**Turkey**	**0.1**	**0.6**	**5.0**
26.	Sweden	1.5	4.7	4.8
27.	Austria	0.9	3.2	4.7
28.	Yugoslavia	—	—	4.4
29.	Hungary	1.0	2.5	3.7
30.	Bulgaria	—	0.6	3.0
31.	Venezuela	—	0.6	3.0
32.	Argentina	0.1	1.3	2.9
33.	Finland	0.1	0.4	2.5

Sources: UNIDO, 'Industry', p. 274; 1985 *Annual Report,* p. 13.

number of new producers have mastered iron and steel technologies and are internationally competitive. Many countries find themselves saddled with uneconomical plants; they are incapable of producing steel at the same price and quality as South Korea or Taiwan.

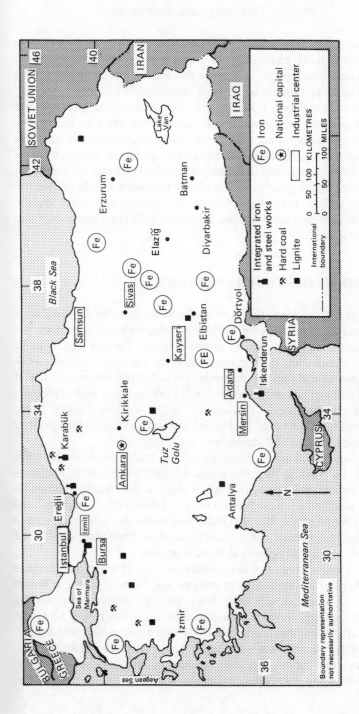

Figure 2.1 Turkey: location of steel mills, iron ore deposits and coal mines.
Adapted from: Federal Research Division, Library of Congress, *Turkey, A Country Study*, 1988.

Many factors have mitigated against the effective transfer of iron and steel making technology to the Third World. These can be divided into two groups: first come the generic problems associated with technology transfer which were discussed in Chapter 1; second, the factors that derive from the specific nature of the industry – its technologies are quite complex, it necessitates much higher investments than many others and, for its successful operation, requires vast quantities of quality raw materials, qualified management, a skilled labor force and an adequate infrastructure, especially in transportation and energy.[21] The rest of this work will illuminate the extent to which Turkey has overcome the generic and sector specific problems and built up a modern, internationally competitive iron and steel industry.

ATATURK'S DEVELOPMENT STRATEGY

It has sought to achieve this position for many decades. Iron and steel have been the backbone of Turkish development strategy since the founding of the Republic over sixty years ago. Turkish leaders of all political persuasions have believed that the nation's economic well-being, power and prestige depended on industrialization, and that if Turkey were to become a modern, self-reliant state it had to produce its own iron and steel. The creator of the modern Turkish state, Mustapha Kemal Ataturk, held this view and accorded a high priority to building an iron and steel plant.

Although the Turkish heritage can be traced back to the sixth century, the Turkish Republic is a new nation forged out of the ashes of the Ottoman Empire, that great state whose boundaries, at its zenith, included all of the Middle East and North Africa (except Iran) and much of Europe. It was transformed into a modern western state by Mustapha Kemal who implemented a dramatic program of political, social and economic transformation.

Such a transformation was an immense task. The Ottoman Empire had collapsed as a result of its exertions and ultimate defeat in World War I. The country was underdeveloped, its people exhausted by years of fighting, most of its meager resources destroyed. Only the largest towns had been affected by Western values and technology most of the society was still highly traditional. Mustapha Kemal however, one of the greatest leaders of the twentieth century embarked upon a sweeping program of modernization designed to change every aspect of Turkish life. He secularized the society, replaced the Ottoman script with the Latin alphabet, eliminated the visual distinction between Muslim and non-Muslim by the passage of the hat law and replaced Islamic laws with European codes. He expanded and modernized the educational system, brought women into political life and, though he ruled through a single party, the republican People's Party (RPP), even attempted to democratize the polity.[22]

In the economic sphere, Ataturk emphasized industrialization and the private sector; during the 1920s several laws to encourage industrial development were passed but, though some progress was made, the great world depression made it obvious that Turkey could not rely on its exports which were almost completely agricultural and that the private sector was too weak to serve as the motor for economic growth. Accordingly, in the thirties, economic policy changed and Turkey became one of the first countries in the non-Communist world to initiate a program of planned development with an emphasis on state action, which was called 'Etatism', to achieve industrialization. In 1932 an Office of Industry was established; the first five-year industrialization plan was prepared in 1933. It stressed textiles (36 per cent of total investments), iron and steel (23 per cent), chemicals, paper and consumer goods and accepted the principle of protecting infant industries. The second five-year plan, published in 1938, accented the production of capital goods. During these years, the weak private sector expanded somewhat, particularly in such areas as food processing, plastics and metal working. The basic strategy remained one of state directed industrialization and import substitution in order to achieve national independence.[23]

THE KARABÜK PLANT

Background

Even before any plan had been drawn up, Ataturk and his colleagues were concerned with building an iron and steel sector. As early as 1923, the new regime discussed the possibility of utilizing the country's mineral resources to support an iron and steel plant, and, in 1925, commissioned an Austrian professor of mining, Dr Granigg, to carry out the necessary analyses. He concluded that a plant could and should be built but that it should rely on imported inputs of iron ore and coking coal. These conclusions were not acceptable to a government seeking to develop its own resources; in 1926 Belgian and German experts were brought in to carry out additional studies. The same year, the Minister of Trade submitted a report to the Prime Minister supporting the establishment of an iron and steel plant and the Grand National Assembly enacted a law endorsing the project and establishing a General Directorate for Iron and Steel. Various attempts were made to implement this law, including consideration of a joint venture with a foreign company – a powerful indicator, given the government's strong nationalist feelings and commitment to absolute national independence, of its eagerness – but this and all other initiatives failed. The Directorate was abolished in 1928.[24]

Despite this set back, the military, which strongly supported construction of an iron and steel complex for reasons of national security, called for additional analyses and for the immediate construction of a plant to meet its pressing needs. Soon thereafter a small facility consisting of two 20-ton capacity Siemens Martin (open hearth) furnaces and a 2-ton capacity electric arc furnace was built in Kirrikale, a small town near Ankara. Production began in 1932; capacity was subsequently increased to 62,000 tons of hot metal and 50,000 tons of ingots and blooms.[25] The plant did not, however, produce enough steel to satisfy either the military which continued to press for the construction of a large integrated complex or those leaders who were committed to the strategy of heavy industrialization.

During these years, Turkey enjoyed friendly relations with the USSR and, in 1932, invited a Soviet delegation to carry out a detailed feasibility study of an iron and steel plant. Its report concluded that a plant was both necessary (it would serve as a catalyst for industrial development) and economically feasible. Its market analysis, based on import statistics, estimated domestic demand to be 150,000 tons a year and increasing rapidly. Accordingly, it recommended a plant with a blast furnace of 300 tons daily capacity which would be fed with a mixture of domestic iron ore and (two-thirds) and scrap metal (one-third). It also suggested that a chemical industry could be built near the plant to take advantage of the coke ovens' by-products.[26] The report strengthened the feeling, shared by all the key political leaders that, regardless of the obstacles, an iron and steel plant represented a fundamental component of the country's development. Discussions continued both domestically and with foreign experts including an American mission that came to study the country's economy and with the German Krupp company which sponsored additional studies. In 1935, the state industrial bank, the Sümerbank, was specificially entrusted with the task of implementing the project and it too carried out a number of studies which showed that even if the plant had to rely on imported iron ore, the foreign exchange savings would amount to TL 9 million per year.[27] Accordingly, the sum of TL 10 million, later increased to TL 30 million was allocated to the project and negotiations were begun with Germany and Great Britain. Fearing that the Krupp company would get the bid, and hence that German influence in Turkey would increase, the British government worked actively to support the H. A. Brassert company. It offered to provide technical experts at no charge and to give two credits, one of £10 million for the plant and another of £6 million for military equipment.[28] Even the royal family was pressed into service. The Prince of Wales made a yachting trip to Istanbul where he met Ataturk.[29] The Germans also made great efforts to obtain the contract and a preliminary agreement according to which Krupp would build the plant was actually initialled but the final contract went to the British firm, because of Ankara's fear of becoming too dependent on Germany, to which it already possessed extensive economic ties.[30]

The formal agreement was signed on 10 November 1936; construction began on 1 March 1938. The contract called for a turnkey project to be designed and built by the British company at a cost of £3 million, about $15 an ingot ton for a plant with a capacity of 175,000 tons. The Turkish investment amounted to TL 33 million; another TL 17 million were subsequently spent on various additional components including a supersphosphate and sulfuric acid plant which began production on 15 June 1944.[31] Work proceeded rapidly, spurred by the gathering clouds of war, and the first components, the coke ovens, were completed by July 1939, the blast furnaces in September 1939, the steel shop by late 1940 and the rolling mills by the end of 1941.[32]

Turkey's first venture into iron and steel had finally been achieved after many years of planning and striving. But, was the plant designed and the technology transferred in such a manner as to stimulate eocnomic growth and fulfill the dreams of its elites?

The design issues

Karabük was conceived as an integrated iron and steel plant. Such a facility is a huge operation; it encompasses all of the activities required to produce steel. It consumes enormous amounts of raw materials – especially coal and iron ore, materials which have to be shipped in – involves various operations which yield several different kinds of products, each of which has to be moved around the plant, and produces large tonnages of finished goods which have to be transported to market. These characteristics require that the mill be located in an area with plenty of space, lots of water (an iron and steel plant requires large amounts of water for its operations), and a good transportation system that makes the plant easily accessible to raw materials and markets. Since transportation by sea is the cheapest way by which goods can be shipped in large quantities, most modern iron and steel plants are sited on a coast.[33] The location of an iron and steel plant, like that of any other project, is, as I noted in Chapter 1, of fundamental importance.

Unfortunately, Karabük's location met few of these criteria though discussions of where to build the plant can be traced back to 1925 when the first studies were undertaken. Both the Russian and the American delegations had concluded that Ereğli, a small port on the Black Sea coast, was the most suitable location. Economic considerations, however, were secondary to strategic ones; the General Staff insisted that the site had to be out of range of hostile warships operating in the Black Sea. The military leaders settled on a valley 100 kilometers inland where thirteen families resided in a small village called Karabük, because of, according to an official source, its proximity to the coal fields at Zonguldak, its location on a rail-line, its potential attractiveness to the workforce (sic), its geological suitability, and its closeness to the coast where iron ore would be shipped.[34]

The site's transportation problems were further aggravated when, in 1936, after work on the plant had begun, an important body of iron ore was discovered near Sivas, a town 600 miles from Karabük, in the course of the construction of a rail line to Erzerum.[35] Transportation facilities thus assumed an even greater significance but these were not accorded a high priority. Only a single-track rail-line linked the plant to its coal source, 60 miles away, to its iron ore deposits located ten times further away, and to its markets many miles distant. It could meet the heavy demands placed upon it only with difficulty and the plant often had to contend with inadequate supplies of raw materials and was saddled permanently with high transportation costs. Further offsetting the supposed advantages of the site was the small size of the valley. As the plant operated over the years its slag took up more and more of the limited ground available and less and less space remained for expansion and the addition of ancillary units which could increase he productivity of the plant. Today there is no space to build an ore preparation plant there. Moreover, because of the topography of the site, pollution became a growing problem that was expensive and difficult to deal with.[36]

An iron and steel plant is not only large, it is complex as well because its numerous activities have to be integrated into a coherent enterprise. Essentially there are four basic stages of production in an integrated plant: (1) raw materials preparation, (2) raw iron manufacturing, (3) the conversion of iron to steel, and (4) the finishing of the steel products in the rolling mills. Various technologies are available for each of these activities so that the design process involves numerous decisions.[37] In this case, these decisions were shaped by the available financing and the size of the estimated market, both of which dictated that a small plant be built at a low capital cost.

The first set of decisions involved the acquisition and preparation of raw materials, especially coal and iron ore, which are consumed in huge quantities.[38] Coal, or at least part of it, is washed, usually at the mine, to improve its quality by removing clays and rocks. At the mill it is transformed into coke, the fuel and reactive agent required for use in the blast furnace. This takes place in the coke ovens where the coal is heated, without air, to a temperature (2,000°F) that eliminates its non-carbon content. The process produces considerable quantities of gas which can be used as fuel and from which such valuable by-products as tar, ammonia, sulfur, light oil and phenol can be removed. If the coal possesses a high ash content (18 per cent for the Zonguldak fields), coke with a low carbon content will be produced and the productivity of the blast furnace will be lowered significantly.

The second basic input, iron ore, also varies in quality. Good ore has a high iron content and possesses few impurities such as sulfur. The newly discovered Divriği iron ore deposits were of varying quality. The best had an iron content of over 60 per cent but this vein was expected to run out by the mid fifties; the remainder of the deposit, which totalled over 30 million tons, contained a very high percentage of sulfur.[39]

The third essential raw material is a flux, usually limestone or dolomite, which combines with the silica in the lime and coke to produce slag. Without the flux, the furnace would soon be filled with silica ash. A plentiful supply of limestone was readily available.

The second set of activities, the manufacture of raw iron, is carried out in a blast furnace. There, the iron oxide is reduced to raw iron by being subjected to high temperatures. Coke (produced in the coke ovens) fuels the furnace and provides the carbon for the reduction. Productivity is dependent upon the size of the furnace, the quality of the ore and coke, the sizing of the material and the chemical analyses that are performed. The process involves blowing preheated air under pressure into the bottom of the blast furnace, igniting the coke, and thus forming carbon monoxide which combines with the oxygen in the iron ore which has been dumped into the top of the furnace by skip cars or, in modern plants, by conveyors, to yield carbon dioxide, melted iron and a cap of molten slag. The gas is drawn off the top and used to heat the incoming blast and for other purposes, the slag skimmed off and transported by slag ladles (thimbles) to railroad cars, and the hot metal is tapped from the bottom and transported by iron ladles into railroad cars. Water cooling is an essential part of the process; cooling towers for the blast furnace consume large amounts of water each day. The raw iron may be sold cast in the form of 'pig' but is usually used to manufacture steel in the plant.

The Brassert Company's technological choices were influenced to some extent by a concern with the future operation of the plant. It therefore tended to select equipment which was relatively simple (and inexpensive) and could be repaired easily. Instead of building one large 120-foot furnace, two blast furnaces, each with a capacity of 300 tons a day, were constructed so that production could be maintained in case one had to be shut down, a not unlikely event in a country that had never operated such a plant before. This proved to be a wise decision because of the difficulties created by the war. Overall, the two furnaces had a capacity of about 300,000 tons of pig iron per year, making Turkey the fifteenth largest producer of iron in the world at the time.

The third activity in an integrated plant involves the transformation of the hot metal into steel. This occurs in the steel melt shop where the carbon content of the molten iron is reduced and the impurities which remain are oxidized. Today three processes are available. The first is the open hearth furnace (Siemens Martin) which had displaced the venerable Bessemer process by the 1900s. It consists of a large rectangular room with openings at each end which are used to inject air and evacuate gases. Next to these are fuel oil burners or inlet gas pipes. The entire room sits on four chambers where air is heated. The charge of molten pig iron, scrap, ferro-alloys, flux and iron ore sits in a large shallow furnace.

The second, the basic oxygen furnace (BOF), was first introduced in the fifties as the LD converter, named after Linz and Donawitz, the two Austrian works which built it. The technology involves the injection of oxygen into a charge of melted iron and steel scrap contained in a cylindrical vessel (lined with refractories) open at one end. The vessel is tilted for charging and brought to a vertical position. Originally the oxygen was injected from the top; later refinements permitted it to be inserted through a lance inserted in the bottom or side of the furnace. Fluxes are then added. Various materials may be also be added to produce special steels. Temperature readings and analyses of slag and refined metal samples indicate the composition of the steel. When the desired quality has been achieved, the vessel is tilted and its contents poured into a ladle. Two vessels are required so that one can always be available for use while the other is being relined with new refractories.[40]

The third and newest method, the electric arc furnace, uses electricity to melt and refine a cold charge. This process makes for flexible operation and close quality control and is, therefore, used to manufacture speciality and carbon steels. The process requires very large quantities of energy and places enormous demands upon the electrical system.

The Brassert Company installed four 65-ton Siemens Martin furnaces, the commonly used technology of the time, which could produce 150,000 tons of steel billets a year. These were later replaced by 75-ton units which increased capacity to 180,000 tons.

The final set of activities involves the transformation of the raw steel into finished products. This takes place in three steps – casting, hot forming and finishing. Until the seventies, casting was accomplished by pouring the molten steel into ingot molds. These ingots which weigh up to twenty tons, would be reheated in soaking pits and run through the primary breakdown mill which, by gradually compressing the hot ingot between rotating rollers, strengthens the steel, reduces it and forms it into intermediate shapes – blooms and slabs.

Since World War II, a new process called continuous casting has eliminated some of these steps (ingots, casting, reheating and ingots in the soaking pits, and their conversion into semi-finished form in the primary breakdown mills) because the molten steel is transferred directly from the ladle into copper molds which are water cooled and then into an area where it is flame cut into the desired length.

The next step, hot forming, represents the last phase of the steel–making process. It can be accomplished in three different types of operations – forging, extrusion or rolling. Forging involves hot forming between dies of various configurations. Extrusion requires pushing the metal through a chamber with an opening of the desired shape. Rolling – by far the most common and the most important method of hot forming steel – is the almost exclusive process in manufacturing flat shapes such as steel plates and sheets.

The basic intermediate forms of steel are either slabs which are used to produce flat products (plate, strip) or blooms which are square or rectangular and are processed into heavy structural steels. Billets, which are generally square, are produced from blooms and are converted to wire, rods and light structurals. Bars, structurals, rails and plates need only little rolling, but if the finished product is to be sheet, the slabs are first hot rolled into strips and subsequently finished in a cold rolling mill. Wire is manufactured from rods by 'drawing' them successively through a series of dies, with inter-mediate heat treatments. Seamless tubes are made from blooms by piercing and a series of drawing operations. Welded pipe, however, is made from hot rolled strip (skelp), or hot rolled plate, by one of several welding processes.

Rolling mills for flat shapes are of two basic types – plate mills and strip mills which deliver their product recoiled. Modern heavy plate mills are usually of the reversing types and consist sometimes of one- or two-stand machines, more commonly four-high, i.e. each stand consists of two work rolls which actually deform the strip and which are, in turn, supported by two very much larger back-up rolls. Hot strip mills and combination mills, which can produce lighter plate, are multi-stand installations and typically consist of a four-stand roughing train and a six- or seven-stand finishing train. Hot strip mills are normally continuous, one-way-through machines. Heavy plate mills are followed by water-cooled runout tables and cooling beds, hot strip mills by water-cooled runout tables and recoilers. Coils from ten to forty tons in weight may be produced. Both types of mills are supplied with slabs, reheated in specialized slab-reheating furnaces to the metallurgically desirable rolling temperature. Control of metal temperature throughout the rolling operation (e.g. slab, roughing, finishing and coiling temperatures) is an essential parameter in developing a final product with the desired properties.

An oxide coating, known as scale, forms on the surface of the steel strip during hot rolling, and has to be removed if the hot rolled coils are to undergo further processing into cold-reduced projects. This operation is performed on 'pickling' lines where the strip is immersed in hydrochloric or sulfuric acid baths. It is then rinsed, dried, trimmed to the desired final width by means of rotary-knife machines commonly referred to as side-trimmers, oiled and recoiled for further processing. Hot rolled picked strip may be sold as coils, or sheared to sheet length to be sold as 'hot rolled, picked and oiled' product.

Most hot rolled strip is further processed in multi-stand tandem, or single-stand reversing, cold reduction mills, in order to reduce the thickness and to impart superior properties to the metal. The end products may be tinplate or cold rolled sheets which may be further processed by annealing (heating the cold reduced steel to soften it), skin-pass or temper rolling to improve the surface and flatness, and coating quality. Sheet products may also be galvanized.

The Karabük plant was designed to produce large sections and heavy plates. Accordingly three rolling mills and a plate mill with a total capacity of 70,000 tons of steel products a year were installed.

Generally, the individual choices of machinery were sound ones [41] but the plant suffered from two significant design shortcomings. First, its various elements did not comprise an integrated whole. The capacity of the blast furnaces (350,000 tons) was double that of the steel shop which could produce 150,000 tons, which in turn was double that of the rolling mills. Second, the products which the plant was designed to fabricate were not those for which Turkey had the greatest need, construction and related steel products. [42]

The impact issues

Since the decision process was driven by considerations of national security, political symbolism and a specific view of the modernization process, the impact aspects received only minimal attention. Essentially the available resources determined the kind of plant that could be built and little attention was paid to the economic aspects of the project. Costs and benefits and trade-offs were never analyzed in any sophisticated manner because of the assumptions that were involved. Its construction would save precious foreign exchange, serve as a catalyst for the country's development, promote national security and serve as a powerful symbol of the great strides that the Republic had achieved. Questions of regional development, pollution and the like, as was the case everywhere in those years, were not part of the range of discourse.

Management issues

Managerial issues are of great importance in any transfer but they are especially critical when a 'greenfield' transfer is involved. In the Turkey of the thirties and forties skilled administrators and technical workers were in short supply; problems of effectively utilizing and maintaining machinery were endemic to all enterprises. Nor did the prevailing organizational culture promote the kind of harmonious relationship between management and workers that leads to high productivity and quality. The World Bank's mission, which studied Turkey's economy in 1948, defined these issues as follows:[43]

> One of the greatest deficiencies in Turkish enterprise is lack of managerial competence. This element is essential to efficient operation of any undertaking . . . We mean by management, not only the top-level officials, but also all levels of supervisors, foremen and crew bosses. In Turkey, and particularly in state enterprises, those who direct labor have been preoccupied with technology and rarely know the workers' jobs. Between top management and workers there is at present an almost complete lack of liaison.

This was certainly the situation at Karabük where administrative issues of all kinds were not accorded the attention that they require. The Turkish Iron and Steel Works was organized as a state enterprise to run the plant; many Turks were sent over to Great Britain to visit various steel works, but this arrangement did not suffice to provide the skilled manpower to operate the plant. The British firm ran it for 18 months with managers and foremen from the UK, along British lines. Each expatriate had a Turkish counterpart who was expected to learn by watching and doing. These informal arrangements were not supplemented by any kind of formal training program.[44] Nevertheless, the on the job training did ultimately create a labor force that could operate the plant.

It proved more difficult to train professional staff and limited managerial competence adversely affected such areas as financial control, marketing and maintenance in the fifties and after. By 1950 63 Turkish engineers were employed by Karabük but many qualified persons left Karabük as soon as they could find positions elsewhere because of poor salaries and inadequate housing. As a result poor management practices continued to limit the plan's effectiveness for many years. Productivity was also hampered by the continuing stratification and rigid hierarchy within the plant. Administrative costs were high, labor efficiency low, and the costs and quality of the finished products not internationally competitive.[45]

The outbreak of World War II greatly exacerbated the normal problems that are encountered in bringing a new plant, especially one involving a 'greenfield transfer', into production. Needed parts and raw materials such as refractories could be obtained only with difficulty and foreign and local managers struggled to achieve anticipated levels of production. To do so they often had to improvise; in one case, chrome ore was ground and mixed with other materials to make ladles and doors. Only one blast furnace operated during the war, the second, though completed in 1939, had to be stripped to keep the other running. Even after the war ended, necessary supplies were unavailable for some time. Adverse weather further hampered the start-up and operation of the plant. One winter was so cold that the river froze making it impossible to generate power.[46] That the plant operated at all under these conditions is a tribute to those involved; that it produce the tonnages listed in Table 2.2 is remarkable.

Table 2.2 Production of the Karabük plant (tons)

Year	Blast furnace	Steel mills	Rolling mills
1941	86,000	33,000	3,000
1944	70,000	60,000	41,000

Source: Muntz, op. cit., p. 52.

Evaluation

Under these circumstances it should not be surprising that Turkey's first venture into iron and steel yielded a plant that was neither commercially profitable nor the hoped for contributor to the country's economic development. Why this should have been the case is by no means clear. The plant had, after all, been the subject of numerous studies by experts from many countries. The location decision is understandable if one accepts the assumptions that the Turkish military elite made concerning the nature of modern warfare. What is more difficult to explain is why the infrastructural aspects were neglected, why the plant was designed with such imbalances, and, above all, why it was designed to produce the particular kinds of products. A considerable part of the responsibility must rest with the foreign experts, apparently with the Krupp Company which provided the basic design for the plant, a design that the Brassert Company was expected to adhere to. Why did Krupp generate such a design? One expert has cynically suggested that Germany wished to continue its steel exports to Turkey.[47] But if this is true, why did the Turkish planners have such faith in the German company as to follow its design to closely? Whatever the truth of this matter, the Karabük case demonstrates the importance of a domestic knowledge base and the difficulty of achieving a successful transfer. Even if a high degree of technological mastery had been achieved, the plant, because of its design, would always remain a deficient project.

The story of Karabük was, unfortunately, replicated in numerous other technology transfer projects that were launched during these years. Scarce capital and manpower resources made only a limited industrialization possible, and that which was so painfully achieved was not as productive as might have been anticipated owing, in large part, to weak project planning and poor implementation.[48] Moreover, the strategy itself has been severely criticized for its internal contradictions – promoting monopoly at the expense of private initiative and entrepreneurship, creating a new state elite that came to represent its own interests as those of the state, and establishing a situation wherein the majority of the populace, feeling that its interests diverged from those of the ruling elite, would turn to ideologies, sacred and secular, that conflicted with those advocated by state elites.[49] And, as we shall see, this situation did indeed come to pass, though whether such an outcome was inevitable or whether it occurred as a result of subsequent political developments is debatable.

THE EMERGENCE OF A MULTI-PARTY SYSTEM

During World War II, the Turkish government pursued a strict policy of neutrality. Looking forward to the end of the conflict, it prepared a plan for future economic development which continued to emphasize heavy industrialization, including the establishment of a second iron and steel plant. When the war ended, the Turkish government hoped that the USA would provide the necessary financing to enable it to industrialize rapidly and asked for a $500 million loan but the USA provided only $53 million through 1947. Then, because of the growth of the cold war, Washington established a program of aid to Greece and Turkey and in 1948 initiated the Marshall Plan. The Turkish government again hoped that it could obtain financing for its ambitious program of industrialization which called for the investment of $100 million per year.[50]

As the USA became actively involved in Turkish affairs it sent a number of experts to evaluate the state of the Turkish economy and identify ways in which it could further its development. The most famous of these missions, headed by M. W. Thornburg (1946), strongly criticized the past strategy of state-sponsored heavy industrialization and argued for the support of private enterprise and an emphasis on agriculture and infrastructural development. A World Bank study undertaken two years later reached similar conclusions and argued strongly against the further development of heavy industry.[51]

Thornburg was especially critical of the Karabük plant, calling it an 'economic monstrosity', a 'white elephant', an 'industrial Moloch' which consumed scarce resources of capital, skills and materials which could have been better spent elsewhere. His report dwelt on all the shortcomings discussed above – its poor location, the raw material situation, the imbalances of the design, the type of products, as well as their poor quality and high prices. He recommended that the steel producing elements of the plant be closed, a recommendation that he himself recognized to be unrealistic in view of the government's continuing commitment to an autarchic development strategy based on heavy industry, a commitment strengthened by the economic difficulties it had encountered during the war.[52]

Rather than follow his advice, Ankara moved as rapidly as it could to remedy some of Karabük's major shortcomings. Its 1947 Development Plan allocated 3.4 per cent of total expenditures of TL 3.8 billion to improving its performance.[53] An oxygen plant was constructed and a 3.5-ton electric arc furnace was placed in operation. The second blast furnace which had been completed in 1939 was finally inaugurated in 1950; in 1952 a sinter plant and a second battery of coke ovens came on stream, and a pipe factory began production in 1954.

While these developments were underway, the domestic political scene was being transformed. The changes that had occurred in Turkey since the founding of the republic led to the emergence of new groups and intra elite conflict over the future of the state. For various reasons, including the desirability of gaining Western support, the expectations that the ruling Republican People's Party with its strong institutional base and proud heritage would remain the dominant party, and a genuine acceptance of Ataturk's ideal of democracy, President Inonu made a momentous decision. He declared on 1 November 1945 that the country had achieved political maturity and expressed the hope that an opposition party would be founded. Shortly thereafter the Democrat Party (DP) was formally established by four leading members of the RPP to contest the elections which were held in July 1946. It elected 61 deputies and promptly raised charges of fraud, calling for reforms to ensure fair and honest elections. The next election, held in 1950, was without precedent and marked a turning point in Turkey's political development. Eighty-nine per cent of the eligible voters went to the polls and the DP, which had established a powerful and effective organization throughout the country won 54 per cent of the vote, electing 416 deputies out of a total of 487. The RPP won 40 per cent of the vote and 76 seats. It was turned out of office after 27 years.

Many groups united under the banner of the DP to voice their discontent with the RPP and its policies. Joining the business community, who demanded a move away from etatism to private enterprise, were intellectuals who wanted democracy, religious conservatives who hoped for a return to Islamic principles, elements of the rural elite, and the peasantry which felt neglected and abused by a tyrannical administration – in short, all those persons and groups (and after 27 years there were many) who harbored resentments against or who had suffered from or disapproved of the policies of the RPP.

Once in power, the DP moved to carry out its campaign promises. It embarked upon an ambitious program of economic development, financed to a large degree by US aid. At first, its development strategy differed from that of its predecessors. Various institutional measures were taken to encourage private enterprise, including the establishment of an industrial development bank and the passage of a foreign private investment law in August 1951. Moreover, the emphasis was now upon agriculture and production boomed as a result of the price supports, the mechanization of farming, and very favorable weather. The highway building program and the concomitant availabilty of transportation and new communications facilitated the shipment of inputs to and produce from the rural areas and integrated the country as never before.

Quite naturally, the DP won an even larger victory in the 1954 election than four years earlier. It emerged with almost 57 per cent of the vote and 503 seats as compared with the RPP which won only 35 per cent of the vote and 31 seats in parliament. Now a series of poor harvests combined with a fall in world prices for agricultural produce led to a profound foreign exchange crisis and forced the government to reconsider its development strategy. It made two fundamental changes. First, it expanded its investments in the public sector, thus abandoning its previous commitment to private enterprise. Second, believing that agricultural output had expanded as far as it could, it switched to an emphasis on industrialization within an import substitution framework.

Essentially, it returned to the development strategy of the Ataturk era, though with one difference. Menderes was convinced that his electoral fortunes depended on economic prosperity. Accordingly, from then on, he determined to achieve economic growth at all costs and his government sought to maximize investments in as many fields as possible, as quickly as possible, using whatever source of financing was available, including inflation.[54] Two other factors influenced the policy process. Much of the financing took the shape of US foreign aid and the pattern of US foreign aid appropriations made it desirable for Turkey to spend fully any given year's appropriations to ensure that the next year's levels not be cut. Second, although the USA tried consistently to moderate his policies, Menderes believed, probably correctly, that the USA could not afford to let Turkey's economy disintegrate and would always come to his rescue.[55]

Given such a policy process few if any projects could emerge as a result of detailed, rational analyses; short-term political considerations, primarily a desire to win votes, usually dictated all project decisions. As a result, inefficiencies in terms of site selections, production techniques, price policies, market appraisals, linkages and infrastructural developments were commonplace. One expert has summarized the situation as follows: 'The economic advance of the 1950s . . . simply proceeded in an unplanned, uncoordinated manner on as many fronts as possible.'[56]

Some fronts were accorded a high priority – sugar, cement, textiles, paper, and, quite naturally, iron and steel where Menderes continued and expanded the Inonu government's previous efforts to modernize Karabük and increase its output. He initiated a second major expansion which affected all parts of the plant. A third, large blast furnace and ancillary facilities increased blast furnace capacity to 600,000 tons per year, a third battery of coke ovens raised coke production capacity to 980,000 tons and the sinter plant was improved to increase its capacity from 225,000 to 475,000 tons per year. The four 75-ton Siemens Martin furnaces were replaced by six 150-ton machines thus raising steel melt capacity by over 300 per cent to 600,000 tons per year.[57] New rolling mills were also installed, including a continuous one with a capacity of 230,000 tons, which increased production to a total of 530,000 tons per year. In addition machine and steel construction shops were added or expanded. As a result of these and the other post World War II investments which totalled over TL 1.5 billion, the major imbalances within the plant were eliminated or greatly reduced and production rose dramatically, as is shown in Table 2.3.

Table 2.3 Production of the Karabük plant 1940–70 (000 tons)

Year	Coke ovens	Blast furnace	Steel mill	Rolling mills
1940	100	82	38	9.1
1945	227	71.4	65	48
1950	308	118	92	76
1955	508	202	190	150
1960	529	248	270	215
1965	728	426	435	381
1970	823	601	620	516

Source: Karabük, p. 12; TDÇI, pp.26 ff.

Given the political context and the limited level of technological mastery that had been achieved at Karabük, one should not be surprised that this expansion, which boosted Karabük's output considerably, was not managed properly and encountered numerous problems. Moreover, the plant remained plagued by administrative shortcomings of all kinds which limited its efficiency in numerous ways. Its deficiencies were enhanced by the same problems that plagued the other State Economic Enterprises, including politicization which aggravated the tendency of qualified administrators to seek employment elsewhere (in a ten-year period, seven different men served as director) and expanded its labor force unecessarily.[58]

The government exhibited little concern with issues of quality and productivity. Instead, always eager to increase production, especially of iron and steel, it focused its efforts on establishing the second iron and steel facility that had been called for in the 1944 plan.[59] On 13 May 1955, Prime Minister Menderes formally declared his intention of doing so with the aid of private capital and parliament passed Law No. 6538 which, in Article II, stated that the Turkish iron and steel industry should produce all kinds of iron and iron products.[60]

The hope that private domestic and foreign capital would finance the plant was not to be realized easily in view of the country's serious economic difficulties. Balance of payment problems were already visible in 1952, and as early as 1954 relations with the World Bank, which was unwilling to finance more projects until the government moderated its economic policy, began to deteriorate rapidly. Ankara complained of external interference in its domestic affairs and even asked the World Bank to terminate its permanent mission. Menderes proved equally insensitive to warnings from other sources for he believed that Turkey was so important to the west that it was bound to be rescued. He therefore continued his policy of growth at any cost and, not surprisingly, the economic situation deteriorated even further.[61]

By 1958 a state of crisis had been reached; the World Bank remained aloof and the Western countries were unwilling to provide further assistance unless he initiated a major change in policy. He finally yielded in August 1958, accepting a stabilization program which called for additional aid to Turkey in return for anti-inflationary measures. This policy, which ran counter to Menderes' perceptions of how development could best be achieved, lasted less than a year.

This was the context in which he sought to implement his cherished dream of a second iron and steel plant. For its realization he was dependent on foreign aid, an area controlled by the Ministry of Foreign Affairs headed by a close associate, Mr F. R. Zorlu. In 1952 he was assigned control of the independent international economic agency that had been established to work with foreign donors and charged with obtaining as much aid as possible.[62] He was personally responsible for successfully negotiating the proposed new iron and steel plant with the USA which, though concerned about the state of the Turkish economy and the impact of such a large project upon it, finally agreed to provide the necessary financial assistance. I shall discuss why it did so and all the other aspects of this project in Chapter 3.

THE ARRIVAL OF NATIONAL PLANNING

The proliferation of weak projects and the steady deterioration of the economic situation aroused considerable opposition. Prime Minister Menderes reacted by imposing various curbs on his opponents. Feelings ran high and the country became increasingly polarized between those who supported Menderes and those who believed that he was planning to establish a dictatorship. Finally, in May 1960, the military overthrew his government. One of its first steps was to rationalize economic policy-making by establishing the State Planning Office and initiating national planning. It also undertook a review of all of the Menderes government's projects to determine which made economic sense. It approved 196, cancelled 35, and postponed a decision on another 65. Some of those which it approved were acknowledged to be of doubtful economic validity but were nevertheless accepted because of potentially mitigating factors such as heavy sunk costs. The iron and steel plant (ERDEMIR) was not only approved, it was accorded 'first priority for completion'.[63] Designed to produce 268,000 tons of flat products plus another 110,000 tons of steel ingots, it was expected to cost $245 million. Construction began in May 1961; the plant was completed 36 months later. The opening ceremony was held in May 1965.

Meanwhile, the newly established State Planning Office was busily analyzing the country's overall economic situation and preparing its First Five Year Plan (1963–1967). In that and in each of the subsequent plans the traditional policy of industrialization through import substitution, with the public sector playing the leading role, was enshrined; potential export possibilities received minimal attention. And, in the seventies, the emphasis came to be placed increasingly upon capital intensive projects that would meet the country's needs for the products of heavy industry.

Iron and steel, along with aluminium and petrochemicals, remained one of the priority sectors. Estimates were made, in the First Plan, of demand for particular items over the next fifteen years, of production quantities and values, and even of export possibilities. Demand was expected to rise from 560,000 tons in 1962 to 1,800,000 tons in 1977, but this increase would be met by the expanded capacity at Karabük which was scheduled to come on stream in 1964 and the output of ERDEMIR. Accordingly, after 1965, 'only limited quantities of products of special quality and size will be imported. In order to utilize fully the facilities of the sector, export possibilities must be sought.'[64] The only problem areas cited were raw materials (the high ash content of the coal made it difficult to produce high quality coke) and the high costs of production which should be reduced to international levels.[65]

This optimistic scenario was soon proven completely wrong. Actual production never reached the expected levels and imports greatly exceeded estimates as demand grew faster than anticipated. Moreover, detailed new studies for the Second Five Year Plan (1968–1972) showed that per capita consumption would rise from 32 to 130 kg[66] so that demand, which the First Plan had estimated at 560,000 tons in 1962 and 1.8 million tons in 1977, was now calculated to reach 765,000 tons in 1962, 3.7 million tons in 1977 and 7 million tons in 1982. The two existing integrated mills, Karabük and ERDE-MIR, would not have the capacity after 1968 to meet the country's needs, especially for the kinds of items that Karabük produced. Accordingly, the plan called for the construction of a third plant to produce sections, rails, bars and rounds, and the further expansion of ERDEMIR's capacity in order to avoid a heavy dependence on imports. The planners acknowledged that costs of production were still higher than international levels, and called for studies on ways to deal with this problem and for the establishment of a board that would coordinate the activities of the plants, sponsor research and collect relevant data.[67]

The Second Five Year Plan was prepared while Prime Minister Suleyman Demirel was in power. Having emerged as the leader of the Justice Party, the successor to the Democratic Party of former Prime Minister Adnan Menderes, he had led it to victory in the 1965 elections. As committed to the strategy of heavy industrialization as any of his predecessors, he acted forcefully to implement these projects. He opened negotiations with the USA and others to expand ERDEMIR and reached an agreement according to which the USA and Turkey agreed to spend almost $30 million to increase the plant's capacity to 435,000 tons of flat products. Subsequently, the World Bank agreed to participate in a massive new expansion project that would raise annual crude steel capacity to 2 million tons at an estimated cost of almost $300 million. I shall discuss these projects in Chapters 4 and 5.

Plans were also laid for yet another major modernization program at Karabük, this one costing over TL2.6 billion. Implemented from

1972 on, this project, which I shall discuss in Chapter 6, was designed to increase blast furnace capacity to 900,000 tons, steel shop capacity to 1 million tons and produce 850,000 tons of finished goods per year.

Prime Minister Demirel also strove vigorously to obtain foreign financing for the third integrated plant that the Second Plan had called for. The USA (which was already committed to ERDEMIR's expansion) and other western governments were unwilling to provide support so he turned to the USSR which, wishing to improve its relations with Turkey, had indicated that it would be willing to help finance as many as seven industrial projects. The iron and steel plant quickly emerged as one of these, the formal understanding being signed in October 1969. Originally designed as a plant of 1 million ton capacity to be located in Iskenderun, the project (ISDEMIR) was revised several times until its rated capacity reached 2 million tons. I shall discuss these developments in Chapter 6.

The Third Five Year Plan (1973–1977) was prepared under a different political regime. The political situation deteriorated rapidly during the late sixties and the military made it clear, in a famous telegram to Mr Demirel in 1971, that he had lost their confidence. Accordingly he resigned and was replaced by a number of short-term governments led by technocrats. These governments found it difficult to govern because Mr Demirel continued to enjoy the support of a majority in the Grand National Assembly which remained in session. The planners, however, were relatively free to prepare a sound economic plan and they produced one that contained long-term projections through 1995 and established a new strategy that evidenced, in contrast to the preceding plans, a specific and explicit concern with qualitative improvements as well as with quantitative growth. Although the Second Five Year Plan had called for measures to improve the sector's performance, including measures for the establishment of a central coordinating agency, very limited results had been achieved. Productivity remained low, costs high, and there was no coordination. Now specific targets for improved iron ore and lower coke usage were established. New calculations projected that demand for steel products would climb from 2.2 million tons in 1972 to 4.2 million in 1977 (instead of 3.5 million as previously estimated), and reach 20.5 million by 1995. This huge demand was to be met, for the next decade, by new, very large investments, totalling TL15.4 billion. These represented a 50 per cent increase over the investments (at 1971 prices) in the first two plan periods combined (TL 4.4 billion during the First Plan, TL 5.7 billion during the Second) and would pay for projects that I will discuss in Chapters 5 and 6, massive expansions at ERDEMIR, ISDEMIR and Karabük. The private sector was also expected to continue growing. Since even these huge investments would not suffice to satisfy demand in the 1990s the planners, recognizing that new technologies made only mini mills or very large plants competitive internationally, expected to build, beginning in 1987, a gigantic new plant with a 10 million ton capacity.[68]

This project never moved beyond the pages of the plan but the expansions of Karabük, ERDEMIR and ISDEMIR were implemented, though, like many of the Third Plan's projections, the goals were never realized, either qualitatively or quantitatively, as each project ran into troubles of one sort or another. Overall, pig iron production reached only 46 per cent of the target, melted steel 41 per cent (because of problems with ERDEMIR's expansion which I shall discuss in Chapter 5) while demand doubled. As a result, the bill for iron and steel imports climbed precipitously, by 250 per cent, from TL 4.6 billion in 1972 to TL 11.6 billion in 1977.[69] Turkish decision-makers reacted in the traditional manner. Unfazed by the problems encountered by expanding and improving production at the existing plants, they made ambitious plans to boost iron and steel capacity even further.

They did so during a period of weak and unstable coalition governments. When, following the military intervention of 1971, democratic processes were restored and elections held in 1973, neither of the two major parties, the RPP nor the JP, emerged with a clear majority. The former won 185 seats, the latter 145, out of a total of 450. Hence, neither could form a government without the participation of smaller parties. The most significant of these was the National Salvation Party (NSP), a party committed both to fundamentalist Islam and heavy industrialization, which won 48 seats. Following lengthy and involved discussions, it agreed in January 1974 to participate in a rather remarkable coalition government with the left of center RPP; it lasted nine months. Forming a new coalition proved to be even more complicated but finally in early 1975 Mr Demirel, the leader of the right of center JP, worked out an arrangement with the NSP that permitted him to become Prime Minister. New elections, held in 1977, failed to break the deadlock. Although the RPP and the JP each increased the number of their seats neither gained an absolute majority. The NSP won only half as many seats as before (its vote dropped from 12 per cent to 8.6 per cent of the total) but it retained its pivotal role in any attempt to form a new government.[70]

Although the plants that were in operation and under construction had encountered and continued to confront such serious problems that a World Bank team studying the Turkish economy had raised the question 'whether investments in steel represent the best use of the country's capital resources',[71] Turkish decision-makers were not swayed. On the contrary the Fourth Five Year Plan (1979–1983), prepared while the RPP, headed by Prime Minister Bulent Ecevit, was in power for a short time, called for massive new investments in this sector in order to make Turkey into a major iron and steel producer. Like the Third Five Year Plan, this plan called for construction of new facilities that would produce 10 million tons. Now, however, two plants were to be built. The first, for which no location was specified, and which never advanced beyond the pages of the plan, would produce 2 million tons by 1993. The second, to be located in Sivas, would have a capacity of 2 million tons, and would come on stream by 1988. I will discuss this project (SIDEMIR), for which studies were carried out, in Chapter 6. Nor were the existing plants overlooked. Karabük was to be modernized once again; ERDEMIR's capacity was to double to 4 million tons by 1983, and ISDEMIR's was to increase – not to 4 million tons as had been originally anticipated, but by almost 400 per cent to 7.6 million tons by 1988. Altogether hot metal production was scheduled to increase ninefold within fifteen years, from 2.1 million tons per year in 1978 to 18.6 million tons by 1993.[72]

The quality of the analyses that underlay these projects is, perhaps, best exemplified by the manner in which the critical question of raw material availability was handled. This level of production would require 40.7 million tons of iron ore but 'total reserves in iron ore deposits currently being exploited and suitable for exploitation will barely meet the iron requirement up to 1992'. Nevertheless, this situation did not deter the plan's architects who simply argued that: 'it is imperative that iron ore beds having total deposits of over 1,000 million tonnes and suitable for enriching and operation must be taken up from now and their technological problems be resolved soonest'.[73] To move from the pages of a plan into a successful project has often proven a challenging task. Since none of these ambitious projects were ever implemented, the iron ore problem did not have to be confronted seriously.

Thus, by the end of the seventies, Turkey had built up a considerable industry in a relatively short time and was eager to expand it much further. Between 1963 and 1977, the iron and steel sector accounted for a large part (18.6 per cent) of the country's investments in manufacturing, which itself accounted for 4.5 per cent of total investments in that period. Now further gigantic investments were being planned, almost TL 40 billion by 1980 alone.[74]

The development of the iron and steel sector until the late 1970s and its projected growth is summarized in Table 2.4.

Table 2.4 Development and projected growth of the Turkish iron and steel sector

Name	Crude steel Capacity	Completion date	Cost
Karabük:			
Original plant	150	1940	£3m; TL 3.3m
1950s expansion	650	1960	TL 1.5b
1970s expansion	1,000	1984	TL 2.6b
ERDEMIR:			
Original plant	378	1964	$260m
Interim expansion	435	1967	$30m
Stage I expansion	1,500	1981	$300m
Stage II expansion	2,000	1985	$240m
Stage III expansion*	(6,800)	(1988)	—
ISDEMIR:			
Original plant	1,000	1974	TL 4.7b
First stage expansion	2,200	1984	TL 14b
Second stage expansion*	(7,600)	(1986)	—
SIDEMIR:			
Original plant*	2,000	1984	—
Private sector	6,200 – (1979 actual)		—

* Projects were never implemented.
Sources: 1979 Annual Report, p.11; 1982 Annual Report, p.10.

All of the projects were economically validated, in the eyes of the decision-makers, by a rapidly growing demand which increased at a faster rate than domestic production and thus had to be met through imports that consumed scarce foreign exchange. Between 1948 and

1975 Turkey's GNP increased by 500 per cent, its consumption of
steel products, by 1,500 per cent.[75] The value of its iron and steel
imports rose from TL 800,000, (8 per cent of total imports) in 1950 to
TL 52.3 million, (13 per cent) in 1974.[76] How the gap between
production and consumption exploded in the seventies is depicted in
Table 2.5.

Table 2.5 Iron and steel production and consumption 1930–1983
(millions of tons)

Year	Production	Consumption	Per capita consumption (kg)
1939	0.04		
1945	0.07		
1950	0.09	0.3 (1951)	14.4 (1951)
1955	0.2	0.4 (1954)	18.0 (1954)
1960	0.3	0.5	19.0
1964	0.8	0.8 (1963)	26.0 (1963)
1970	1.5	1.7 (1969)	50.0 (1967)
1973	1.7	2.0	54.0
1976	2.0	3.7	82.0
1983	3.8	9.0	90.0

Sources: Barutçugil, op. cit., pp. 25, 28;
Ereğli Annual Report, 1976, p. 6; Ereğli Annual Report, 1985, p. 13.

Iron and steel was now one of the country's major industries and
played a critical role in the economy. Its share of GNP increased from
1.29 per cent in 1963 to 3.17 per cent in 1971, 3.43 per cent in 1975
and 3.62 per cent in 1983.[77] And, as far as backward and forward
linkages are concerned, the Turkish iron and steel sector ranked
high; its backward linkages (coal mining, iron ore production and
energy) climbed in value from TL 757 million in 1963 to TL 2,000
million in 1968 and TL 7,400 million in 1973. Its forward linkages to
agriculture, food processing, metal products, construction and other
sectors also rose sharply, from TL 1,800 million in 1963 to TL 3,750
million in 1968 to TL 13,590 million in 1973.[78] The industry had also
emerged as a major employer: the number of persons working in the
integrated plants went from 5,700 in 1963 to 29,000 in the mid
seventies. This was a significant part of the country's total employment in manufacturing – 0.6 per cent in 1963, 2.0 per cent a decade
later.[79]

TURKEY'S DEVELOPMENT STRATEGY AND ITS CONSEQUENCES

At first, the strategy of heavy industrialization with a powerful import substitution bias yielded a surprisingly good rate of economic growth, one that compared favorably with the 6 per cent rate that 'middle income' countries averaged. GNP rose at a 6.4 per cent annual rate through the First Plan period (1963–1967), 6.7 per cent during the Second Plan period (1968–1972) and 7.2 per cent during the Third Plan period (1973–1977). Industry grew at a 9.2 per cent rate during these years, a rate that also compared favorably with many other 'middle income' countries including Brazil (10.7 per cent), Mexico (8 per cent) and Yugoslavia (7.5 per cent).[80] The share of industrial value added grew from 21 per cent in 1950 to 44 per cent in 1976 as manufacturing, which absorbed 26 per cent of total investments, emerged as a leading sector, providing consumer goods of all sorts. Industries such as machinery, chemicals, transport equipment and basic metals, however, remained dependent on imports.[81]

These impressive gains, which one should emphasize, were achieved by a democratic system that enjoyed few natural resources (though it did benefit from the remittances of Turkish workers abroad and from significant foreign loans) were offset by important structural weaknesses. Since it was implemented in a labor rich country that suffered from capital and foreign exchange shortages, the strategy placed a heavy burden on limited resources and did little to promote employment opportunities. When compared to the other 'middle income' countries, exports, imports and gross domestic investment all occupied a lower share of GDP than the average. In terms of exports Turkey ranked last; they accounted for 5.6 per cent of GDP in 1977 as compared to an 18.5 per cent average.[82] The 'virtually closed' Turkish economy was marked by a low rate of domestic savings, a high rate of disguised unemployment and a low export capability and was vulnerable to inflationary pressures and balance of payment difficulties.[83]

Turkey's failure to develop an export base commensurate with its level of development[84] had important consequences for domestic growth rates. Krueger's careful analysis suggested that with a different pattern of investments – one that emphasized exports – the country's GNP could have grown by as much as another 3 per cent per year and that the economy would have benefitted in many ways: less imported technology, increased employment, greater export earnings, and increases in productivity and entrepreneurship since producers would have been forced to exhibit a greater concern with competitiveness and quality control.[85] Most experts accept these findings which are reinforced by another study which demonstrated that the emphasis on capital intensive industrialization within a domestic orientation resulted in an industrial sector marked by high capital output ratios.[86] And:

> The protectionist system, which featured an anti export bias in the past, and provided greater effective protection at higher stages of fabrication . . . [led to] the emergence of high-cost private firms that produce equivalent products for the domestic market under different technological agreements and that exhibit no particular tendencies for the horizontal and/or vertical specialization needed for trade oriented sustainable growth in the 1980s.[87]

CONCLUSION

Thus, by the late seventies Turkey had consistently followed a particular development strategy for over forty years, a strategy which led to great accomplishments but also entailed heavy opportunity costs. That strategy, import substitution industrialization, was implemented remorselessly. Unlike many other countries that had initially pursued similar policies, Turkey never made the necessary adjustments to meet changing conditions or to take advantages of new opportunities. It continued on an inward-looking path, ignoring the examples of those countries who oriented at least part of their economies outwards and thereby achieved powerful results. The consequences were disastrous. After years of striving to become economically independent and to build an industrial base that would permit the achievement of self-sustaining growth, Turkey had failed to achieve the first objective and, at most, had partially achieved the second, due in significant degree to the functioning of the iron and steel industry.

Clearly, from a quantitative perspective, the dreams of Ataturk had been fulfilled – the country had built up a significant iron and steel capacity. Yet, it had not created a forge for development. Its emergence had not proceeded smoothly even after the era of national planning had been inaugurated. Many of the planners' projections had proven woefully erroneous and the sector's performance never met any of the goals which were established for it, with adverse consequences, given the sector's extensive forward linkages for numerous industries. The process of technology transfer had obviously not proceeded smoothly; Turkey had failed to build sound projects or to master the technologies involved. Why was this the case? Why had the lessons of Karabük apparently not been learnt? What had gone wrong? To answer questions such as these it is necessary to turn to a consideration of the nature of the decisions that were made in the case of each major project and how these were implemented. I begin with the saga of ERDEMIR.

3 The Decision to Build ERDEMIR

AID Agrees to Build a Steel Mill

THE NEGOTIATIONS

The news that the government of Prime Minister Menderes wished to build Turkey's second integrated iron and steel works soon reached the Swiss representative of the Koppers Company, Inc. of Pittsburgh, a majoring engineering firm specializing in iron and steel. He promptly flew to Ankara where he discussed the proposed project with various Turkish officials. On 8 November 1958, the Turkish government contracted with Koppers to carry out a feasibility study for a plant that would meet the country's need for the kind of iron and steel products that were not manufactured at Karabük. The report which was delivered to the Turkish government on 1 September 1959 found that the project was quite feasible. It suggested the establishment of a consortium with Westinghouse Electric and Blaw Knox to construct a plant which would cost about $208 million, $158 million of which would be foreign exchange, the remainder would be in local currency. Equity, in the form of common stock, would total about $50 million, the remaining $158 million would be in the form of long-term debt. The plant, like the existing facility at Karabük would be owned and operated by the state.[1]

The Turkish government readily accepted the study's conclusions and moved decisively to implement them. On 11 November it sent formal letters of intent to Kopppers and its associates asking them to establish a working committee. Koppers responded promptly and the committee arrived in Ankara on 23 November. An agreement in principle was signed twenty-four hours later. That same day, the Turkish cabinet met and formally approved a proposal that the plant be exempt from custom duties. Prime Minister Menderes continued to act expeditiously, convening an emergency session of the Grand National Assembly to secure legislation authorizing the project. During the debate, the opposition party, the Republican People's

Party, criticized the special concessions given to the foreign investors and the haste with which the legislation was debated but did not oppose the project which was approved by a vote of 385 to 1.

From the outset the Turkish government looked to the USA for the foreign currency requirements. On 30 September (less than a month after the original Koppers report) Mr F. R. Zorlu, the Foreign Minister, who was responsible for all projects involving foreign aid, visited the USA and, while there, met with Development Loan Fund (DLF) officials to discuss the project. Additional meeting were held on 9 and 14 October. Prime Minister Adnan Menderes, who was also in the USA at this time, participated actively in these discussions, emphasizing the importance that his government attached to building the plant. He stated formally that the 'steel mill was Turkey's highest priority industrial project.'

Washington policy-makers were well disposed toward any project that would strengthen an important ally. They also tended to look favorably upon projects that promoted industrialization for they subscribed to the conventional wisdom of the time, that the developing countries could achieve rapid growth only by building up their industrial base. But, it evidenced several reservations about supporting this particular project.

The most important of these derived from another widely held belief. US officials, from President Eisenhower on down, were convinced of the overriding importance of a dynamic private sector for development and regarded public enterprises as burdens upon the state. A report prepared for AID clearly reflected these themes. It emphasized the need to promote industrialization in the developing countries but also stressed that the private sector had to play the leading role because state enterprises were less efficient, responsive and entrepreneurial. If a state failed to restrain its public sector, it would face a dismal future:[2]

Unless ways are found of channeling public funds into privately operated industrial establishments and of otherwise encouraging private enterprise, the pace of economic and industrial development may not be fast enough to keep up with rising demands for better living standards.

Such views were particularly relevant in regard to this project because the Turkish state enterprises, which had expanded despite Prime Minister Menderes' rhetoric about private entrepreneurship, were widely acknowledged to be inefficient and in need of reform. Yet there were few indications that any changes would be implemented. By sponsoring a major private company that would be well managed and economically competitive, Washington hoped to provide a catalyst for the development of the private sector and a magnet that would attract private capital from abroad. The DLF's position was also influenced by another important consideration. Although it was fully committed to supporting development based on industrialization and had in fact financed a government-owned iron and steel mill in India,that loan had encountered significant opposition from conservative congressmen, who, believing that America, a bastion of capitalism, was engaged in a global struggle with socialism in its many forms, strongly opposed any action by the US government that promoted the spread of state enterprises. The Eisenhower administration did not relish a battle in Congress over the Turkish proposal.

Accordingly, Washington decided that it would only support a plant that was privately owned and controlled. That message was conveyed unambiguously to the Turkish government by Mr Brand, the managing director of the DLF, who, while attending a meeting in Istanbul in the fall of 1959, informed Mr Zorlu that the DLF would be willing to entertain a proposal only if two conditions were met. First, although vast amounts of state financing would necessarily be involved, the mill would have to be privately owned; second, private US investors would have to participate in the financing. President Eisenhower, who visited Turkey in December 1959, reaffirmed his willingness to support the project but emphasized that he would do so only if it were a private enterprise.

Realizing that the USA was adamant, Turkish policy-makers acceded to its conditions and worked actively with Koppers to hammer out a formal proposal as quickly as possible. Chase International Incorporated, a subsidiary of the Chase Manhattan Bank, which was interested in purchasing and marketing $2 million worth of securities in the mill, and the First Boston Corporation which was willing to help place a DLF guaranteed loan among private investors, were invited to join the consortium. Within a month the Turkish government and the American firms had agreed on numerous details and, when Mr Brand visited Turkey again in late January 1960, the talks now dealt with the acceptibility of the arrangements that had been made, the role of the DLF, and the loan procedures. Shortly thereafter, on 28 January 1960, Prime Minister Menderes sent a personal letter to President Eisenhower reiterating his eagerness for the project. He wrote:

During the course of this visit, there have been constructive negotiations of the second steel plant to be erected in Turkey which will be financed and managed mostly by Turkish and American private investors. I have been very happy to learn that important progress has been made on the subject.

The accomplishments of this monumental effort will constitute a shining example of the magnificant cooperation among friendly nations of the free world. I would certainly like to confirm that every possible effort will be made by the Turkish government, as well as the Turkish people, for the realization of this project . . .

A month later, on 25 February 1960, the DLF received a formal proposal from a committee representing the three major parties involved in the project as defined by the agreement of 29 November – the Turkish government, the US investors, and the Turkish private group. Three days later, the Turkish parliament passed a bill establishing a new private company, ERDEMIR.

The Turkish government lobbied actively to ensure that the USA would actually provide the necessary financing. Its ambassador met with various high administration officials on 29 April and reiterated his government's interest in moving expeditiously. He was assured that the USA remained favorably disposed. Under Secretary of State A. Guy Hope told him that he understood that satisfactory progress was being made and that Mr Brand was very interested in the project. Mr Dillon stated that 'The US government is particularly interested in this project because it brings together private and public financing in both countries, a pattern we have very much wanted to develop.'

Despite these assurances, the basic soundness of the project was being questioned by officials within AID who had analyzed Koppers' feasibility study. These doubts were formally expressed on 18 December 1959 by the Chief Engineer of the DLF who, in a memorandum to the Director, pointed out that the study did not demonstrate the availability of adequate iron ore reserves, or of sufficient supplies of coal at the volume required, discuss the issue of water or of limestone, or deal with the major transportation problems involved. He concluded that additional investments totalling $50 million might be required.

Neither he, nor any other high official, however, raised any questions about the project's financing. As was noted in Chapter 1, a sound project is one that is not burdened with a heavy debt which it may find difficult to support. Yet, although this principle was clearly violated – somebody noted, perhaps cynically, in the margin of one copy of the loan document, 'Damned small equity, isn't it'; and a financial analyst who subsequently joined AID was 'absolutely astounded when he asked about the equity and was proudly given the figures' – the project's capital structure did not receive the detailed scrutiny that it obviously deserved. I shall return to this point when I analyze the project's impact dimension.

The practical difficulties that arose during the lengthy and difficult negotiations between the two governments represented another significant obstacle. The Turkish government was reluctant to agree to a 30 per cent return on equity as requested by Koppers because such a return meant that ERDEMIR's products would have to sell at 33 per cent above world prices. Moreover, it was difficult to arrive at a formula that would permit the Turkish government to divest itself of its shares in ERDEMIR so as to ensure that the mill would be privately owned. Finally, the Turkish government was concerned that the plant would cost more than necessary because US foreign aid was 'tied' to purchases of American machinery which was higher priced than comparable equipment from other countries.

While it was engaged in these negotiations, the Turkish government had to resolve a fundamental difficulty, it had to find the amount of local capital that had been agreed upon. News of the project had leaked out in November 1959 but the private sector evidenced little enthusiasm for it. The US embassy reported that:

> The project is considered to be one which the government has espoused at this time for primarily political reasons . . . (the forthcoming election); it will base its appeal to the electorate in large part on its industrial achievements and plans and the government has taken the initiative in obtaining private sector financing.

Prime Minister Menderes reacted strongly. He summoned key investors to Ankara on 6–7 December 1959 to discuss their involvement. There, according to an embassy memorandum, he 'made abundantly clear that this plant was not only of paramount importance to the country but a venture of profitable nature insofar as the shareholders were concerned . . .'

More than rhetoric was required to convince the skeptical businessmen present. They criticized the project on the following grounds: (1) the Turkish government could not furnish $24 million without borrowing from the central bank; (2) the cost of the project did not include large infrastructural costs for transportation and port facilities nor working capital for the mill – additional investments will be necessary, resulting in increased inflation; (3) this and other proposed new projects would absorb so much new capital that inflationary financing would be necessary.

Prime Minister Menderes was not the type of leader who could be persuaded to abandon a cherished project on the basis of such arguments. According to the US embassy, he 'exerted considerable persuasive powers' and, to enhance the project's attractiveness, agreed on a number of compromises on such issues as the base on which interest would be paid, a government guarantee of profit, a promise of a monopoly on the distribution of the plant's products. He also moved actively to discourage criticism of the project. When an Industrial Development Bank official in a meeting with some potential Turkish private investors, expressed serious doubt about the possibilty of obtaining the required financing, he soon received a sharply critical telephone call from the Finance Ministry.

The Turkish businessmen's fear of inflationary financing was shared by Washington which was unwilling to make a formal commitment to support the project until the Turkish government demonstrated its ability and willingness to lower inflation and restore economic vitality. Prime Minister Menderes, however, as noted in Chapter 2, never bothered with economic planning and believed in growth at any price. Accordingly, he did not exhibit the monetary and fiscal restraint that was essential to the success of the 1958 stabilization program which he had reluctantly accepted. He failed to keep public sector investments within the limits established by its fiscal year 1958 budget, exceeding the planned target of $161 million by about 50 per cent.

Hence by late 1959 most foreign experts were expressing serious reservations about the future course of Turkey's economy and the potential impact of such a large project upon its financial situation. Many argued strongly that the loan should not be approved unless the Menderes government proved that it would seriously pursue a stabilization program. Ankara sought to calm such fears by providing assurances of all sorts but these were considered to be far too vague. On 11 May the chief of the AID mission sent a memorandum to the director of the DLF expressing concern that the new plant would jeopardize the stabilization program. He suggested that the Turkish government's proposals, such as limiting future total public sector financing to specific sums, be formally negotiated to ensure that they be actually carried out. Moreover, DLF administrators and many US officials in Ankara felt strongly that the Menderes government's anarchic view of economic development had to be replaced by a more systematic approach, that Turkey needed an overall investment program into which this project could be integrated.

The vagaries of Prime Minister Menderes' economic policy-making ceased to be an issue on 27 May 1960 when his government was overthrown by a military regime which assigned a high priority to restoring the economy and to planning development in a coherent and integrated manner. As a first step, it undertook an evaluation of all the projects that were under construction and in the planning stage. It also called in Professor J. Tinbergen, a Dutch expert, as a consultant and asked him to evaluate the proposed iron and steel plant. Five days later, on 28 June 1960, Koppers' Zurich office was invited to send its technical group to Ankara. Following extensive discussions, Professor Tinbergen concluded that the benefits of the steel mill had been evaluated too optimistically by Koppers and gave serious consideration to recommending temporary postponement of the project.

That such a proposal would have been accepted by Ankara is quite doubtful but the USA too had changed its attitude. By this time, despite all the reservations which had been raised, US policy-makers had become so enamored of the project that they actually began to worry that it might be cancelled and convened a special meeting to discuss how such an outcome might be avoided. They finally concluded that the USA should not appear too eager to finance the plant. A cable to that effect was sent to the US embassy on 23 June 1960, instructing it to '. . . avoid any action which might given the impression of pressing the matter [steel mill] on new regime . . . would prefer intitiative remain with Turks.'

Although the DLF was clearly anxious to see the project implemented, it hoped that other lenders would be willing to participate in the financing. Despite continued efforts to persuade them to help, the two most important sources, the World Bank and the US Export-Import Bank, remained aloof. The former remembered its unfavorable experiences with Prime Minister Menderes who had openly rejected its counsel and had asked it to leave Turkey. AID's report noted: 'The negative position of the IBRD with respect to financing development projects (in Turkey) at this time has not changed.' The EXIM bank was equally unenthusiastic: 'It has no interest in the financing of the project.'[4]

The lack of enthusiasm exhibited by the bank and the IMF deterred neither the DLF nor US officials in Ankara who worked hard to achieve the project's realization. The US ambassador, Fletcher Warren, a vocal and active proponent, forcefully endorsed the plant on many occasions (e.g. in a letter dated 23 August 1960) as did the AID mission which '. . . has been favorable to the project on its merits and has indicated its strong support of DLF financing of it.'[5]

Fears that the project would be abandoned proved illusory; having completed its review of public sector projects, the new military government accorded the plant 'first priority for completion'.[6] By this review and its other economic policies, the new regime signalled to the US that it regarded economic stability as being of prime importance, thus eliminating a major concern of the project's opponents. It also indicated that it would be willing to guarantee a loan amounting to TL 800 million for Ereğli and on 4 October 1960 sent a formal request to the DLF asking for foreign exchange financing in which it stated that: 'It attaches the highest priority to the completion of this project.'[7]

Although both governments were now fully committed, many serious questions still remained, such as the extent to which Ankara would implement the necessary infrastructural requirements (which some experts now estimated would add as much as $100 million to the cost), the limited participation by private Turkish investors, the very low debt-equity ratio, the possibility that the costs might be higher than anticipated, and whether the supply of domestic inputs would suffice for the plant's operation. These actual and potential problems did not deter Washington; it approved a loan (DLF No. 169) for $129.6 million on 8 November 1960; the contract between Koppers associates and ERDEMIR to design and build the mill was signed in December, the formal signing taking place in Ankara on 9 January 1961.

That the agreement was reached despite continuing reservations on the part of many experts is somewhat surprising. That it contains the following three points make it unique. First, the loan was the largest ever made for any industrial project by AID (and even today remains one of the biggest in its history). Second, it was granted to a private Turkish company, ERDEMIR, not to the Turkish government. Third, and most memorably, it was neither guaranteed nor secured.[8] Whether these terms would create problems for the USA would depend on how well the project was planned and implemented.

THE DESIGN ISSUES

Since ERDEMIR would use Zonguldak coal, it was obviously desirable that the plant be located nearby, on the Black Sea. There were few possible sites along the coast and Ereğli, the best of these, had been selected by the US and Russian missions in the thirties as the most suitable spot for the plant that was ultimately located at Karabük. Ereğli's advantages had been further enhanced by the completion of a good, though small, harbor in 1954.[9] The location of Ereğli is shown in Figure 3.1.

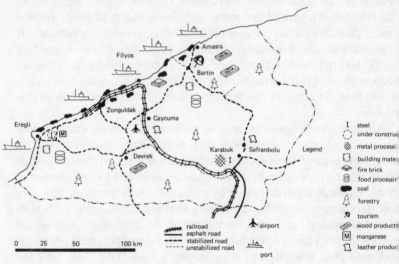

Figure 3.1   Ereğli and its environs.
            Source: Malcolm D. Rivkin, *Area Development for National Growth: The Turkish Precedence* (New York: Prager, 1965), p. 147.

Despite the importance of transportation and the reservations that had been expressed about its adequacy, no consideration was given, in the loan document, to the state of the overall road and rail network, though some specific issues were considered. In particular, the desirability of building a 30 km rail link to the coal mines at Zonguldak was discussed but the topography was such that 20 km of tunnels would have be bored through mountains and the Turkish government was unwilling to bear the high cost ($27.8 million). The local roads, especially the one from the harbor to the plant, were obviously inadequate; the Turkish government agreed to build a new highway and rail link there. The need to expand the harbor and to enlarge the facilities for handling iron ore were also considered but these projects were deemed not essential.

An appropriate location also possesses an extensive water supply, plenty of room and soil bearing conditions that minimize site preparation costs. It is obviously not desirable to locate a plant in a spot where extensive and expensive piling and other construction works are required to support the heavy loads characteristic of the various components of a steel plant complex. But, as will be evident, such activities had to be undertaken.

A desirable site also possesses good educational, health, housing and other public services. This was not the case in Ereğli, a small town of 8,812 inhabitants in 1960. Hence housing for the new employees would have to be built and some public works improvements would be required.

The question of size was more problematic and the final decision was essentially determined by two major considerations: the amount of financing available and the estimated market. Having decided that it could provide only about $128 million, AID asked Koppers to eliminate what it considered to be non-essential items in order to save $40 million.

The importance of the second determinant, the market, was emphasized in Chapter 1. To estimate demand accurately is a challenging task under any circumstances; in this case matters were complicated because the existence of import controls made the available data unreliable. Koppers carried out two studies. First, it surveyed the major potential consumers for flat products and concluded that 1,245,000 tons would be required in 1963. AID was skeptical of this result because 'while the forecast based on this survey may be indicative of potential usage for 1963, it is probably less valid as an indicator of effective demand.' AID was equally critical when Koppers estimated that demand would reach 1,550,000 tons in 1963 on the basis of a statistical projection of consumption figures for those years when imports were relatively free. It felt that 'too much weight was given to the year 1953 when imports were abnormal in anticipation of exchange restrictions.'[10]

AID decided to carry out its own analyses and did so using three different methodologies. The first involved calculating the relation between the ratio of increases in steel consumption and industrial growth and yielded a figure of 1,700,000 tons for 1965. The second estimate was derived from per capita steel consumption in Turkey (about 40 lb in 1952, an extremely low figure); if per capita consumption remained constant, 1965 consumption would be 570,000 tons; if it increased, as was to be expected, demand would also rise. An increase of 25 per cent to 50 lb per capita was therefore posited, yielding a demand of 710,000 tons. The third estimate was developed on the basis of the relationship between steel consumption and national income. UN data indicated that Latin America consumed 30-35 lb per $100 of national income; the more industrialized countries, 50 lb per $100. Accordingly, Turkish demand in 1965 was estimated on the basis of the assumptions that national income would reach $5.8 billion (at 1959 prices) and that consumption would be either 30 or 40 lb per capita. The lower figure yielded a demand of 800,000 tons, the latter one million tons. Thus, the efforts of AID and Koppers yielded projections for Turkey's iron and steel demand that differed quite widely, ranging between 570,000 and 1.7 million tons.

Part of this demand would be met by the Karabük plant which could produce 650,000 tons of structural steel. Hence AID analyzed the relative demand for flat products on the basis of past experience; it concluded that these accounted for 28 per cent of the total demand for iron and steel. According to this calculation the market for the new plant's products would be quite small, between 160,000 and 476,000 tons per year.

All these studies reveal quite clearly the complexities in estimating market demand and the extent to which particular methodologies yield different results. Inevitably assumptions have to be made, assumptions which often turn out to be erroneous. Yet policy-makers must make decisions and the question of which estimate should be accepted is not an easy one. In this case, they had a wide choice since the results varied by 300 per cent, though even the largest figure projected a relatively limited market.

AID decided that the plant should be sized conservatively in order to ensure its profitability. Accordingly, it was designed to produce 268,000 tons of flat products plus another 110,000 tons of steel ingots which it would sell to Karabük. This level of capacity was deemed adequate to meet the projected demand. And, if the estimates proved to be too optimistic, the plant could still operate profitably because the estimated breakeven points were well below the projected capacity. In AID's words '. . . the capacities indicated and the safety factors involved are within reasonable limits.'[11]

The decision to build a small mill at a low capital cost affected technological choices in each component of the plant, beginning with the acquisition and preparation of raw materials. ERDEMIR would use an estimated 840,000 tons of iron ore annually. As early as March 1959, Koppers concluded that Turkey's proven reserves totalled 53 million tons, 35.5 million tons of which, located at Divriği, were owned and reserved for the Karabük plant, and another 10.5 million tons contained too much arsenic to be useful. Thus a mere 7 million tons were available, obviously an inadequate amount. These findings were received with gloom in Ankara and the Turkish Mineral Research and Exploration Institute undertook its own study. It produced more optimistic findings – 21,700,000 tons of suitable iron ore (a 26-year supply) were available for the plant in three different sites and sizeable probable reserves also existed.

Koppers now analyzed the cost of utilizing iron ore from each of these sources. Hekimhan East possessed the largest proven reserves, 11,900,000 tons, but this ore, being limonite, would require sintering for its effective utilization. Its location in a rugged mountainous environment raised development costs to $5.3 million. The second site, Hekimhan West had not yet been analyzed in detail but the preliminary results were deemed to be encouraging in terms of both quality and quantity. The third site, Özkoyuncu, possessed proven reserves of only 2.8 million tons though it was hoped that additional drilling would raise that figure to 10 million tons. The latter two sites would cost $5.9 million to develop. Koppers estimated that the cost of the ore from the three sites ranged between $12.46 and $14.30 per metric ton, 0.213 and 0.270 cents per unit or iron, figures that compared quite favorably to US and European prices. The transportation costs were estimated to be $15.23.

Despite the reservations which had been expressed by its own Chief Engineer, the DLF accepted these optimistic conclusions. Its report stated: '(a) there are ample proven reserves for at least 25 years of operation, (b) ore is of good quality, (c) delivered cost is in line with other countries, (d) there are splendid possibilities of proving-up very substantial additional reserves'.[12] Each of these conclusions, as we shall see, was to prove invalid.

The second major input, coal, was also deemed not to represent a problem. An estimated 640,000 tons of coking coal and 69,500 tons of steam coal would be required each year. The former could readily be supplied by the large Zonguldak field but this coal had a high ash content, and therefore produced coke with a low carbon content (75 per cent as compared to the US standard of 85–87 per cent), thus lowering the productivity of the blast furnace significantly. Steam coal of satisfactory quality and quantity was to come from Armutcuk,

14 km by rail from Ereğli. The estimated delivered cost of the coal was comparable to US prices.

Limestone would be the flux, the third input, and 223,000 tons would be required. The company planned to exploit a nearby property in which it would invest $330,000. The estimated cost per son would be $1.70, similar to US costs. In addition, 60,000 tons of dolomite would be required each year for the lining of the oxygen converters, and this, too, was in ample supply at a reasonable price.

Only one decision had to be made at this stage, whether to build a sinter plant. Koppers had recommended that one be built in order to ameliorate the iron ore problem but AID decided to omit it. After all, one could always build such a plant when additional financing became available.

The second set of activities, the manufacture of raw iron, also involved a decision. Here a choice had to be made between the established coke plant–blast furnace combination and the newly developed direct reduction process. After detailed analyses, Koppers chose the former because of favorable economics and because the latter had not yet been widely commercialized. Accordingly, Koppers would design and construct a battery of 74 coke ovens and auxiliary equipment. This plant would turn 640,000 tons of coal into 405,000 tons of coke and the usual by-products.

The size of the blast furnace represented the next choice. The one selected, 28 feet in hearth diameter, was the largest in common use in the sixties and the largest in the Middle East. Although a standard off-the-shelf design, it was not expected to function at optimal effectiveness because the coke's high ash content (a function of the available coal) would result in a lower carbon content that would, in turn, decrease production by at least 5 per cent to 440,000 tons of iron per year. Moreoever, because unsintered ores would be used, the amount of flue dust produced per ton of hot metal was expected to be higher than in the USA. Nevertheless, AID argued that quality would not be affected, that the 'specifications of the various finished products . . . will be equal in quality to US materials.'[13]

The next stage, the transformation of hot metal into steel, could be carried out using any of the three technologies. Koppers evaluated these as follows:

1. The open hearth furnace process accounted for about 90 per cent of US steel production in 1957. Its popularity was due to the fact that it can accept a wide variety of charge methods and produce a

range of products. On the other hand, large furnaces are required for high production rates which means that heavy construction is involved and that potential customers are limited to those who can order large quantities or who use standard grades of steel that are warehouse. Moreover, the open hearth furnace requires fuel with low sulfur content and therefore liquid fuel oil is most commonly used.

2. The electric arc furnace generates higher temperatures than the other methods and these can be controlled precisely and easily. Moreoever, one can achieve consistency in chemical and physical properties. However, this process entails higher operating costs, requires large inputs of electrical power and is of limited size.

3. The basic oxygen furnace, although in commercial operation for only about ten years, was growing rapidly in popularity because units of equivalent capacity capable of producing steel of equal quality to open hearth furnaces were smaller and simpler to build and maintain and, hence, the cost of construction and operation was much lower. Two negative factors were noted – that higher skill levels were required to operate this process and that the plant would be the first to function on hot metal with the particular phosphorous content anticipated at Ereğli.

Koppers made a forward looking recommendation arguing that:

> . . . the most satisfactory and economical steel making process for Turkey . . . is the oxygen converter process. This process is cap-able of producing an excellent product in the qualities required for hot and cold rolling into sheets and strip, can utilize the iron produced from Turkish ores, will not require the purchase of scrap from outside sources, and does not need liquid fuels.[14]

For the transfer of this technology to be successful, however, particular attention would obviously have to be paid to management and training. And, as is so often the case in technology transfer, some adaptation of the technology might be required because of the nature of the local inputs. I shall consider these points below.

Finally, the raw steel had to be transformed into finished products. Here too options were available because various kinds of rolling mills could be installed. The choice was profoundly affected by the previous decisions as to the size of the plant and the amount and type of flat goods that it should produce. These were (in metric tonnes):

Plates	55,000
Cold rolled sheets	77,000
Hot rolled sheets	28,000
Tin plate	50,000
Strip	8,000
Skelp	50,000
Total	268,000

Normally three separate mills are utilized to produce such goods but, because of the low quantities involved, Koppers recommended an ingenious solution – the use of a Steckel mill, a piece of machinery that carried out all the operations. Steckel mills are quite rare because modern plants use semi-continuous or continuous rolling equipment, but its installation would permit ERDEMIR to become a flat steel producer at minimum cost. If demand subsequently increased, other rolling equipment could be installed. Even a Steckel mill, however, could produce double the projected tonnage. Hence, while the other units were to operate for three eight-hour shifts, six or seven days a week, the rolling mill plant would be running for only two to fifteen shifts a week.

All these decisions meant that ERDEMIR was deliberately built with imbalances among its various components. Yet every aspect of the plant was subject to detailed analyses. Elaborate flow charts and practice diagrams showing the capacity of each unit and their interrelationships were prepared by Koppers personnel and discussed in detail. Hence, though imbalances existed, these were consciously accepted by designers who were unwilling to build the major components (e.g. the blast furnace) smaller than was economically sound. Moreover, Koppers envisaged the future expansion of the plant to a million ton capacity and regarded this project as merely the first stage. Even the DLF accepted the wisdom of expansion, though on a smaller scale, noting that with the addition of a coke oven battery, a second blast furnace and an expansion of the power plant, the rolling mills could produce 470,000 tons, thus greatly lowering operating costs.[15]

THE IMPACT ISSUES

A large section of the study was devoted to a consideration of the costs and benefits of this design and of the plant's potential contribution to Turkey's economic development. The first and most comprehensive set of analyses dealt with economic feasibility, the costs of the project, its potential profitability and international competitiveness.

Altogether it was now estimated that the mill would require investments totalling $244,875,000 – $168,652,000 in foreign exchange, the remainder, $76,233,000, in local currency – about $26 million more than originally estimated. The foreign exchange costs were to be provided by a variety of sources, the most important being the DLF which would provide $98.7 million and guarantee a private loan ($31 million) to be placed by the First Boston Corporation at an interest rate of about 4.5 per cent. In return for goods and services, the Chase International Corporation would receive $5 million in convertible debentures, and some European countries would provide $20 million in credits for equipment purchases. The local currency requirements would be met largely through public sector contributions. The Turkish government would loan the company the equivalent of $20.7 million, and State Economic Enterprises would purchase $34 million of stock in the corporation. Turkish private investors who, as noted earlier, had been persuaded to participate in the project only with difficulty, were expected to subscribe $11 million.

Although most of the capital was to be provided in the form of loans, the document dealt cursorily with the magnitude of the debt burden. As I have noted, this critical point was never formally raised when the project's shortcomings were discussed prior to the DLF's decision to provide the financing. Nor was it accorded any greater consideration in the feasibility study. Even though a pencilled-in calculation showed that the debt–equity ratio stood at a very high 3.09 : 1 the report dismissed the matter summarily in the following words: '. . . the ratio of long-term senior debt to equity is not excessive for a project of this type and magnitude.'[16] No evidence was provided to substantiate this rather startling assertion and the authors of the document included, elsewhere, a caution that was to prove prophetic: 'It should be noted that the debt structure is extremely heavy and fixed charges constitute a large percentage of sales. If sales do not meet forecasts, Ereğli will have difficulty in meeting its commitments.'[17]

A successful project needs not only a certain level of sales, it must earn a profit. The loan document devoted much attention to all aspects of profitability. First Koppers' estimates of the costs of converting the inputs at every stage were compared with data from three plants of roughly similar capacity in the USA, Taiwan and the Philippines. The DLF concluded that '. . . Koppers operating costs are in line and acceptable'.[18]

Second, the actual costs of production after a two-year breaking-in period were calculated. Here Koppers' original estimates had to be increased because it was already obvious that both the coal and the iron ore would be more expensive than originally anticipated. These costs were also compared with US and European prices, though it was noted that accurate comparisons are difficult to make owing to wide variations in prices and great differences in specifications, tonnages, packaging, etc. Nevertheless, AID concluded that the cost of ERDEMIR's steel (including depreciation and debt servicing) would be $145 per metric tonne, a price only slightly higher than the cost of imports, $142 per ton, that the cost to the Turkish consumer of imported steel (including customs duties, importers' profits, etc.) would be $209 as compared to a $212 figure for ERDEMIR steel (including a 30 per cent return). Accordingly, the Turkish consumer would not pay higher prices than he would for imports and the mill could even compete for Middle Eastern markets. The confident conclusion read as follows: 'The ability of the corporation to meets its obligations and realize a reasonable return on investment appears assured . . .'[19]

The third set of calculations analyzed the capital costs. The mill would cost $217 million and produce 378,000 tons of steel. The investment cost was estimated to be an expensive $570 per ton of produce, $460 per ton of ingot capacity because of the imbalances within the plant, particularly the low level of operation of the rolling mill units.[20] In the words of the report: 'This unit cost is high because the plant is designed for a much larger output of rolled products.' The DLF acknowledged that these costs meant that the project represented a very inefficient use of capital resources but it was not fazed by this condition. On the contrary, it sought to justify its decision in several ways. It began by arguing that high capital costs are 'common to all similar projects'. It then pointed out that with an additional investment of $60 million, the production of flat products could be increased to 470,000 tons, thus lowering the costs per ton of product of $320. Finally it noted that even at $570, the cost per ton of produce compared very favorably with costs elsewhere, about $600 in Latin America and $470 in the USA. Accordingly it concluded: '. . . the cost estimates for Ereğli are definitely in line.'[21]

Finally the cost of various components was compared with their costs in other plants. The coke plant and blast furnace, for example, would run about $56 million; in a Canadian plant, units of about the same capacity cost about $70 million. No comparison was made for the rolling mills because the low level of capacity at which these mills would operate would make the results meaningless. As a result of these computations, the report found that: 'Costs . . . appear fair and reasonable . . .' To ensure that these would be the ones actually charged, the Turkish government was urgd to hire an independent consultant 'to evaluate the lump sum proposals submitted by the three organizations' because:

> It must be remembered that Koppers Associates . . . will have exclusive, non-competitive contracts to supply engineering, services, construction, erection, and initial operation at prices no higher than those in effect for comparable goods and services in the U.S. . . . This cannot be verified solely by a comparison of invoices . . .'[22]

The next step was to calculate commercial profitability. First, revenues had to be estimated and this involved certain important assumptions, that (1) the plant would operate at capacity, and (2) all the products would be sold. Under these conditions annual revenues would amount to roughly $79 million, total costs to $61 million, leaving a net income of $18 million. Overall the plant would yield a gross income on sales of 33 per cent, a net income on sales of 23 per cent, a net income on capital assets of 8.3 per cent and a net income on the equity ($50 million) of 36 per cent. The Turkish stockholders would earn a 20 per cent return on their investments, and if the 110,000 tons of ingots to be sold to Karabük were to be needed to satisfy a larger than anticipated demand, then profits would be 25 per cent greater.

The breakeven point was also calculated. Below capacity operation was estimated to reduce efficiency by 25 per cent, raising the cost of production from $95 to $119 a ton. Given the estimated average selling price of $209 a ton, a margin of $90 per ton would still remain to cover the fixed costs and, since fixed costs were about $20 million, the breakeven point would be 222,000 tons (20 million divided by 90) or 60 per cent of capacity.

All these calculations culminated in the profit and loss statement which was based on highly questionable assumptions: the first year, sales were expected to reach 87 per cent of capacity (332,000 tons); in the second year, 96 per cent (363,400 tons); and in the third year, the plant was expected to operate at full capacity, producing and selling

378,000 tons. Yet, as I noted in Chapter 1, experts believe that a new plant that achieves 50 per cent, 75 per cent and 90 per cent of capacity in the first three years of operation is performing above the norm. The analysts recognized this point for they stated: 'These estimates indicate a substantial return based on the assumption of efficient operation at capacity beginning in the third year of operation. This, of course, is an optimistic assumption.' But, it never explained why its assumptions were justified and dismissed the issue cursorily: 'It is clear, however, that the breakeven point of 60% of capacity leaves ample room for adjustments to varying conditions.'[23] The profit and loss statement is presented in Table. 3.1.

Table 3.1 Profit and loss statement for ERDEMIR (US$000)

	Operating years		
	1	2	3
Sales value of products[1]	69,400	76,000	79,000
Estimated expenses:			
Cost of manufacture	31,000	33,300	32,500
Selling, general admin. expenses	3,078	2,585	2,533
Depreciation (at 4%)	8,694	8,649	8,694
Operating period interest	11,147	10,800	10,425
Amortization of deferred interest	380	365	350
Allowance doubtful accounts	260	40	—
Total expenses	54,559	55,739	54,502
Net income – Before bonuses & taxes	14,841	20,261	24,498
Bonuses & incentives (5%)	742	1,013	1,225
Taxable income	14,099	19,248	23,273
Provision for income tax (23.5%)	3,313	4,523	5,469
Net income	10,786	14,625	17,804
Legal reserves (5%)	539	731	890
Transfer to earned surplus	10,247	13,894	16,914

1. Assumes sales of 332,000 tons, 363,640 tons and 378,000 tons for the first, second and third years, respectively at $209 per ton.
Sources: P262, p. 52.

The analysts also calculated the benefits which the Turkish economy would derive from the project. These can be summarized as follows:[24]

1. Turkey lacked a facility to produce flat rolled steel products and therefore had to import them. The cost of these imports was about $7 million per year between 1955 and 1959. The actual cost to the Turkish economy was much higher, however, because needed imports were limited by a shortage of foreign exchange.
2. In addition to the foreign exchange savings, the ratio of value added in steel-making, about four or five to one, means that the output of Ereğli, valued at $74 million, would actually contribute about $300 million to the country's GNP.
3. The new plant would have a beneficial impact on employment because three to four thousand persons would be hired and additional indirect employment in steel consuming sectors would be generated.
4. Moreover, given that foreign exchange was expected to remain in short supply, the country's ability to import steel products would be limited. Thus, ERDEMIR, by insuring a constant supply of essential steel products, would permit development to occur in ways that would not otherwise be possible, particularly in the steel fabricating industry which is characterized by relatively short construction periods and quite high capital output ratios.

Clearly the national value of the project was never analyzed in any detail. It was taken for granted that an iron and steel plant would be of great value, not least because of the country's foreign exchange situation.

The only potential negative that was foreseen was an issue that had been in the minds of US officials since the project's initiation, 'whether or not it will have an inflationary impact'. The large lira expenditures (the equivalent of $60.2 million, about 12 per cent of total public sector investments at its peak[25]) could easily wreak havoc upon the new government's efforts to balance the budget and stabilize the economy. Hence the DLF representatives discussed this issue at length with Turkish officials and the latter prepared invest-ment and budgetary plants 'that would permit the carrying out of the Ereğli project without jeopardizing efforts to maintain the stability of the Turkish economy . . .' Moreover, since the IMF and the OEEC were again attempting to secure the implementation of the 1958 stabilization agreement the DLF managing director discussed the project with high officials of the agencies and countries involved.

Other potential impacts were ignored. Ecological considerations were totally neglected (as was the case for the iron and steel industry everywhere at this time). Nor did questions of the social, cultural, physical, political or economic consequences of establishing such a huge project in a quiet, small town receive any attention apart from mention of the need to construct housing for the workers. And, no attention was paid to the possibility of integrating this project into the region's overall development despite its catalytic potential.

THE MANAGEMENT ISSUES

As noted earlier, the USA had successfully insisted that ERDEMIR be a private sector firm. Technically a 'mixed enterprise' because its ownership was both governmental and private, ERDEMIR was organized in such a way as to ensure that, even though the Turkish government would, by contributing $24 million, own over half the shares, actual control would lie with the private Turkish shareholders (whose share amounted to $11 million) and the American share-holders ($10 million) by giving them 28.2 per cent and 25.7 per cent of the voting power, respectively. Moreover, not more than four of the nine members of the Board of Directors were to be representa-tives of the Turkish government, and the government was required to seek to sell its shares to private investors, on the basis of an agreed upon formula, within seven years.[26]

These were the only management issues that received any detailed attention. The more prosaic yet vital area of the plant's operation and administration was dealt with cursorily. Koppers would provide the supervisory personnel and would receive a contract for management training and supervision extending over the life of the loan. The labor force was to be recruited from Karabük and elsewhere and some personnel would be sent to the USA for training.[27]

THE IMPLEMENTATION

Initial funds for construction were released in September 1961 and the first foundation piles were sunk in August 1962.[28] Though all the engineering and scheduling details were worked out in Pittsburgh in advance, numerous changes and much engineering had to be carried out at the site because of unforeseen eventualities, including a very harsh winter in 1962.

Originally, about fifty Americans came to Ereğli and found a small town of about 8,000 inhabitants with few amenities. The town's hotel provided rudimentary accommodation, a handful of restaurants prepared simple meals, and a few stores stocked essential goods. All facilities had to be constructed – housing, a restaurant and a hospital. Arrangements were made for electricity and water – the latter had to be supplied by truck. Life under these conditions was quite difficult; when wives and children began to arrive, the issue of creature comforts became even more troublesome.

Not surprisingly, the degree of culture shock was quite high. This was enhanced by the relative isolation of Ereğli which did not possess easy access to the big cities of Istanbul and Ankara. Veterans of that period still relish recounting stories of the hazards of the five-hour trip that was involved, three of which were on a narrow, winding dirt road.

The short construction schedule dictated a frenetic pace; everything was done quickly and many activities were carried out simultaneously. Over 10,000 Turkish workers were employed on the project and hundreds of trucks roared back and forth along dirt roads with supplies and construction materials. Everything passed through the town, creating innumerable traffic jams. Nor were there any warehousing facilities – materials were simply laid out in piles in the fields. Problems with supplies were constant.

Stories about conditions at Ereğli have probably become more exciting and awesome as the years have passed but one cannot doubt that tensions often ran high. Nevertheless, there were many mitigating factors, including vacations not only in Istanbul and Ankara but, often, in Paris and Beirut. One veteran summarized the situation well, 'I don't care to minimize the frustration and exasperation that we encountered. But this is true of any major construction project, no matter where it is located. It might have been a little more true in Ereğli, but the relief from the drudgery also had a higher quality.'

The key man on the site, the project manager, was a mechanical engineer who found himself dealing with engineering issues – piling, foundations, roofing, etc. – for which he had no formal preparation. Today he recalls that 'the experience was a shock at first but it spoiled me for everything else'. One of his first duties was to recruit and train the workforce. Some crafts were not a problem, others proved troublesome. Qualified carpenters were readily available but few welders were to be found and men had to be trained on the site. Bricklayers were plentiful but of poor quality. Coke ovens involve a critical design which demand a high degree of accuracy in brick placement, but few of the bricklayers on the site had ever worked to such exacting standards. Eventually about fifty of the best were given further training.

Local personnel were unable to handle the foundation work, as had been planned, partly because the soil conditions turned out to be quite different from what had been anticipated. Twelve test holes had been drilled, but the results proved to be invalid because the borings were too far apart. Extensive foundation work was necessary and, after some debate, the Turkish government, because of its fervent desire to see the plant completed as rapidly as possible, agreed to bring in Morrison Knudson and Foster Wheeler, two large US construction firms, to carry out the work. Laying the foundations proved more difficult than even Morrison Knudsen had foreseen (some piles had to be sunk 1,500 feet); though the company started working around the clock, it lost money on the project. This experience illustrates both how any project encounters numerous unexpected difficulties as well as the risks involved in bidding for such contracts.

As construction proceeded, the AID mission in Ankara became increasingly aware that it required additional expertise if it were to overseee the project effectively. Accordingly an experienced steel man was hired and sent to Ereğli where he soon found that various issues were threatening the viability of the project. Washington began to receive memoranda such as the one dated 1 September 1962, which stated: 'Certain questions come to mind which need investigation and follow up to ensure the establishment of a profitably operating company.'

The first of these was the iron ore situation. The DLF's original feasibility study had concluded that there were 'ample proved reserves for at least twenty-five years of operation' but, only a few short months later, in January 1961, ERDEMIR requested that the iron ore situation be analyzed again. A new committee consisting of Turkish and foreign experts was established and their report published five months later seriously challenged the previous findings. Additional drilling had revealed that none of the deposits which the DLF had analyzed in detail could be utilized; Özkoyuncu possessed limited reserves with a high sulfur content, Hekimhan West very small proven reserves, and Hekimhan East's ore had a high manganese content which made the use of large quantities undesirable. Suitable ore was available for only twenty instead of the twenty-five years which had previously been anticipated and would have to come in small quantities from a large number of different sources. Surprisingly, the cost projections remained the same, per ton $12.70, per iron unit 22.5 cents.[29]

The second issue concerned the accuracy of the demand projections. Here the very viability of Ereğli was at stake for, as the DLF itself had noted earlier, given its heavy debt structure, unless the sales projections were met, Ereğli would be forced into bankruptcy. Accordingly ERDEMIR commissioned a product specific market study (July 1963). It yielded startling results, finding that the demand structure was quite different from what had been planned for. The anticipated demand for cold rolled sheets was far smaller than the projected production whereas that for pig iron, skelp and hot rolled sheets was higher. The survey also indicated a new difficulty, that many potential customers were not familiar with the technology of cold rolled sheets and that the company would have to offer a program of technical assistance as part of the marketing effort.

The third issue of concern was the management of the mill. As noted above this topic was addressed very cursorily in the original feasibility study. Now doubts were expressed as to whether Turkish personnel could administer such a complex operation. Accordingly, after various negotiations, Koppers signed two new contracts with ERDEMIR in October 1963 to provide management assistance for five years after the plant began commercial operation. The first, for $100,000, called for Koppers to provide five full-time advisors to Ereğli – a general manager, a financial expert, an advisor to the plant manager, a sales and procurement specialist, and a specialist in the development and application of modern metallurgical technologies. Under the second contract, ($200,000) per year, Koppers would provide assistance for all stages of planning, management and production.

The administrative structure of the enterprise represented the fourth problem area. The original rationale for the project had been to create a plant that would serve as a shining example of free enterprise in a developing society. For this to occur, however, private investors had to purchase a large percentage of the shares but, from the earliest days of the project, Turkish capitalists had sought to minimize their involvement. If the necessary local capital were to be raised, new measures were necessary and it was now decided to appeal to small investors throughout the country. A Koppers press release entitled 'Stock Market in the Street – Turkish Style' describes one of the methods used in this effort:

Mainly, it has been done through the efforts of stock sales caravans which make a direct but simple approach to the 'man in the street' in various Turkish cities. Into these cities and towns comes a small bus, loaded with display panels, a motion picture machine, a small electric generator (in case no electricity is readily available) and a professionally produced colour film entitled 'Opportunity of a Lifetime – Investment in Ereğli.'

Usually the Ereğli representative first visits the local bankers who aid in dealing with local officials and often appear personally for the film showing and take part in the discussions that follow. Frequently, the bankers order 'bearer shares' in anticipation of future sales. The sale 'show' may go on in a building – or outdoors in the town market place at night. The film itself is tastefully done, low pressure selling. Around a story theme, it shows colourful views of the Ereğli plant and finally takes the viewer into the homes of Turkish workers who have purchased stock – their investment in the future industrial might of Turkey.

Even these strenuous and innovative measures failed to provoke an enthusiastic response. Investors, large and small, continued to evidence little interest even though the military government that had assumed power after the 1960 revolution had enthusiastically endorsed the project. Nor was their interest ignited by the decision, when sales began in 1962, to pay a dividend to shareholders until the plant went into operation. By late 1963, only $4 million of stock had been sold instead of the $11 million which had been projected. US investors were proving equally cautious; they too had acquired little stock. Overall the shortfall amounted to about $13 million and almost three-quarters of the shares that had been sold were owned by the Turkish government – an anomalous situation for a plant that was supposed to serve as the flagship of Turkish free enterprise. The difference between the original expectations and the reality that confronted the policy-makers at the end of 1963 is depicted in Table 3.2.

Problems such as these could be dealt with in time but there was one that had to be tackled immediately. ERDEMIR possessed no cash reserves to deal with unexpected expenditures. And the harsh winter, the poor soil conditions and other difficulties during construction meant that local currency expenditures were exceeding budgetary allocations at an alarming rate. Koppers officially informed the DLF and ERDEMIR of this situation in mid 1963 and ERDEMIR, in

Table 3.2 Stock ownership of ERDEMIR (end 1963)

	Projected distribution		Actual situation	
	Stock owned ($ million)	% of voting rights	Stock owned ($ million)	% of voting rights
Turkish public sector	34	52.5	34.0	71.5
Koppers Assoc.	10	20.6	5.32	14.9
Other US	2	4.1	0.76	2.1
Turkish private sector	11	22.8	4.13	11.5
Total	57	100.0	44.21	100.0

Source: P262, p. 2.

turn, notified the Turkish government which disclaimed any responsibility even though, according to the original loan document, it had agreed 'unconditionally to provide or cause to be provided any additional local currency costs not provided for in the Financing Plan which may be necessary to complete the project.'[30] Despite this commitment, Turkish policy-makers refused to provide any additional resources. The DLF tried to persuade Ankara to change its decision but numerous meetings merely demonstrated that the Turkish government was obdurate. It relented only after brutal negotiations – in the gentle words of the official memorandum 'after strong representation by the US government on the highest levels'. The new agreement called for Ankara to pay for part of the overruns, TL 250 million ($27.8 million), the USA would supply another TL 100 million ($11.1 million).

The DLF accepted this compromise reluctantly but made the 'Cooley' (local currency) loan because it feared that the only alternative would be to shut down the project. In such an eventuality the credit position of the company would be seriously damaged; it might even be forced into bankruptcy and the DLF would lose its investment. Even if that dismal prospect did not materialize, the cost of starting up construction again would be very high. The DLF summarized its dilemma as follows:[31]

> The U.S. has a large investment in this project and a strong interest in its timely completion. The DLF loan is *not guaranteed* and possible operations are required to generate funds for repayment. These considerations amply justify AID participation in financing the overruns. [My emphasis.]

The new loan at 8 per cent was to be repaid in four semi-annual instalments beginning 30 June 1966.

When the final calculations had been made, the local currency overruns totalled $34 million. They fell into three general categories.[32] The first involved service items which had been included in the original budget but which cost more than projected, such as land appropriation (an overrun of TL 7 million, about 20 per cent) and organizational and pre-operational expenditures (an overrun of TL 46 million about 1,500 per cent). Overall, TL 70 million (about $7 million) instead of the anticipated TL 16.2 million were spent.

The second consisted of items that were not originally included in the budget such as all the auxiliary facilities which had to be constructed to accommodate key personnel. This involved the construction of houses, bachelors' quarters, guest housing, furnishings and fixtures, a hospital and a cafeteria. The hotel in Ereğli was improved, an apartment furnished in Ankara, and so forth. Into this category also fell such unanticipated expenditures as the cost of constructing a dam and hiring expatriates. Altogether such costs accounted for another TL 118 million ($13 million).

The third comprised all the items relating directly to the construction and erection of the plant which had been foreseen but which cost more than originally projected. Because of the problems encountered with the soil conditions, these costs exceeded estimates by almost 80 per cent. In addition, such tasks as improving roads, building loading and unloading docks, and maintaining buildings and other structures also involved overruns. Overall, these costs totalled almost $20 million, about 40 per cent over the budget.

These overruns were due in part to the problems described above and in part to the attitudes of the major parties involved. Lira expenditures were controlled by Turkish officials who were usually more concerned about ensuring that the necessary facilities be built than with accepting budgetary ceilings. Thus Koppers personnel have claimed that Turkish officials often insisted that they carry out some project or other without regard to its cost. The Koppers representatives were probably willing accomplices since their primary motivation was to construct a good plant. They believed that many items which had been excluded from the original contract represented necessary and useful expenditures which AID could subsidize because it had access to significant amounts of local currency funds that could not be taken out of Turkey. The Koppers people felt that these 'Cooley' funds would be well spent if they were utilized for projects related to the plant. Needless to say, Washington did not share this cavalier view and strove strenuously to avoid having to increase its already huge financial commitment.

Nor was the Turkish government willing to allocate additional resources to the project and the new agreement proved as difficult to enforce as the original loan document. Ankara did not provide the TL 95 million for the 1963 fiscal year and the Ministry of Finance did not make $4.7 million in foreign exchange available to buy semi-finished materials. Moreover, by 1964, it appeared that an additional TL 210 million would be required if construction were to be completed on schedule. And it was also apparent by this time that ERDEMIR did not have any of the working capital (about TL 200–300 million) which would probably be needed to finance operations during its first two years. ERDEMIR's management apparently hoped to secure that sum from sales, a belief that was called 'fantastic' by AID's field supervisor. In his words: 'There still lingers the fantastic notion that in 2–3 months of operations, sales income will match cash outgo.' He ominously warned that there would be 'rough weather ahead'.

Evidently, another infusion of local currency was required to keep the project alive, and AID again had no alternative but to embark upon difficult negotiations with the Turkish government. It finally succeeded, in 1965, in reaching an agreement whereby Ankara released the promised funds and lent the company another TL 100 million ($11.1 million). For its part, Washington increased the amount of its Cooley Loan by TL 50 million ($5.6 million). ERDE-MIR also arranged for another TL 100 million in credits.[33]

CONCLUSION

Obviously ERDEMIR was a 'typical' development project, one with serious flaws that had not been anticipated, despite the numerous studies that had been carried out. How can this state of affairs be explained?

The original decision to build ERDEMIR was obviously made on the basis of Turkey's national aspirations as defined first by Prime Minister Menderes and, later, by the new military regime. Its roots were to be found in Ataturk's views on how to achieve national development: through import substitution industrialization with an emphasis on heavy industry. That perspective was shared by Turkish leaders of all political persuasions. They were willing to make significant concessions to obtain the necessary external support to make the dream of a second iron and steel plant a reality. Similarly the USA agreed to support the project for reasons that were primarily political and ideological. The Eisenhower administration shared the belief that development could be be achieved by a strategy of industrialization, especially one that emphasized the private sector, and became extremely committed to a project that could demonstrate the validity of its position. Accordingly, neither the US nor the Turkish government considered any alternatives or carried out any detailed analyses. The latter was content to leave the design-related issues to Koppers and the USA. The former was essentially willing to accept the Turkish government's definition of its needs and priorities; Turkey was a valuable and valued ally and its economic well-being was an important consideration. Washington's primary concern was not with the desirability of building a small iron and steel plant but, rather, with its impact on the country's economy, especially its inflationary potential and its profitability.

The US decision, however, represented a major departure from past practice by the DLF. That it behaved in this way can best be explained by the bureaucratic politics model – powerful actors within the administration were committed to the project, even though AID's own experts were questioning many of its elements. Koppers, which wanted to obtain the contract to build the plant, made its decisions according to its standard procedures and conformed to the organizational process model. During the implementation stage, the numerous problems that were encountered and which led to cost overruns were resolved on the basis of its experience and past practice.

Given this context it is not surprising that important areas such as management and impact issues (other than economic feasibility) were essentially ignored and that only the design issues were analyzed in detail. Furthermore, it was already obvious that many of the analyses were seriously flawed and that the planners had not foreseen numerous problems. They had overlooked the need for the dam and for housing, miscalculated the nature of domestic demand, and reached conclusions about the iron ore situation that were not warranted.

Defective studies are endemic to large technological projects and I shall return to the question of why this should be the case in Chapter 7, for an understanding of how they are prepared, used and abused can contribute greatly to an understanding of how and why projects so seldom achieve their goals. Suffice it here to point out that some errors can be attributed to a lack of expertise or to simple errors (the soil conditions), methodological weaknesses, and the genuine difficulties involved in making certain estimates, especially of market demand. Others, however, resulted from the ways in which the decision processes worked within specific organizations and the interactions between them. Sometimes an organization had to produce a particular result – a good example being the Turkish agency's analysis of the iron ore situation which indicated that Turkey possessed 22 million tons of usable iron ore, three times more than Koppers had estimated a short time before. And, other actors, seeking to achieve particular outcomes, were willing to accept such findings, at least until the final commitments had been made. Then ERDEMIR requested a new study which produced quite different results.

This behavior reflects but one of the ways in which political factors influence project outcomes. Another is to be found in the very nature of the transfer process which inevitably requires bargaining between various actors. In this case the interactions did not proceed smoothly; difficult negotiations were required for the Turkish government, despite its eagerness to see the project implemented, was not a dependent or a passive actor. It consistently fought hard to secure the best possible terms and, when additional financial investments were required, was unwilling to divert any more of its scarce resources to the plant than it absolutely had to.

Still, despite the many obstacles, the plant had been built in record time and was ready for operation. All the problems had merely resulted in unanticipated expenses and additional costs. What now remained to be seen was how well the transfer process had worked. Was the project fundamentally sound? Would it operate successfully? Had the base been laid for Turkish managers and workers to acquire technological mastery? The answers to such questions would soon be forthcoming; they would reveal the extent to which the doubts that many were expressing about that plant's very viability were justified.

4 Salvaging the Project

All It Takes is Money . . .

INTRODUCTION

ERDEMIR began operation in early 1965 in a relatively trouble-free atmosphere with the Koppers personnel essentially running the plant. The most serious difficulty involved the reversing hot mill, a complex machine, but this and some other difficulties were quickly overcome.[1] Soon all of the units were exceeding guaranteed production levels by significant margins.

Other aspects of the operation, however, were not meeting, let alone surpassing, the goals which had been set. Sales ran about 50 per cent of capacity, about 60 per cent and 55 per cent respectively of the projections for the first and second years of operation. The size of the market had been estimated accurately (the backlog of unfilled orders actually rose during this period) but the assumptions that had been made about the production levels that the plant would achieve in its first years of operation proved to be wildly optimistic. As a subsequent AID report noted: '. . . even US steel plants cannot safely be expected to produce (and sell) at 90 per cent of capacity in the first year of operation and 99 per cent in the second.'[2] Further aggravating the plant's problems was the collapse of the plan to sell 110,000 tons of ingots to Karabük annually.

The original cost estimates also proved to be quite wrong. These had been accorded the greatest attention in the original study because the loan could be defended only if the project did not constitute a burden on the Turkish economy. Yet, as early as 1963, AID and ERDEMIR became aware that the plant could not produce at a price that would be competitive with imports. Hence, a fundamental part of the analysis, one on which the rationale for building the plant in the first place essentially rested, now proved to be in error by a significant margin.

ERDEMIR's management responded to these troublesome developments in a manner typical of entrepreneurs in all countries that follow an import substitution strategy – it raised its prices and sought protection from foreign competition by applying to the Turkish government for a decree that would forbid the importation of those items that it would be producing.[3] And, like any government following that strategy, Ankara acceded to this request. As a result, although income did not meet expectations, the company was able to earn 78 per cent and 72 per cent of what had been projected for the first two years. Overall this meant a shortfall of about $46 million.

AID officials were naturally concerned about this situation for both practical and intellectual reasons. First, the plant in which Washington had made such a huge investment in order to create an international model of what free enterprise could accomplish was in serious financial trouble; second, the original analyses which had legitimized the project were obviously flawed and it was important to pinpoint why these errors had occurred so that future projects would not be plagued by similar difficulties.

Accordingly AID set out to identify the shortcomings in the feasibility study and to account for the shortfall. It quickly found several significant discrepancies between the original estimates and the actual situation. The first, reduced sales, accounted for $17 million. The second, higher interest expenses (about 50 per cent higher than planned because of the infusions of new capital necessitated by the cost overruns) entailed additional expenses of $5.6 million. Increased depreciation and amortization expenses added another $2.1 million to the total. The raw material costs, the third item, were also higher than anticipated by another $4.1 million. Koppers had revised its original 1960 estimate upwards by about 15 per cent by 1965 but the actual cost turned out to be 22 per cent higher, though the cost of coal declined slightly.[4] All these items sufficed to explain part of the shortfall but, because of inadequacies in the original document, AID found it impossible to account for the remaining $17.5 million: '. . . the estimates of costs of sales in the DLF loan paper does not detail the individual costs'.[5]

AID also sought to identify an economic rationale that could have justified the original loan. After considerable effort, it finally concluded that: 'Economic advisability of the Ereğli steel mill project was . . . based on the assumption that low manufacturing costs would offset high capital costs . . .'[6] But by 1966, it was obvious that this assumption was completely invalid and that manufacturing costs at Ereğli would be at least as high as in other iron and steel plants. Hence, the project was caught in a financial vise; it could not generate enough revenues to pay off its high financial obligations.

AID was forced to an inexorable conclusion: 'It appears that the Ereğli Steel Mill is not very economic . . .'[7] The prediction of 'rough weather ahead' had indeed come true; actually the storm was of such a magnitude that the project was in danger of capsizing completely.

Clearly AID was confronted with a major crisis – it had sponsored and financed an iron and steel mill that could not, if it continued to operate in its existing form, pay off its large debt and might even be forced into bankruptcy, a sad fate for a project that was to demonstrate the viability of using private capital as a catalyst for national development. The possible solutions were limited: raise prices and/or expand the plant.

A further increase in prices was out of the question because, by this time, ERDEMIR's prices were already well above what had been projected. Instead of $212, the Istanbul consumer was actually paying $305 for a ton of steel products. And, imported steel cost 10 per cent less, $275 per ton. Hence the only answer was to increase the plant's capacity, a move that was desired by both ERDEMIR and Koppers. At ERDEMIR's request, Koppers analyzed the situation and, in October 1965, submitted a report that called for removing the imbalances within the plant, thus expanding production to meet the increased market demands that were now projected for 1970.

It suggested that the capacity of the iron and steel producing units be expanded so as to permit the hot rolling and cold rolling facilities to operate at or near capacity. Specifically, Koppers called for a sinter plant, the use of fuel oil in the blast furnace and installing hi-top pressure equipment there. These measures would increase hot metal production by an estimated 41 per cent from 440,000 tons to 620,000 tons. The addition of a second oxygen plant would increase steel production by 43 per cent. Koppers also suggested installing a continuous billet casting unit to process the 110,000 tons of ingots which were not being sold to Karabük as well as a continous type galvanizing line, a corrugator and a hot dip tinning line. The purchase of some additional rolling mill equipment was also recommended.[8]

This study, too, contained careful analyses of market demand. Koppers defended its original estimates made in 1959 and again used a customer survey to estimate 1970 needs because consumption reflected, as in 1959, 'availability not demand'. Demand was also estimated for specific product groups. Overall, it concluded that demand would rise by 8.5 per cent per year and made projections at 9.5 per cent and 13 per cent (growth rates experienced by other countries) as well. All these projections, however, were '. . . intended as indicators, not forecasts.'[9] This caution aside, the additions were expected to increase the amount of flat products from 350,000 to 401,000 tons per year and thus satisfy the anticipated 1970 demand. The total costs of these improvements was estimated at almost $42 million of which $36 million represented foreign exchange costs and $6 million local currency expenditures.[10]

The raw material situation was once again studied in detail. No problems were foreseen with coal and limestone but the iron ore situation was viewed in more negative terms than ever. Reserves of this material were now considered sufficient only to maintain the existing level of production and could not support any additional blast furnace capacity. In addition, the ore that was being used was of such poor quality that large amounts of fines were being generated (which meant that that an inferior blast furnace charge had to be used, thus leading to lower productivity) and transportation costs '. . . are exorbitant.' Koppers concluded: 'In view of these disadvantages and consequent uncertainty of ore quality, hot metal production for the long term is unpredictable.' It therefore called for an ore exploration program preferably along the coast where reserves (if found!) would reduce transportation and ore degradation problems which should be addressed in any case. And, if these efforts should prove unsuccessful, as was likely to be the case, recourse to imported ore should be considered.[11]

This report was submitted to AID which was again confronted with unpleasant choices. Further commitments were required in order to ensure that its 'show-case' project continue to operate at all. Moreover, many of the fundamental assumptions on which the original loan had been based were demonstrably false, e.g. the availability of an adequate supply of good quality iron ore, transportation costs, the private sector involvement, the costs of production, and so on, so that if the plant were to be salvaged, it would be a very different project indeed from the original conception.

TURKISH PERSPECTIVES

The Turkish government was equally concerned about these developments for it was under strong, continuing pressure from Washington. But Ankara was not at all certain that it should make any additional allocations or any further concessions concerning loan repayments.

After all, if it refused to cooperate it would inevitably inherit the entire works. And, by 'nationalizing' the plant, it could still the considerable domestic opposition which the project had aroused.

The return to civilian rule following the 1960 military coup was accompanied by a free, democratic atmosphere in which ideologies of all kinds were discussed for the first time. Various groups on the extreme left, including the Marxist Turkish Labor Party, organized in 1961, found ready support for an ideological stance which included bitter attacks on the USA for its 'imperialism' and hence, upon ERDEMIR as well. As one expert on US–Turkish relations has noted, '. . . from the moment that the agreement was concluded . . . [it] was assailed as prejudicial to Turkish interests.'[12]

Leftist intellectuals attacked the project on many grounds. They particularly disliked its private sector status and denounced ERDE-MIR as a project designed to promote international capitalism at the expense of Turkey's development. They argued that private capital should not be permitted to have any control over the production of such a basic component of the country's economy as iron and steel. Indeed, they believed that the Government had acted illegally because the 1960 Turkish constitution repealed the private invest-ment law of 1954 and provided for the nationalization of sectors that did not contribute to the national welfare. Accordingly, ERDEMIR should be nationalized because capitalists in Turkey and abroad would be earning the profits.[13]

Moreover, the original agreement was seriously flawed. Having been reached within an imperialist framework, it subordinated Turkey to the interests of the United States. It made concessions to foreign capital that did not meet Turkish needs and were destructive of the national interest. The agreement stripped the Turkish govern-ment of its sovereignty; the DLF had to approve all equipment and technical assistance decisions and these were made to benefit Ameri-can capitalists. The fact that the United States offered the most credits was proof that it wanted to make the most profits. In the words of one critic:

> Why do we have to give all these concessions? There is a $234.3 million investment of which $129.6 million comes from the DLF . . . at a 5.75% interest rate. Because the US firms have control over the pricing and because technology is going to be mainly transferred from the United States, Turkey is going to return that $129.6 million to the US with accrued interest.[14]

The critics calculated the consequences of these decisions for the plant's operation and severely criticized the high costs. They pointed out that ERDEMIR had emerged as a very expensive plant by international standards. Costing $250 million, it would produce 268,000 tons of sheet plus 110,000 tons of ingot whereas the Bhillai plant in India which cost $276 million turned out 770,000 tons of steel, and the Rourkeld plant which cost $350 million produced 720,000 tons of sheet. And, though the facility was designed to save foreign exchange, this would not happen in practice because foreign exchange would be spent to import technologies from abroad.[15] Accordingly, production costs would be extremely high – three times more than the average iron and steel plant, $569 per ton of steel product as compared to about $255 in India, $279 in the USA, $187 in France, $128 in West Germany, $113 in Japan. And, these high costs were due to two factors. First, Ereğli's site was badly chosen because it required expensive port development, necessitated high raw material transportation costs and inadequate soil studies had necessitated expensive foundation work. Second, and more importantly, American capitalists controlled the design and had forced Turkey to buy equipment that could be obtained more cheaply elsewhere. 'The high cost of production per ton is directly related to the dictation by foreign firms of the prices.'[16] Actually, as I have demonstrated, the plant's high costs were due neither to its site nor to capitalist rapacity but primarily to its small size.

The plant's travails provided ample ammunition for its opponents. One article, for example, discussed the so-called 'miracle of private enterprise' in ironic terms, pointed out that ERDEMIR had lost TL 210 billion during its first year of operation, that heavy losses were continuing in 1966 and 1967 and that small Turkish shareholders were the major losers:[17]

> Owners of small savings, who greatly favored Ereğli shares, influenced by the extensive propaganda, are angry; 500 Turkish lira shares can be bought for 350 Turkish liras . . . the government should demand an explanation for this situation. If ERDEMIR were really a private enterprise firm, it would have closed its doors a long time ago. However, this heavy burden of debt will have to be paid by the government . . . that is, the taxpayer.

The view that ERDEMIR served primarily the interests of private capital in Turkey and abroad, that the project represented a classic case of foreign capitalists taking advantage of low wages to invest in the periphery in order to make great profits, has been articulated most systematically in N. Şeni's recent book,[18] which analyzes ERDEMIR from a dependency perspective. Like other dependency theorists, she argues that multinational industrial monopolies are promoting a new international division of labor based on new production and exchange patterns. These monopolies seek higher profits and a cheap labor market and therefore establish new production units in the periphery. These emerging production units contain the necessary natural resources and, most significantly, have proven more profitably than the production units at the center. The use of highly mechanized technological means of production coupled with cheap labor costs generates higher productivity and greater surplus value, the portion of profits directly appropriated by the capitalists.

Şeni asserts that ERDEMIR provides a classic illustration of how foreign capital flows into the periphery; concerned with a falling rate of profit at the center, the multinational industrial monopolies export them in order to take advantage of the opportunity for greater profits. Şeni argues that the dramatic changes in the global iron and steel industry (discussed in Chapter 2) took place because of the increasing costs of production in the center and the availability of cheap labor in the periphery. As a result capital accumulation occurs not only at the center but also at the international level because of the declining rate of profits at the center. Accordingly, the demands of international capital dictated the decision to build ERDEMIR. The plant was designed to advance these interests by providing a new opportunity for capitalists to produce iron and steel profitably and by introducing a capitalist industrial infrastructure into the Turkish economy which would facilitate Turkey's complete integration into the capitalist world economy.

Unfortunately the author provides little supporting evidence for these assertions. The most significant datum involves the Turkish government's inability to implement its plan to build a second iron and steel plant (which it had first articulated in 1944) for a decade and a half. As I noted in Chapter 2, this project did indeed receive a cold reception from American and other Western experts after World War II. Şeni argues that this rejection was due not to the intrinsic merits of the project but to the interests of international capitalism. Similarly, Washington's willingness to finance the project in 1960 was occasioned by the emergence of the new international division of labor which required peripheral industrialization. The history of ERDEMIR that has been presented above, however, does not substantiate such claims; it certainly does not support a radical explanation of the factors that influenced the US decision to finance ERDEMIR. Nor does it support the argument that the Turkish government was a passive, dependent actor at the mercy of large historical forces and powerful international capitalists.

Equally suspect are the two general criticisms of foreign aid that are commonly made and which were levelled at ERDEMIR. First, because of incompetence and ignorance, aid is inappropriate in terms of the country's needs and does more harm than good. To determine whether the decision to build ERDEMIR yielded more costs than benefits is no easy task. Certainly several Turkish governments believed it to be a highly desirable project. Second, such damage is not accidental but results from the desire of the donors to exploit the recipients. This argument, that international capital structures foreign aid to further its own interests, has been dealt with above for ERDEMIR. In general, it oversimplifies the reasons why countries provide foreign assistance. As one scholar has written:[19]

> It is certainly true that the rich countries' motives are mixed; that foreign policy and export interests play their part. One would be amazed if it were otherwise. Unless one is to assume an exercise in international hypocrisy on an unprecedented scale, however, as a conspiracy among the rich countries of unprecedented complexity, it is clear that developmental interests also play their part. The question, surely, is not whether the aid-givers' motives are entirely pure, but whether in any given situation the combination of interests at work will promote trends that are advantageous or disadvantageous to those whom the critical observers would like to see benefited.

In any event, it is important to realize that the attacks on ERDEMIR were widespread and impacted upon political developments, upon the government's policies, and upon the enterprise itself. Many left of center and even conservative intellectuals were receptive to at least some of the charges, not least because US – Turkish relations were deteriorating rapidly during these years. What had been, in the fities, an extraordinarily warm alliance now entered a new era as Turkish governmental and public opinion was profoundly affected by various events, the most significant being the emergence of the Cyprus question and the widespread belief that the USA supported Greece on this issue.

A strong and wise government might have been able to contain the general disillusionment and minimize the damage to both countries that resulted. Unfortunately, the civilian governments that came to power beginning in the fall of 1961 were weak coalitions between the RPP and the newly formed Justice Party (JP), the heir of the outlawed DP. Tensions within the country were heightened by the emergence of new ideologies and with the realignment of the political parties along a left-right continuum. The JP, which gained strength steadily, because the major right-of-center party, the RPP, after considerable internal struggle, as the left-of-center party. The JP defeated the RPP in the 1965 election but the new Prime Minister, Suleyman Demirel, often made concessions to conservatives to maintain his position. Such moves, especially those involving religious affairs, further polarized the society. The result was only too predictable – fights, even pitched battles, between leftists and rightists and often involving armed students became commonplace.

THE AID RESPONSE

Such was the atmosphere in which AID had to find solutions for the problems of ERDEMIR, solutions that inevitably required the cooperation of the Turkish government. Having received the Koppers study recommending expansion, AID, which by now accepted the view that if ERDEMIR were to be a successful enterprise it had to be enlarged, acted in accordance with its organizational requirements. It called for further analyses and, after discussions with the major US steel companies, awarded a contract to ARMCO Steel Corporation on 3 June 1966 to study the operation and management of the mill. AID also hired Professor R. S. Eckaus of MIT for an economic analysis of the project.

These studies would require time to complete but time was a precious commodity because, unless the immediate financial problems were resolved, questions of long-term viability would become irrelevant. AID had concluded that: 'As the project now stands . . . it would not reach the breakeven point until 1968 and would never show a profit.'[20] ERDEMIR would lose over $35 million: $15.5 million in 1966, $11 million in 1967, and $8 million in 1968. AID feared that such losses would be disastrous from a political as well as a financial perspective. This view was shared by ERDE-MIR's management which felt that these developments:

'. . . would be very deleterious in this critical period . . . the effect on the morale of the company as a whole would be adverse and . . . the hostility on the project among elements in the country, the government and even the Board of Directors would be increased . . .

Even more seriously: '. . . Ereğli would be subject to involuntary (perhaps mandatory) bankruptcy under Turkish law in 1968 (and possibly in 1967) . . .'[21] In other words, the plant could easily collapse before any salvage operation could be mounted.

In order to prevent this eventuality, AID sought the Turkish government's agreement to an emergency program of debt rescheduling that would buttress Ereğli's financial condition so that it could bear the local currency costs of a future expansion. AID proposed that ERDEMIR be permitted to reduce temporarily its interest rate payments and to defer payments on the principal in order '. . . to bring the company's income statement more in line with the realities of its cash flow statement – by not deducting the interest that could not be paid – and thereby obviate the danger of the company being dissolved.' AID would also provide an additional $50 million during the 1967 fiscal year.[22] This meant that the Turkish government would have to adopt similar measures in regard to its outstanding loans, and hopefully, that it would also provide additional funding to ERDEMIR.

Negotiations proved to be extremely difficult, for the Turkish government, not surprisingly given the political environment described above, was more unwilling than ever to make any concessions. Once again considerable efforts by high level US officials who stressed the implications for US–Turkish relations if ERDEMIR were to collapse were required. An agreement was finally reached in February 1967 according to which the Turkish government did not have to advance any more cash to the financially strapped corporation.

THE NEW STUDIES

The specific nature of the expansion now had to be defined. Here design and management issues came to the fore but attention was concentrated on questions of impact, particularly economic profitability. Such calculations were, of course, dependent upon market projections and, as usual, every important actor made his own projections using different methodologies and assumptions and obtaining quite varied results. ARMCO interviewed importers, users and officials and, making assumptions about GNP growth rates, developed a low demand and a high demand scenario. Eckaus built a regression equation that related the historical demand for steel products to alternate assumptions of GNP growth rates. The State Planning Office based its own projections, unlike the others, not on the overall growth rate but on the growth of the manufacturing sector. And, ERDEMIR, with Koppers' cooperation, contributed its own estimates. All these calculations yielded results that once again differed markedly; not unexpectedly the highest, by significant margins, were the ones provided by the SP and ERDEMIR. The results are presented in Table 4.1.[23]

Table 4.1 Demand projections for ERDEMIR (000 tons)

	1970	1975
ARMCO A	384	560
B	402	614
Eckaus 10%	366	691
8%	340	580
6%	313	484
4%	291	400
SPO	450.7	878.8
ERDEMIR	487	813

AID now had a new task – it had to make a choice. It began by deciding that ARMCO's assumption of an annual GNP growth rate of 6 per cent was 'within the realm of probability' even though Eckaus had concluded that such an increase would be difficult to achieve.[24] It then engaged in extensive discussions with ERDEMIR (which wanted as large an expansion as possible) and decided to use the ARMCO 'A' projections as the basis for the financial planning and the 'B' projections for facilities planning. By so doing the company would achieve a significant increase in capacity but it would be forced to pursue a conservative financial policy.

No such disagreements marked the technological choice analyses. ARMCO supported Koppers' proposal to expand the mill and essentially endorsed its recommendations, with some minor modifications such as adding a six-stand billet caster rather than a smaller, three-stand one, and not expanding the power plant because the State Power Authority guaranteed the availability of adequate electricity. Its most important recommendation, using imported iron ore instead of building a sinter plant, was based primarily on the poor quality of the domestic ore which tended to break down easily so the the charge placed on the blast furnace contained about 30 per cent fines, with deleterious consequences for productivity. Hence, ARMCO suggested importing high quality ores to achieve an increase in hot metal production from the present maximum of 410,000 tons a year to 750,000 tons. Although, from an economic perspective, this was an optimal solution, AID and ERDEMIR, concerned with the political consequences of seeking to abandon domestic ores entirely, decided that the company should seek permission to use imported ore to meet only 50 per cent of total requirements. Using this mix meant that the level of blast furnace production would exceed coke production by 25 per cent and hence would necessitate the use of some fuel oil. Overall steel production would be increased from 560,000 tons to 900,000 tons per year by doubling the capacity of the lime kiln and the oxygen plant. Changes in practice that would permit the hot strip mill to be used for longer periods were also recommended by Koppers.

Koppers, ARMCO and ERDEMIR all agreed on the need to add a continuous billet caster to handle the increase in molten steel production that exceeded the capacity of the hot rolling mill and the market demand. The billets produced in this way would fill an established demand. At first, there was some disagreement as to the appropriate size of the billet casting machine, but the three companies subsequently reached an agreement.

The proposed expansion was expected to yield results in 1970 and be fully productive by 1976. Koppers and ERDEMIR, however, did not believe that ARMCO's estimate of 750,000 tons of hot metal production was feasible even though the blast furnace was scheduled to be expanded from 28.5 feet in diameter to 29.5 feet and hi-top pressure facilities added during its relining in 1969. ERDEMIR projected output at 660,000 tons per year; Koppers cautiously suggested that 700,000 tons per year might be possible. This would mean that steel production would be limited to 870,000 tons per year instead of the anticipated 900,000 tons.[25]

Decreased production would obviously lead to lower profits. Moreover, AID delicately noted that all of the ARMCO recommendations could not be implemented because '. . . the company's management is still in the process of learning . . . and the national attention focused on the Ereğli Steel Mill because it is the largest private enterprise and economically one of the largest and most significant public or private undertakings in Turkey does not leave management quite the freedom that it would enjoy in the United States.'[26] Given the extent of the Turkish government's involvement in the project and the nature of the political environment which existed, one must admire the delicate phraseology. In any event, the reference to management underscores the problems that continued to limit the plant's operations. These will be discussed in detail later.

Eckaus, too, had analyzed the iron ore situation but he concluded that, from the viewpoint of the national economy, the use of domestic ore was to be preferred over imported ore. He argued that the high cost of transportation was the fundamental problem and urged that shipping procedures be improved and that the economics of sintering domestic ore be studied further. AID asked Koppers to carry out such a study. The results indicated that (1) the costs of producing sinter would be $7 per ton (including depreciation and interest, (2) the cost of producing hot metal for the blast furnace using a mix of sinter and local ore would be 5–15 per cent higher than if imported and domestic ore were blended, and (3) if the transportation costs of the domestic ore could be reduced, the sinter alternative became more attractive.[27]

When AID analyzed these findings, it entered several qualifications, particularly the impact of using sintered ore upon blast furnace capacity. Koppers and ARMCO had reached significantly different conclusions, the former estimating that sintering would yield 650,000 tons of hot metal, the latter 500,000 as compared to 700,000 tons with imported ore. Such a drop in production would profoundly impact on the company's financial prospects; income would fall by more than $40 million per year.

AID decided, in the face of these findings, that, instead of investing $9 million in a sinter plant, the company should import ore, a solution that required no investment. AID also noted, albeit in a footnote,[28] an additional reason to favor the import option – its mission in Ankara now estimated that the company's major source of iron ore would be exhausted in five to ten years! The reliance upon imports would extend the life of these deposits and provide time to search for and develop new supplies. What had originally been a twenty-five year supply had shrunk to a twenty-year supply by 1961 and now, six years later, to about a third of that estimate.

Eckaus also suggested that, instead of billets, additional flat goods be produced for export. This proposal was also studied in detail, and the cost of increasing the capacity to produce such products was compared to the benefits to the Turkish economy. The results did not favor this alternative.[29]

AID also subjected its own projections to a sensitivity analysis to determine what would happen if its assumptions concerning such variables as the level of sales, the growth rate of the Turkish economy, the time required to complete the expansion, and so on, were proven wrong. This study revealed that further debt rescheduling could compensate adequately for all potential problems except a devaluation of the Turkish lira which would necessitate an increase in prices.[30]

Above all, AID focused on the issue of profitability and concluded that this expansion would permit ERDEMIR to become a viable enterprise. Even though the study's profit estimates were negatively affected by a new increase in coal and labor costs, AID's calculations (using the discounted cash flow method) showed that the expansion would still be desirable. If no expansion took place, the return on investment would be 4 per cent a year – less than the cost of the loans which was about 6 per cent; with the expansion, the return would be about 10 per cent per year and the cost of the product would decrease from $575 to $340 per ton. And, if the additional revenues generated by the new investments were taken into account, the return was estimated at 60 per cent per year. In other words, the cost of expansion could be repaid within the remarkably short period of sixteen months. The expansion was, therefore, essential and profitable.[31]

The 10 per cent return, however, was still a small fraction of the 30 per cent return on equity that had been assumed by the DLF when it had approved the original loan and which had been enshrined in the 'Founder's Agreement'. AID's new analysis noted that this figure was based on a premise of ever-rising prices since return on equity meant the return on a growing base consisting of the capital plus the reinvested earnings. Thus ' . . . highly profitable operations as were originally contemplated . . . will have to await the growth of the market for steel in Turkey to the point where a major expansion of the mill for more economic size will be warranted.'[32] In short, the original return on equity estimates could have been realized only if a much larger mill had been built.

AID also calculated the benefits that would accrue to the Turkish economy, again using the discounted cash flow technique. Taxes were eliminated, the cost of imports was utilized, and a shadow price 50 per cent higher than the official exchange rate adopted for the analysis. Because Ereğli's prices were higher than comparable imports, the analysis showed a zero rate of return for the economy without expansion, a 4 per cent rate with expansion, and a 45 per cent return on the new investment. Accordingly, the report concluded '. . . the national economic profitability of the expanded project is very low, the incremental return on the expansion investment is very good.'[33] The expansion would also lead to significant foreign exchange savings; without expansion the saving was seen as $24 million, with the expansion, the figure would amount to $41 million in 1973 and would increase subsequently.

If these economic benefits were to be fully realized, the plant's management would have to improve. The Americans involved with the project were in unanimous agreement about the type and magnitude of the management problems that prevailed at ERDE-MIR. These can be analyzed at three different levels: (1) the labor force, (2) the supervisory personnel, and (3) the management team.

Koppers had provided five full-time advisors and about 85 men (through a subsidiary, International Consulting Services, Inc.) to fill important supervisory positions. By 1967 their number had declined to 65. ARMCO urged that US supervisory personnel be kept on through 1975, though the numbers involved were to drop sharply from 65 in 1967 to 28 in 1970, twelve in 1972, and three in 1973.[34] It did so because it found that, though the ICSI personnel had been quite successful in training workers involved in production, most of whom had no previous industrial experience, much less progress had been achieved at the higher levels. Few Turks had yet acquired the necessary skills to operate independently, particularly at the level of foreman and above. Several reasons accounted for this weakness, including turnover in the highest position, the division of the company's management between Ankara and Ereğli, the assigning of line responsibility to people with inadequate backgrounds – especially troublesome in this regard was the general manager of operations – and the need of the foreign experts to spend time implementing the decisions that they made. Like the advisors, the supervisors were supposed to train their counterparts but, because the labor force and managerial personnel were so inexperienced, they found themselves forced to assume the burden of actually making and implementing operational decisions and had little time to devote to training.

Because of these shortcomings, the plant's productivity was quite low by international standards. Whereas eight man-hours were required to ship a ton of finished product in the USA, in Turkey the figure was 40 man-hours, more than five times as much.[35] Productivity was also negatively affected by the size of the labor force which had been expanded well beyond that necessary. ARMCO urged that it be reduced by 1,100 persons but this recommendation – which possessed obvious political implications – simply could not be implemented in the existing climate. Accordingly, following extensive discussions, AID, Koppers and ERDEMIR agreed that the labor force would be reduced by 600 men over a three year period.[36] As we shall see, even this goal was never met and problems of overstaffing became even more acute.

THE NEW LOAN

The expansion which was designed to permit the corporation to almost double its production of finished steel, from 268,000 tons to 435,000 tons per year, had already been endorsed by ERDEMIR, and many of the ARMCO recommendations were being implemented while Washington and Ankara engaged in their usual tough negotiations about how to provide the required financing. AID had decided that it could loan ERDEMIR another $22.35 million to implement the proposed interim expansion. For its part, the Turkish government was to provide a loan of $5.05 million. In addition, in order to ensure that the company would remain on a sound financial footing until the expansion project could yield the anticipated benefits, the current local currency loan would have to be rescheduled. Moreover, AID would grant the new loan only if Ankara provided assurances that it would permit ERDEMIR to import the iron ore that it needed. Altogether the new loans, which were formalized in April and authorized in June 1967, meant that AID's total investment would climb to almost $230 million, the Turkish government's to $132 million.[37]

THE SINTER PLANT DECISION

Even though a sinter plant had been, as we have seen, part of the original Koppers design and had been recommended by Professor Eckaus, AID, after careful consideration, had abandoned the idea. Now, ERDEMIR suddenly notified AID that such a facility was of the highest priority and that, because it realized that the size of the loan was fixed, it would substitute the sinter plant for the continuous billet caster even though ARMCO, Koppers, ERDEMIR and AID had all concluded that this piece of machinery was an essential addition if ERDEMIR were to achieve financial solvency.

ERDEMIR's decision was based on several considerations. First, it was not at all certain that, even with imported iron ore, the blast furnace would produce sufficient hot metal to manufacture both flat products and billets. ERDEMIR was, in fact, extremely concerned about the level of hot metal production it could achieve without sintering the local iron ore and was doubtful that it could even meet the flat product requirements. Above all, ERDEMIR, recognizing that it had to function in a turbulent environment, that the political situation could change, that foreign exchange crises could easily arise, wished to protect itself against potential interruptions in the supply of imported iron ore and gain greater flexibility and independence.[38]

Faced with this request, AID again proceeded with its customary attention to detail. It recalculated the economic feasibility of an expansion project that did not include a billet caster and decided to approve a loan of $14.2 million. In the meantime, Koppers executed another study of the iron ore situation, particularly the desirability of sintering. AID then hired the Rust Engineering Company to evaluate the Koppers study.

Koppers had argued that the need for a sinter plant was inescapable because the domestic iron ore picture had deteriorated still further. As noted earlier, the original studies had indicated that, if it consumed 800,000 tons of ore a year, ERDEMIR could rely on a twenty-five year supply, that a subsequent study in 1961 had reduced that estimate to twenty years, and that a later study had concluded that the domestic supply would be depleted within the decade. Moreover, the available iron ore contained a high percentage of sulfur which rendered some ore unusable without sintering. Hence, AID now decided that the company had access to only about

550–600,000 tons of usable domestic iron ore each year, iron ore that was of poor quality. Moreover, as much as 40 per cent of the ore arrived at Ereğli broken down in the form of 'fines' but, because of the shortage of ore, the company had to utilize these even though blast furnace productivity suffered accordingly.

The proposed expansion would greatly exacerbate an already bad situation because the consumption of iron ore would increase to one million tons per year. At best, only 60 per cent of this amount was available (of which more than 30 per cent was in the form of fines) so that ERDEMIR was confronted with a shortage of 600–650,000 tons of ore per year. This shortfall could be reduced to 400-450,000 tons if a sinter plant were built because fines could then be utilized as could high sulfur ores because sintering removed about 65 per cent of this contaminant. Hence, Koppers concluded that a sinter plant would permit the use of more domestic iron ore and the better quality charge would increase the efficiency of the blast furnace and lower production costs.[39] The Rust Engineering Company endorsed the Koppers study and approved the installation of a sinter plant.

AID subjected the proposal to its standard, detailed economic analyses, considering it in terms both of the company and the national economy. It found that although imported ore cost TL 170 and domestic ore cost TL 205 per pound, the difference would be offset by the advantages derived from sintering such as reduced use of coke and limestone and less wear on the blast furnace. Hence, costs were deemed to be roughly equal. And, though the company's profits would decrease because of the added interest charge, its ability to service the debt was judged to be satisfactory since its average debt coverage calculated on a cumulative basis would be about 2:1. [40] These studies sufficed to permit AID to support the project. ERDE-MIR asked the Turkish government on 10 June 1968 for loans of $12.5 million and TL 45.0 million to cover the costs of the sinter plant; two days later, the Turkish government applied for a $12.5 million loan from AID.

The first sinter was actually produced on 25 February 1972. This did not mean, however, that the plant could now operate efficiently. Production was hampered by the necessity to debug various problem areas, by foul weather (which caused the ore to turn to mud), by malfunctioning of the sizing screen, by the inability to use the product in the blast furnace and, most of all, by an attempt to force the machine to produce specified products from unspecified raw materials. All these difficulties which reflect the problems involved in transferring just one of the technologies used in an iron and steel plant took about ten months to resolve.[41]

CONCLUSION

The results of the first years of ERDEMIR's operation demonstrate very vividly the difficulties involved in achieving a successful technology transfer. All the analyses that had been so carefully prepared were now revealed to have contained significant errors which made the project a very flawed one indeed. And, when steps were taken to salvage it, new studies were undertaken, but these too were often compromised by errors of various kinds since most of the reasons that accounted for the analytical deficiencies were still operative. Changing conditions, sometimes resulting from the calculations of key actors as in the case of the sinter plant, were an important factor. Fearing the foreign exchange would not always be available to import ore, ERDEMIR wished to ensure a minimal supply under any conditions. The role of such studies was also unchanged; AID dutifully carried out the necessary work to validate a decision to support this change.

Every decision was made in the context of complex interactions as each actor strove to achieve its particular objectives. And these activities were influenced by changes in the domestic Turkish political environment where powerful forces were now attacking the project and the government for having agreed to its private sector status (thus supposedly making the plant a beach-head for capitalist exploitation of Turkey) and for the manner in which it had been implemented. Several decisions were affected by this development, including the one not to abandon domestic ore entirely (despite the high costs involved), and ERDEMIR's position on surplus workers. Relations between the USA and the Turkish government remained quite acrimonious, for the latter, seeking to protect itself from political attacks by demonstrating that it was not a captive of US interests, sought to obtain as much financing as possible and to minimize its own investments in the project. Nevertheless, compromises were always reached in the end because it also wished to prevent a complete breakdown in its relations with the USA. AID, concerned with saving the project, consistently made its decisions according to organizational norms and sought to resolve whatever problems arose in an incremental manner. It had few options for it wished neither to abandon the project nor to increase its already sizeable investments more than was absolutely necessary to ensure a successful outcome. ERDEMIR, on the other hand, wanted above all to ensure that it could continue to operate under any political conditions and to expand still further.

Clearly the level of technological mastery that was achieved was quite limited. Only scant learning had taken place at any level. The workers were the most advanced; they were becoming familiar with the equipment and how to operate it. But, from the foreman level upwards, serious weaknesses were apparent. Like other Turkish enterprises, the plant was organized hierarchically and its culture was not conducive to independent decision-making. Almost every decision had to be approved by higher management, overburdening persons (some of whom were unqualified) with unnecessary details, and making it more difficult for key personnel to learn how to manage the plant effectively. These conditions would obviously have to change if ERDEMIR were to operate at international levels in its existing configuration, let alone accommodate a major expansion.

5 The Expansion of ERDEMIR
Enter the World Bank

INTRODUCTION

The projects that were implemented during the 'Interim Expansion' led to a profound change in the condition of ERDEMIR and in its performance. Sales, profits and productivity all improved steadily and ERDEMIR became a thriving enterprise. This remarkable transformation was due partly to the continued learning that was taking place and to the increased level of mastery that was being achieved but also, more importantly, to the elimination of bottle-necks which had previously limited the plant's ability to operate successfully. Now the plant could produce at levels that ensured profitability since it possessed a monopoly in a protected market. Although its quality and productivity levels were not high, these shortcomings were overshadowed by a structural flaw: its debt–equity ratio still stood at a very high level. It had declined somewhat in the late sixties as a result of the restructuring but increased again in 1970 owing to the devaluation of the Turkish lira. These developments are summarized in Table 5.1.[1]

As a result, despite all of AID's efforts, ERDEMIR'S financial situation remained precarious. Although a profitable operation, the company was unable to generate sufficient cash to service its debts; these obligations now totalled TL 200 million, 50 per cent of which was in the form of interest. In 1970 its cash resources were TL 50 million short of the principal and interest that was due and, unless its debt structure were once again reorganized, default would occur in 1971.[2]

Accordingly, AID undertook yet another major review of ERDE-MIR'S financial situation. It commissioned the development of a sophisticated computer model to test the impact of over 400 variables (the cost and quality of such inputs as iron ore, different levels of productivity, fluctuations in exchange rates, and like) upon the

126

Table 5.1 Production (000 tons) and financial data 1966–70

	1966	1967	1968	1969	1970
Production of steel ingots	325	446	546	568	702
Production of flat-rolled products	211	267	402	384	503
Production of non-flat products	91	82	54	49	16
Net sales (million TL)	487	689	869	987	1,105
Net profit (million TL)	(16)	52	110	134	132
Debt–equity ratio	82:18	80:20	78:22	76:24	82:18

company's operation. The results clearly demonstrated that the plant, despite all the progress that had been achieved, remained a seriously flawed project because of its small size: 'The conclusion of this seven month study was that the company would eventually be unable to meet its debt service unless the plant were expanded and thus could profit from economies of size.'[3]

These findings were received with varying degrees of enthusiasm by the various actors. ERDEMIR and Koppers welcomed the findings. In fact, ERDEMIR had already commissioned Koppers to study the feasibility of an expansion and negotiations were underway between AID, the Turkish government and the World Bank which ERDEMIR had approached in November 1969. AID, on the other hand, which was cutting back on its involvement in Turkey, was unwilling to commit itself to any additional investments in ERDE-MIR. The Turkish government, naturally, vigorously supported all efforts to expand ERDEMIR; as one of its embassy officials stated in a letter to AID: 'My government considers this project to be of the first priority for the Turkish economy.'

The Koppers study, completed in late 1969, called for a major expansion program to be carried out in four stages over a ten-year period. After analyzing the study with the help of outside consultants, AID suggested that ERDEMIR contract with a company with extensive knowledge of the steel industry for a more detailed review. In April 1970, ERDEMIR commissioned United States Steel

Engineers and Consultants, Inc. (UEC), a division of US Steel, to analyze all aspects of the proposed expansion, including its economic justification. UEC ran numerous scenarios with various alternative assumptions.

The results which were submitted to AID in August were quite unexpected. Several startling conclusions emerged from all the computer runs. First, ERDEMIR was a very profitable enterprise – future after-tax profits would be no less than those achieved in 1969 and usually would be much greater. This finding had serious and adverse implications for the proposed expansion; in the words of the report:[4] 'This relatively high level of profitability (15%) is surprising and also has unfortunate effects on Stage I expansion justification.' Second, the return on investment calculations also did not favor the expansion for these were quite low, ranging between 12.5 per cent and 14 per cent for all the scenarios. Third, not only would the project expansion yield a low incremental return, but increasing ERDEMIR's capacity would not enhance its capacity to service its existing and new debts. This was, of course, a critical consideration for, as noted earlier, ERDEMIR was and would remain in serious financial trouble. The computer runs showed that the expansion would not change this situation. If the first stage of the expansion were to be completed in 1974, ERDEMIR could not meet its financial obligations until 1977 – a mere three years earlier than would otherwise be the case. Hence, UEC noted, '. . . a three-year advance in debt service coverage is in itself insufficient justification for the expenditure of $190 million.' And, taking all these considerations into account, UEC concluded: 'If the case is to be made for expanding ERDEMIR at this time, it must be based primarily on national economic grounds.' In other words, the projected expansion simply could not be justified on financial grounds; other considerations would have to be introduced.

The formal report which was delivered by UEC in September 1970 covered such topics as market demand through 1980, an evaluation of the existing facilities and the proposed expansion program, the raw material situation, financial projections including annual income and cash flow statements under different scenarios, and the economic benefits that would accrue to Turkey.[5] Shortly thereafter, UEC was commissioned to carry out additional studies. These reports were submitted in January 1971 and June 1971. All these studies served as the basis for the IBRD and AID appraisals of the project.

PROJECT APPROVAL

Despite the UEC's conclusions, the World Bank and AID remained willing to support ERDEMIR's expansion, each for its own reasons. AID's motivations were simple and easy to understand; it was influenced by a continuing desire to make a success of its investment. The Bank's motivations were far more complex but its interest was essentially due to a perception that the project was consonant with its goals and values. Its loans to Turkey had been extremely modest over the past decade because of the country's balance of payment problems and heavy foreign debt service obligations. In the late sixties, however, the Turkish government began discussions with the Bank which indicated its willingness to change its policy if Turkey would amend its traditional, inward-oriented, protectionist stance and emphasize export-oriented projects, initiate certain reforms in its international trade regime, and improve its ability to formulate specific priority project proposals.

The ERDEMIR project was especially appealing because the Bank felt that its expansion might help Turkey improve the competitiveness of its industry and its export performance in particular. Most importantly, believing that private enterprise could and should play a leading role in Turkey's development efforts and recognizing that, to date, little if any progress had been achieved in this regard, it looked with favor upon a company that had been established for that specific purpose. In its words:[6]

> The private sector has so far been unable to mobilize capital resources required for large scale industrial operations which, as a result, have been left mostly to the government. The establishment of ERDEMIR as a company which, despite a majority government ownership, is operated as a private enterprise and eventually to be transferred to private ownership, represents an effort to resolve this problem . . . The proposed loan would finance steel production and be the first direct lending operation to industry.

The Bank's renewed interest may also have been influenced by the political and economic developments that were taking place within Turkey. The Justice Party which had emerged as the major party in the sixties under the leadership of Suleyman Demirel, proved unable to provide strong leadership. The political scene came increasingly to be marked by growing polarization and fragmentation of various groups within the society and by growing violence between opposing elements. The 1969 election did not halt this trend and, though the Justice Party retained its position as the majority party, violence continued.

The government's economic policy, however, was consistent with the Bank's orientation and the Second Five Year Plan (1968–1972), as noted in Chapter 2, accorded to the private sector a new and important role for industrial development.[7] The state was to provide incentives for private sector investments, particularly export oriented industries. The plan did not provide, as had heretofore always been the case, for the continuing growth of state enterprises, but rather for the creation of mixed enterprises in which private capital would play an important role. Moreover, it adopted the kinds of policies that the Bank had been urging, including a major devaluation of the lira in August 1970.

That move led to an intensification in the negotiations and by late that year, the Bank decided that it should give detailed consideration to supporting several new projects in Turkey, including the ERDE-MIR expansion. On the basis of the UEC study, the Turkish government in December 1970 formally requested AID, the EXIM Bank (which it hoped would become a major participant) and the IBRD to cover the foreign exchange costs of the project whose total budget now came to $230 million.

During these months, Turkey's domestic political scene remained violent and unstable. In early 1971, the military forced Prime Minister Demirel to resign and sponsored the formation of a technocratic government that could restore law and order and rationalize the economic situation. The Bank now increased the level of its operations in Turkey significantly, began a detailed analysis of the ERDEMIR project, and sent a mission to Ankara in April 1971 to meet with the State Planning Organization and AID officials. In September, another mission visited Turkey, principally to consider the environmental implications. Their reports together with the UEC studies served as the basis for the loans documents that were prepared by the World Bank, AID and the EXIM Bank.[8]

The World Bank, however, did not wish to commit itself to a project that would not improve ERDEMIR's financial viability. Recognizing that the corporation labored under a very heavy debt–equity ratio (4 : 1), it sought to ensure that ERDEMIR would indeed become a financially sound enterprise if the project were implemented. Such a transformation could be achieved in one of two ways. Preferably, an infusion of new capital from either the Turkish private or public sector could be arranged, but the Bank acknowledged the unreality of such an expectation. Or ERDEMIR's existing obligations could be reduced. Accordingly the Bank entered into negotiations with AID and the Turkish government, seeking to persuade them to change the conditions of their loans. These negotiations did not proceed any more smoothly than any of the previous ones. At first, the Bank proposed that the hard currency AID interim expansion loan ($14.2 million at 5.7 per cent interest) and the AID sinter loan ($12.5 million at 6 per cent) be restructured, but AID objected strongly to making such concessions. Eventually, it was agreed that these would not be changed; only the hard currency interest payments due in 1972 and 1973 (TL 193.5 million) would be postponed. Prepayment of the Turkish lira loans would also be deferred for five years.

The terms of the new loan represented another troublesome issue. The Bank wanted AID to charge only 2.5 per cent on its loan, a concession which it somewhat snidely argued 'would in a way compensate for the low equity base in the existing capital structure.'[9] Not surprisingly, AID did not welcome either the suggestion or its rationale and retorted 'that the bank should . . . also waive its requirements for a "guarantee" [of 2 percent] on its loan.'[10] The Bank, however, was only willing to lower the fee to 1.5 per cent and thus charge ERDEMIR 8.75 per cent interest over fifteen years, including a four-year grace period. It argued that this rate (lower than existing rates in Turkey of 12–14 per cent) was appropriate for an iron and steel plant but was 'not so low as to endow its subsidy to ERDEMIR.'[11]

Negotiation between AID, the IBRD and the Turkish government were equally, if not more, troublesome. AID and the World Bank shared a common concern, that 'the government not increase its already large ownership of ERDEMIR and thereby create a danger that ERDEMIR become a state economic enterprise'.[12] They disagreed, however, on the question of the Turkish government's guarantees. The World Bank, aware of the problems that AID has encountered, sought to ensure that these be absolutely binding. AID officials, on the other hand, were quite sensitive to the political implications of such demands. One person noted that the original draft guarantee agreement contained an 'almost dictatorial tone'. Moreover:

. . . the terms and conditions the guarantor is expected to accept are so extreme in some cases that we are convinced that the Turks would feel that they are faced with a situation where they had absolutely no right to any defenses . . . this would be politically impossible to accept especially in today's environment.[13]

Nor did negotiations among the US participants proceed easily. AID objected to the EXIM Bank's financing package of supply credits became it would increase ERDEMIR's debt service problems and because it deviated from US policy concerning Turkey.

All these difficulties were finally ironed out after months of intense negotiations. The Turkish government agreed to guarantee payment of AID loans totaling TL 2,128.8 million and to give ERDEMIR financial relief by granting it a price increase, an accelerated depreciation schedule, and to reschedule some of its loans. AID, for its part, agreed to defer principal repayments on its original loan and on its 'Cooley' loan.[14]

Almost as soon as these carefully worked out arrangements had been agreed upon, the package fell apart. Changed conditions in 1971 – a fall in the value of the Turkish lira, an increase in the price of coal and of ERDEMIR's products and, most importantly, a decision by the Turkish government that it could not commit $30 million in foreign exchange to the project – forced a new round of bargaining. Finally AID agreed to increase its contribution significantly, from $15 million to $40 million, the EXIM Bank would contribute $70 million, and the IBRD $76 million instead of $65 million.[15] By the time that the new agreement was arrived at, the cost of the project had climbed to over $295 million. All of the local expenditures were to be provided by the company itself out of its retained earnings.[16]

THE IMPACT ISSUES

The new agreement did, however, address a heretofore ignored topic – the plant's environmental impacts. In fairness to AID one should bear in mind that environmental considerations were of little concern anywhere in the world until this period, even though each activity within an integrated iron and steel plant generates residuals that can cause severe or even irreparable damage to the environment. The quantity and type of pollution does vary greatly from plant to plant, depending particularly upon the quality of inputs, the technologies used and the type of end product.

The Bank's interest in pollution control was not shared by either ERDEMIR or the Turkish government and even AID evidenced little interest. After much debate an on-site study of the environmental situation was finally carried out in September 1971, and, a few months later, an analysis of the expansion's environmental quality implications was also undertaken. These studies revealed water pollution to be a major problem. Coke plants yield phenol and cyanides, which had been diluted by being washed with sea water before being discharged into the bay. Pickle line operations produce contaminated sulfuric acid and rolling plants yield water contaminated with oil and solids. These pollutants were simply dumped into the bay. As a result, marine life may have been seriously damaged and no bathing or washing of clothing was permitted. The rolling plant's waste water had coated the shorelines with oil and the basic oxygen furnace had produced high quantities of suspended solids. Even the company's beach was in danger of becoming contaminated and the acid pickle line waste water was temporarily diverted to the river.[17]

Other environmental problems involved air pollution (much dust was generated by the basic oxygen furnaces and the blast furnaces), noise, especially in the pickling operation and the calcing plant, and smoke and fumes in the form of sulfur dioxide. Overall 70 tons of this chemical were being discharged daily into the atmosphere.

When the loan application was being processed, only the preliminary results of the study were available. These permitted the Bank to assess the environmental damage to date as 'minor'. Nevertheless, $3 million was included in the budget for anti-pollution equipment – a new 160 meter high stack to deal with the air pollution problem, a biological treatment plant for the coke plant effluents and an acid regeneration system for the pickle line.[18]

AID's analysis also contained a section dealing with the environment. Its assessment of the situation was similar to the Bank's – no great damage had yet occurred. It noted that 'gaseous emissions . . . have had no particular impact on the township . . .' but that: 'Liquid wastes are proving troublesome in the existing plant and will be compounded by plant expansion in the absence of corrective measures.' These had had an 'adverse effect on recreational facilities.' Not surprisingly, AID's recommendations were extremely modest. They consisted of a formal request to ERDEMIR to incorporate environmental issues into the design of its new facilities and a suggestion that management consult an AID publication, *Environmental Considerations* for helpful advice on how to deal with the problem.[19]

Even these modest suggestions were not acceptable to ERDEMIR. Its management may have been willing to read the AID booklet but it was not prepared to deal with the causes of the pollution. It argued that no ecology standards existed in Turkey and that the company could not act until these had been prepared. ERDEMIR's attitude was consonant with that of the Turkish government which never expressed any concern about pollution by the plant. No occupational health service was available. The prevailing attitude has been described as being: 'If something happens, nobody will know what really caused it.' The IBRD, however, was equally intransigent and, after some tough negotiations, ERDEMIR formally requested, on 11 July 1973, that UEC prepare plans to deal with the pollution problem.[20]

This request sufficed to delay significant action for many months, until November 1974, when an IBRD pollution specialist became personally involved. After checking the situation, he sought to persuade AID and Koppers to force ERDEMIR to remedy the situation, but they refused to do much on the grounds that there were no applicable Turkish regulations. He then worked to get the Bank to take further steps and, finally, the Turkish government indicated that it would establish some standards. ERDEMIR agreed to install pollution control equipment, but the level of its commitment is indicated by the fact that it never bothered to send specific data to the bidders or seek any guarantees.

In November 1975, the Bank finally obtained figures on the concentration of cyanides and phenol in the Black Sea. The data revealed that the cyanide was disappearing but that some phenol concentrations were still too high. In 1976, the IBRD specialist visited the plant himself and found that the effluent treatment system was appropriate if it were operated properly. The coke oven plant, however, continued to operate as before, merely diluting the waste so that eight tons of phenol and two tons of cyanide were still being discharged daily into the Black Sea. At his insistence, Koppers and ERDEMIR carried out new analyses of the sea water; these showed that the toxic concentrations of cyanide and of phenol were higher than those tolerated by fish. Since the bidding documents had already been sent out by ERDEMIR it was difficult for the World Bank to do very much but the Stage II expansion, discussed below, did include a biological treatment plant for the coke ovens and a dust collection system for the sinter plant.

How productive these measures will be is not at all clear. An effective anti-pollution program requires more than the installation of some equipment; monitoring is a necessary and vital function. Even though monies were set aside for this purpose, it is not at all certain that they were properly utilized. Moreover, chemicals have to be obtained from abroad at a cost of about $300,000 a year; during a foreign exchange crisis, a not unknown event, this item would probably be accorded a low priority.

Nor was the plant the only polluter. Since Ereğli possessed no sewage treatment plant the town's garbage was simply discharged into the Black Sea. This procedure may have been adequate when Ereğli was only a small village but its rapid growth had created a new situation. One beach had already been condemned and cholera was a possibility, but the Turkish government and ERDEMIR were indifferent. Ankara was unwilling to provide any funding for sewage treatment arguing that Ereğli should not be accorded a higher priority than the numerous other communities which lacked such facilities. ERDEMIR was equally apathetic, claiming that the town's problems were outside its jurisdiction; it was most reluctant to cooperate even though one plant could handle Ereğli's sewage and ERDEMIR's effluents.

Although the IBRD raised the issue of pollution control at ERDEMIR, it essentially did so according to its organizational procedures. It probably was not, at first, very serious, for environmental considerations seldom occupied a central role in its project analyses. This was due to several factors. First, under McNamara the volume of bank lending increased from $800 million to $12 billion, but the staff dealing with environmental issues only tripled. Hence, it was overworked and under much pressure. Moreover, only 180 days could elapse between the appraisal by the mission in the field and the submission of the final report. It is during this period that the environmental aspects must be checked to see if they have been dealt with properly. Yet projects have increased in number, size and complexity and thus require more time for analysis. Hence it is possible only to concentrate on the most important cases and, given the structure of the organization and the prevailing norms which, dominated by orthodox economic thought, are not very sympathetic to environmental concerns, it is easier to go along with than to oppose a project or suggest major changes within it. Aggravating these difficulties is the reliance on external consultants – many of whom had had little, if any, relevant experience.[21]

Despite such constraints the Bank did play an important role in this case, though largely because of the zeal and dedication of one specialist. His efforts to ensure that adequate pollution controls be established and maintained created a controversy that became so heated that the Bank actually threatened to cut off funds for the Stage II expansion unless its recommendations were put into effect.

THE DESIGN ISSUES

The proposed expansion, which closely followed the UEC recommendations, was a major undertaking. Overall, production of hot metal was expected almost to double, rising from 860,000 to 1,654,000 metric tonnes, and sales to more than double from 621,000 to 1,500,000 metric tonnes per year. This would be achieved by the addition of a second blast furnace, a third battery of coke ovens, a third basic oxygen furnace vessel, a semi-continuous hot strip mill to replace the original reversing Steckel mill, additional cold rolling capacity –(doubling the horsepower and speed of the existing tandem mill) and various auxiliary facilities. The expansion also provided for that continuous billet caster whose desirability had previously been analyzed at length. In the second stage, a new coke plant, a third large blast furnace, and a new basic oxygen furnace would be added and the semi-continuous mill would be converted to continuous operation.

The two phases were to be arranged so as to maximize the output of existing facilities and to add new facilities to meet the projected increases in market demand. During Stage I (1972–76), the emphasis would be on expanding the raw steel production, during Stage II (1976–80), on the finishing capacity to process the surplus production which would be created.[22]

Primarily designed to increase capacity and achieve economies of scale, this major expansion had several subsidiary goals. These included the achievement of (1) operational advantages – the capacity of the existing slabbing/plate mill would increase because it would be producing slabs and plates only and would not be required to roll slabs to bar thickness for the reversing mill; (2) quality improvements because the new machines would permit the production of coil with close tolerances and improved surfaces; and (3) greater operating security and flexibility because of the duplication of various facilities.[23]

As before, questions of market size occupied a prominent place in all the studies. UEC had analyzed the market demand using two different methodologies. First, it carried out a simple regression analysis of the relation between flat steel and GNP in various countries. This 'global' approach method indicated that steel demand in Turkey would grow at 1.43 times the growth in GNP and, assuming that the proportion of flat steel to total steel demand would remain steady at 31 per cent, UEC projected a 10 per cent annual increase in demand during the seventies. Second, UEC studied the estimated requirements by major users and concluded that the results were contaminated by prevailing high demand and did not reflect accurately the longer term situation. Accordingly, in planning the expansion, UEC relied on the results of its 'global' approach which showed the demand for flat products to be 855,000 tons in 1975, 1,310,000 tons in 1980.[24]

The bank also undertook its own market projections, using the same methodologies as UEC. Though its staff doubted the validity of the 'global approach', it concluded that the UEC figure of 10 per cent growth in steel demand 'may seem overly conservative.' The end use approach was received more positively because of its sectoral emphasis which rendered it 'an indispensible tool in sales strategy and in facilities and production planning.' The analyses of possible demand in the major sectors which Ereğli supplied – water, gas and other pipe, the oil and gas industries, container and bottle corporations, household appliances, automobile manufacturing, etc. – yielded a somewhat large demand estimate. The possibility that steel might be displaced by other materials was also considered. The former methodology yielded a market of 1,310,000 tons by 1980, the latter one of 1,543,000 tons.[25]

ERDEMIR, which as always was anxious to expand as much as possible, was not pleased by any of these estimates, all of which it considered to be too low. The Bank's experts, however, were not swayed; they concluded that UEC had erred on the low side but that this was desirable since by doing so it provided a margin of safety for the expansion. Its detailed analysis of how the Stage I expansion would relate to the market demand is present in Table 5.2.[26]

138

Table 5.2 Available Market and Output Projections for the ERDEMIR expansion projects (000 tons)

	1971	1972	1973	1974	1975	1976	1977	1978	1979	1980
*Available Domestic Market**										
Plates	121	130	145	160	175	190	210	235	260	290
Skelp	62	75	80	90	100	110	120	130	145	160
HR sheets	117	120	135	145	155	170	185	205	225	240
CR sheets, black plate	154	180	205	230	265	295	330	370	410	450
Tin plate	56	65	70	75	85	90	100	110	120	130
Total Flat Rolled	510	570	635	700	780	855	945	1050	1160	1270
Billets[6]	—	—	60	200	300	300	300	300	300	300
Ingots (for sale)[6]	—	60	60	60	60	60	60	60	60	60
Total Steel Products	510	630	755	860	1140	1215	1305	1410	1520	1630
Output Projections – 'Project'										
Plate	121	127	127	160	175	190	190	190	190	190
Skelp	62	65	65	90	100	110	110	110	110	110
HR sheets	117	119	119	145	185	220	220	220	220	220
CR sheets, black plate	154	154	154	230	265	305	305	305	305	305
Tin plate	56	56	56	75	85	90	90	90	90	90
Total Flat Rolled	510	521	521	700	810	915	915	915	915	915
Billets	—	—	60	200	300	300	300	300	300	300
Ingots (for sale)	—	60	60	—	60	60	60	60	60	60
Total Steel Products	510	581	641	900	1170[1]	1275[2]	1275[3]	1275	1275	1275
Ingot equivalent	729	804	864	1182	1495	1648	1648	1648	1648	1646

Purchased slabs or ingots (ingot equivalent)									
(179)		(132)	(124)	62	(124)	62	(124)	124	(124)
Ingots to or from inventory	96	—	—	—	—	—	—	—	—
ingot production: 550**	900	900	1050	1560	1710	1524**	1648	1772	1526**
Ingot capacity 800	900	900	1050	2000	2000	2000	2000	2000	2000
Ingot operating rate[4] 69%	100%	100%	100%	78%	86%	76%	82%	89%	76%
Hot metal requirements 473	774	774	903	1390	1520	1340	1470	1580	1330
Pig iron sales —	—	87	250	180	180	180	180	180	
Iron output: 473	774	862	903	1640	1700	1520	1650	1760	1510
Iron capacity 475**	778	872	1209[5]	1654	1654	1448**	1654	1654	1448**
Blast furnace utilisation[7] 100%	99%	99%	74%	100%	103%	105%	100%	106%	104%

* UEC November 1970. Total market growth as estimated by both ERDEMIR and the Bank Staff would be somewhat higher.

** Years of blast furnace relining.

1. Includes 30,000 tons of assumed exports.
2. Includes 60,000 tons of assumed exports.
3. Includes 35,000 exports in 1977, and small quantities in 1978.
4. Ingot production divided by ingot capacity.
5. No. 1 Furnace plus 90 days of No. 2 Furnace at 60% of capacity.
6. The figures for ingots and billets represent projected sales by ERDEMIR rather than the total market which could exceed the projected sales.
7. The fact that projected output would exceed normal blast furnace capacity is not highly significant, since the projected output could be reached, if necessary, by various expedients, including a higher admixture of rich imported ores or pellets. Alternatively hot metal ratio in the BOF could be reduced slightly.

A plan to increase output to this magnitude clearly necessitated a vast increase in the quantities of raw materials to be consumed and, once again, much attention was paid to this topic. Surprisingly, in the light of the previous history of the iron ore situation (the 1965 forecast has been that the supply would be exhausted in five to ten years) and the coming on stream of ISDEMIR, the IBRD's major concern was not the quantity of domestic iron ore but its quality and cost. In its words: 'There was enough proven domestic ore reserves to meet the requirements of the Turkish steel industry through an expansion of state owned mines . . .' It did, however, acknowledge that whether production could be expanded rapidly enough was problematic and, since ERDEMIR had started to import iron ore in 1971, the Bank urged it to enter into long-term commitments for a specific percentage (about 25 per cent) of its iron ore requirements.[27]

UEC had carefully calculated the cost differential to ERDEMIR of using domestic versus imported iron ore and concluded that reliance on domestic ores imposed a heavy burden on the company. This was partly due to price (26 cents per unit of iron as compared to 22–23 cents for imported ore) but more importantly, the lower quality of the domestic ore meant lower production and higher operating costs. As a result, the real cost of using domestic iron ore was increased by a factor of 40–50 per cent. The advantages of using imported ore, however, were negated to some extent because of the relatively small quantities that ERDEMIR required and especially because of the small ships (40–50,000 tons) that had to be utilized since Ereğli's harbor had never been expanded to accommodate modern large ore carriers.[28]

The other major raw material, coal, did not present any difficulties. ERDEMIR received about 90 per cent of its coal from Zonguldak, the other 10 per cent from a nearby mine. Moreover, the coal was competitively priced running about 3 per cent more than imported coal. It was noted, however, that the Turkish coal industry was characterized by escalating labor costs and problems of management and development. Hence, the price of coal was likely to rise in the future.

Questions of costs were of major concern to the Bank's analysts who sought to ensure that the company become profitable and internationally competitive. Existing costs were extremely high, partly because of the relatively high prices that the plant paid for its raw materials. In 1970 these accounted for 54 per cent of ERDEMIR's average before-sales price, a very high figure by international standards.

The expansion was expected to improve this situation greatly and to lower the costs of production and sales significantly through economies of scale and the elimination of bottlenecks that prevented various units of the mill from operating at capacity. The overall costs were expected to decrease by 21 per cent from $2,414 per ton in 1972 to $1,897 in 1976.[29]

These projections were based on an important assumption – that a 95 per cent operating rate would be achieved.[30] Although this was acknowledged to be a high rate (in the West, the average was 80–90 per cent), the Bank accepted it because of three mitigating factors: (1) a protected market, (2) the potential for exports, and (3) the future investments that would be undertaken by the company to increase productivity. But this was not the only significant assumption that the Bank decided to accept – at least five others can be identified, about each of which serious questions could be raised. First, the blast furnace was expected to produce 1,545,000 tons of iron per year based on a mix of 43 per cent domestic ore, 39 per cent sinter and 12 per cent foreign ore. Second, the BOF shop, after the installation of the third vessel, would produce at its capacity of two million tons per year even though this level of production could be achieved only if existing practice improved. Third, because of improvements to upgrade ERDEMIR's quality to international standards, rolling mill yields would decrease slightly. Fourth, although output would rise by 25 per cent, the number of workers was expected to decrease by about one-third. Fifth, productivity was expected to improve from 17.5 man-hours per ton for all products in 1971 to 8.3 in 1976–80, an increase that was deemed reasonable because it '. . . assumed essentially only a continuation of present practices . . .' Yet the analysts went on to point out that 'they assumed strict managerial controls and the maintenance of successful labor relations with emphasis on productivity.'[31]

If all these assumptions proved to be valid, then the production cost estimates would be accurate and ERDEMIR would become financially viable. The Bank computed the internal rate of return on the incremental investment to be 20.2 per cent, and on the basis of sensitivity analysis, that the lowest reasonable rate would be 12.3 per cent. The debt coverage was also carefully calculated; at its lowest point in 1977, ERDEMIR could safely pay off its obligations even if income were to drop by 20 per cent and operating costs rise by 30 per cent provided that (1) dividends be paid only to the individual Turkish shareholders at a 9.5 per cent rate and that no further cash allocations of any sort be made until the debt–equity ratio reached

60 : 40 and, (2) the company not borrow or invest more than $2.5 million in any year without IBRD approval.[32]

Even though the plant would yield a satisfactory rate of return, the question of international competitiveness remained. In its present state, ERDEMIR simply could not compete with foreign plants. If its cost performance improved as anticipated, however, it would operate on a level with European ones though it would not be competitive with Japanese steel producers. ERDEMIR's average domestic price would be only 12 per cent higher than comparable imports and would require an effective protection rate of 22.17 per cent, a figure which the bank found acceptable.[33]

This, in effect, was the cost that Turkish consumers would bear – the benefits that would flow from the expansion, foreign exchange savings (an estimated $38 million per year),[34] secure supplies of steel, skill development, forward and backward linkages, etc., had to exceed this amount for the expansion to be justified.

All these comprehensive calculations were based, however, not only on numerous doubtful assumptions but also on costs that were estimated conservatively. As one of the bank's own analysts has written:[35]

> The price level . . . is one that would have allowed a reasonable rate of return on the historical book value of the plant rather than on the replacement value. Application of the latter more proper and more stringent standard would make the economics of the project even less favorable.

Equally questionable were the calculations that showed that if one considered merely the new investments and price structure only 5.6 per cent higher than comparable imports, the company could earn a 12 per cent return: this level of protection '. . . would not allow full coverage of costs and a reasonable return on the total investment, including the original plant. In 1970–72 this would have required a further price increase of about 8 per cent.'[36] In short, even with all the assumptions that were made about costs of production, etc., the new expansion could be justified only with difficulty and, if more stringent standards were applied, the project could hardly be defended at all.

Nevertheless, all these analyses served their function; like so many studies they were designed to legitimize a decision that the Bank wished to reach. This is quite apparent if one considers the rationale that President McNamara provided to the Executive Directors when he recommended that the loan be approved. He wrote:[37]

> The justification for an expanded Turkish steel industry is based primarily on its ability to operate on an economic scale at competitive prices and on Turkey's virtual self-sufficiency in coal and iron ore. The relatively sophisticated industrial sector includes major steel consumers for whom a competitive steel price is essential, such as machinery and metal fabrication, appliances, automotive and tractor manufacture, and all types of pipe for water, gas and electricity. Much of the production is for domestic consumption but Turkey's increasing links with the Common Market may provide export potential and the favorable wage rates of Turkish labor offer sub-contracting opportunities to Common Market firms in the metal fabrication sector. Competitive prices for steel supplies may also enable Turkish tractor and appliance manufacturs to compete in regional export markets. It is in this context of achieving an input at reasonable prices for the Turkish steel consuming industry, that the ERDEMIR expansion project has its main significance.

Whether ERDEMIR could, in fact, provide steel at 'reasonable prices' became the subject of new studies almost as soon as the financial arrangements had been formalized. Changed conditions (ERDEMIR's decision to import semi-finished and finished steel products to satisfy a greater than expected market demand), devaluation of the US dollar, higher unit prices for several major items) had rendered obsolete many of the financial projections which had been so carefully worked out.

Accordingly, UEC undertook another new comprehensive study that incorporated these factors. The report, submitted in June 1973, now estimated the domestic market for flat products available to ERDEMIR in 1973 to be 775,000 rather than 635,000 metric tonnes and to reach, in 1977, 1,300,000 metric tonnes rather than 945,000 metric tonnes.[38] Various amendments to the facilities plan were recommended in order to increase output which raised the cost of the project to $268.6 million and TL 3,760.4 million.

All these changes inevitably meant that the production costs had to be refigured. Two scenarios were analyzed in detail, one in which ERDEMIR continued to import steel products, and one in which it did not. Sensitivity analysis was also used. The results may be summarized as follows:[39] (1) the current ratio (current assets to current liabilities) was about 1.6 or 1.7 to 1, though it was generally accepted that an appropriate ratio was 2 : 1; (2) the debt to equity ratio 'is not especially attractive', and (3) the debt service ratio was essentially marginal. Or, to put it more simply, the project's economic justification remained as questionable as it had always been.

THE MANAGEMENT ISSUES

In all of the reports little attention was accorded to issues of management. Surprisingly, no major difficulties were anticipated in this area, despite all the problems that had existed in the past. ERDEMIR's management had indeed improved somewhat and had actually initiated an innovative program to deal with the shortage of technical personnel that it confronted in the late sixties. Many of its engineers were seeking more desirable opportunities in the major metropolitan areas. To solve the turnover problem ERDEMIR's management implemented a number of measures to make life in Ereğli more attractive and inaugurated a training program that permitted the best workers to prepare themselves to fill such positions by studying at night and on weekends. The project was apparently quite successful – its graduates were able 'to execute quite satisfactorily the duties of many engineering posts. Moreover, it was discovered that these "upgraded" workers . . . had far fewer problems of working with (or under) foreign counterpart steelmen . . .'[40]

Still, few experts would have agreed with the Bank's conclusion that: 'With the exception of the continuous billet caster and, to a lesser extent, the semi-continuous hot strip mill, ERDEMIR personnel are well experienced in operating the general type of plant included in the project.' It did go on to emphasize the need for thorough training on the new equipment and the desirability of having the company maintain an ongoing relationship with an experienced foreign steel producer in order to keep the company abreast of technological developments. Above all, the Bank sought, like AID had since ERDEMIR's inception, to ensure that ERDEMIR retain its private sector character and not become a State Economic Enterprise.[41]

THE IMPLEMENTATION

Koppers served as the consulting engineers for the Stage I expansion but implementation did not proceed smoothly. The conflicts that rose were due to several factors. First, and most important, ERDEMIR, which by now considered itself a mature company that needed only advice from Koppers, insisted upon managing the expansion itself. The final contract, agreed upon after extensive discussions, specified that Koppers' responsibilities would not involve any operational control. As a result it was far less expensive than would otherwise have been the case but the savings proved illusory because ERDEMIR's management proved unable to handle the expansion.

Secondly, each of the actors had its own interests, some of which conflicted. Koppers, which had worked closely with ERDEMIR since the earliest days, had expected to be involved in a major way. It planned to bid for some of the facilities because, although the IBRD had a rule that consulting engineers could not bid on equipment (to avoid potential conflicts of interest), the EXIM Bank had a different philosophy. Koppers gambled that those units in which it was interested such as the blast furnace, the basic oxygen furnace shop, materials handling and casting would be financed by the EXIM Bank. ERDEMIR, however, decided to Koppers' great dismay that the rolling plant should be financed by the EXIM Bank because of the superior quality of US machinery of this type. Thus Koppers, which did not compete in this area, was effectively excluded from providing any of the equipment.

ERDEMIR and the Turkish government also had a private agenda – they were interested (as had been the case during other stages of the plant's development) in obtaining equipment that met their private specifications regardless of cost. Mesta, for example, one of the major mill builders in the USA, quoted a semi-continuous mill. Although they were the low bidders, ERDEMIR wanted a more elaborate facility, and when Mesta overdesigned their mill in an attempt to make its bid comparable, it was no longer the low bidder and ERDEMIR acquired an unnecessarily embellished mill. Although Koppers, concerned with rising costs, made representations to the Turkish purchasing mission, its engineers were told not to worry, that the mission had been instructed to buy the very best equipment that was available, regardless of price, because overruns would be taken care of by the Turkish government. AID's files contain numerous documents indicating its concern about this state of affairs in particular and, more generally, with the way that the expansion was being handled. One such communication to ERDE-MIR noted that: (1) ERDEMIR was deviating from the original UEC report on which the IBRD loans were based by enlarging the facilities that it was purchasing; (2) no project budget or financial plan had been prepared by ERDEMIR and it appeared that the local currency budget was being exceeded; (3) no PERT chart had been drawn up, partly because of indecision by ERDEMIR concerning various technology choices; (4) ERDEMIR had not planned adequately for future needs, particularly in terms of the electric power that would be available.

Given these managerial shortcomings it might be expected that implementation of the Stage I expansion would not proceed smoothly. Koppers had drawn up an organizational chart and the Bank too, concerned about the quality of project management, had prepared a detailed schedule of all the positions which should be filled by ERDEMIR and the skills necessary for each. But ERDE-MIR paid little attention to such managerial techniques and neither of these plans was ever implemented. Construction started haphazardly and, before long, the project was in disarray. By the end of 1972 it was encountering major difficulties and significant tensions between the major actors, especially between Koppers and ERDE-MIR, were evident.

The situation continued to deteriorate, and in late 1973 UEC was commissioned to evaluate the project's management and to suggest corrective measures. It quickly learnt that Koppers and ERDEMIR accorded very different interpretations to their agreements. ERDE-MIR had asked Koppers, in 1972, to set up a group in Turkey for project management, but Koppers refused on the grounds that its contract did not provide for such an arrangement. It proved so difficult to reconcile these two positions that not until April 1974, at Koppers suggestion, was an amendment to the contract finally agreed upon.

Not surprisingly, therefore, UEC found that responsibilities were not clearly delineated, that control systems were almost non-existent, and that manpower requirements had not been estimated correctly. Accordingly it recommended organizational changes and the establishment of a project management system. It spelled out ERDE-MIR's responsibilities in detail. These included the maintenance of a cost control and accounting system in order to control income and expenditure for the project, coordination of the work being done, monitoring its quality, prompt unloading, storage and delivery of goods, the maintenance of schedules for locally purchased materials, and so forth. Although ERDEMIR's management had obviously displayed rather limited capabilities in all these areas, UEC was quite diplomatic and careful not to place the blame entirely on the Turkish company's shoulders. Hence its conclusion contained the following section:[42]

> . . . it is recommended that ERDEMIR take the initiative and responsibility of the owner to assure that Koppers lives up to its contractual responsibility to meet schedule requirements. If the cause for delay is the fault of ERDEMIR, internal corrective steps should be taken . . . The case is that usually both parties are at fault . . .

THE STAGE II EXPANSION – THE DECISION PROCESS

Even before the first expansion project was completed, ERDEMIR and the Turkish government sought to secure an IBRD commitment for the second stage. The World Bank had already approved the project in principle but it now held back because of all the implementation and other problems that ERDEMIR was encountering. In late 1976 the Bank informed the President of ERDEMIR that its willingness to consider financing Stage II depended upon successful completion of the expansion then underway and also on the company and the government undertaking certain initial measures and committing themselves to policies that would permit: (1) a speedy return to and continued maintenance of the financial viability of the company, (2) re-establishment and continuance of efficient project implementation management, and (3) re-establishment and continuance of the efficient management of the company. The Bank was obviously signalling its discontent not only with the conduct of the implementation but, more fundamentally, with the internal developments that had taken place within the company during these years. These developments, due to increasing politicization, had adversely affected all aspects of the company's operations, including its efforts to handle the expansion. I shall discuss this problem in some detail later in this chapter.

Negotiations over these points were protracted and complex and Turkey's unfavorable balance of trade greatly complicated efforts to secure the other necessary foreign financing. In the end, the Turkish government agreed to cover all cost overruns, to strive for more stable management, and not to expand by more than 10 per cent the highly inflated labor force which was already large enough to handle the capacity projected for 1982. Finally, various agreements were reached for the foreign financing: the Bank would provide $95 million, West Germany $20 million, the USA $22 million (in the form of supplier credits) and Japan $16 million. The Japanese contribution may well have been considerably larger for a Japanese company submitted a very low bid – $16 million, half that of Krupp ($32 million), and significantly less than the US bid of $24 million. Some experts believe that the Japanese company lost money on the contract itself but gained considerably from the spillover benefits. Construction of the new addition began in June 1978, and was scheduled for completion in August 1981.

THE DESIGN OF THE EXPANSION

A new UEC feasibility study was prepared for this project and was completed in March 1976. It called for rounding out the facilities in order to eliminate the bottleneck in steel-making so as to permit ERDEMIR to produce 2 million tons of liquid steel per year.[43] Like all the other studies this one analyzed the raw material situation, production and operating costs, and the financial implications. The Turkish authorities were not satisfied with the report and UEC therefore prepared a 'Final Version' which it submitted in December 1976.

A comparison of the content and conclusions of the two studies reveals quite clearly why the original did not appeal to Ankara. There the market was estimated to reach 4.8 million tons by 1987. Total expenditures would amount to $203 million; the discounted rate of return was estimated at 22.2 per cent. Nine months later ERDE-MIR's market was calculated to be 7.2 million tons by 1987, a 50 per cent increase over the earlier estimate, and the cost had climbed to $239 million, $175 million of which – the local currency costs – were to be covered by ERDEMIR from its profits. The rate of return had increased slightly to 22.4 per cent. And whereas the March study had cautiously concluded that the expansion projected 'appears to be feasible', by December UEC had reached the unequivocal conclusion that the expansion 'is feasible'.[44]

The cost increase can be accounted for quite easily – the Turkish government, concerned with its military requirements, wanted larger tinning and cleaning lines in the cold finishing facilities in order to ensure that the navy would be guaranteed an adequate supply of normalizing plate and other items. But how can the large discrepancy in demand estimates by explained? In March UEC made its own calculations using a projected growth rate of 7 per cent per year. It noted that this rate was less than that estimated by the State Planning Organization but argued that the 7 per cent figure was more 'realistic'. In its revised report UEC simply worked with the Turkish government's estimates, merely noting that 'UEC has accepted these data, subject to UEC's review at a later date.'[45]

Obviously UEC behaved like most consulting firms – it sought to please its clients. Yet it did have a problem. In order to do so and still justify the expansion it had to accept projections of future demand which were considerably higher than those calculated by its own experts. Essentially UEC was confronted with the task of demonstrating the feasibility of an expansion that was desired by the Turkish parties but which its own analysis had shown to be questionable.

Some experienced steel men believed that the project was fundamentally flawed. The expansion rested on providing ERDEMIR with the ability to produce 2 million tons of liquid steel but it was not at all clear that such an output could be achieved. Critics of the project argued that, at best, ERDEMIR would be able to produce 1.6 million tons, too little to justify the expansion. In their view certain elements of the project were reasonable and necessary – the improved raw material handling facilities, the hot shearing lines, the annealing units, and the improved scrap preparation – but the other parts did not represent a wise use of resources. One expert summarized this view in a personal communication as follows: 'The Stage II plan is based on defective and delusive concepts so the projected benefits will not be reached. The investment is over $100 million upon which there can be no return as ERDEMIR was led to anticipate.' What the writer overlooked, of course, was that ERDEMIR eagerly sought the expansion. In any event there is little doubt that the goal of two million tons was highly optimistic. ERDEMIR never came close to producing even 1.6 million tons of liquid steel until 1984 when it produced 1.54 million tons.[46]

THE IMPLEMENTATION

The Stage II expansion did not proceed any more easily than the previous one and also ran well behind schedule. Moreover, by 1979 ERDEMIR was incurring problems with the sinter plant and the basic oxygen furnace, the new coke ovens had not yet been tested and it was suffering from a severe shortage of both coal and ore. As a result the plant was operating at only 50 per cent of capacity.

ERDEMIR's problems were exacerbated by two important external developments – the inadequate energy supply which was available to it and the start of ISDEMIR, Turkey's third iron and steel plant at Iskenderun, which I will discuss in Chapter 6. Turkey's energy situation was affected very adversely by the sharp increases in oil prices that began in 1973 and adequate supplies of energy were simply not available in sufficient quantities to feed the energy hungry iron and steel sector. In 1977, for example, even though the country's three iron and steel plants were not functioning at anywhere near capacity, they still accounted for 24 per cent of the country's total consumption of 21,649,000,000 kWh.[47]

The inauguration of ISDEMIR added to ERDEMIR's woes. It had been optimistically assumed that the coal mines at Zonguldak could increase their production to supply both ISDEMIR and ERDEMIR. As in the case of iron ore, Turkey's foreign exchange difficulties – difficulties which became especially acute from 1974 onwards – drove the assumption. It was soon proven wrong and ERDEMIR was starved for coal. Moreover, the decision to ship Zonguldak coal to ISDEMIR was not a wise one given the proximity of this coal source to ERDEMIR and Iskenderun's excellent port facilities which could easily handle coal imports.

The availability of inputs and their price were not the only aspects of ERDEMIR's functioning determined by the key actor in its environment, the Turkish government. More generally, the character of the political system led to certain kinds of governments which adopted policies that had a profound impact upon all aspects of its operations, notably the size of the workforce and the quality of management. Though ERDEMIR was not legally a state enterprise, it came increasingly to be treated like one by the government with the following consequences:[48]

The first is the lack of continuity, since the board is changed whenever there is change in the government. The second is the intrusion of politics. Since board members are politically appointed, they are vulnerable to political influence. The third weakness is the lack of industrial experience of the boards of state manufacturing enterprises . . . The fourth and perhaps the most serious flaw of the system is that it leads to the board's interfering with and second guessing the general manager . . . Another way of looking at this is that the board of managers is not really a board in the traditional sense but an executive committee.

In theory, and to a substantial degree in fact – with respect to pricing, investments, and personnel policies, for example – the Council of Ministers acts as an overall board of directors – an impossible task for them.

Under these conditions it should not be surprising that most executives were inadequately trained in both technical and managerial areas, that they exhibited an exclusive concern with the domestic market and had little interest in exports, or that the most able and qualified managers moved to the private sector where they could enjoy higher salaries and greater latitude in decision making as soon as they acquired the necessary qualifications.[49]

These chronic problems were aggravated by the political developments that took place during the seventies. During this decade the political system was characterized by weak and unstable coalition governments. Neither of the major parties (Mr Demirel's Justice Party or Mr Ecevit's Republican People's Party) was able to gain a clear majority in parliament so that minor parties, especially the National Salvation Party, often held the decisive votes that made governments possible. For its participation the NSP demanded, and usually received, the Ministry of Industry. Once in power, the NSP would place its own men not only in the ministry but in the many enterprises that it controlled as well. ERDEMIR was one of these and it suffered particularly from such political interference as NSP loyalists were placed into administrative and managerial posts even though they had little or no experience in iron and steel. By early 1975 the situation at the highest levels of management was so poor that an AID official utterly frustrated from his dealings with these men, scribbled on the margin of a telegram that he received from the President of ERDEMIR, a man in his late sixties, 'I hereby declare the Ereğli board a basket case!'

The turnover among the company's board of directors was extremely high. An analysis of the annual reports from 1972 onwards indicates that none of those who served as board members in 1972 remained on the board in 1980. The ten-member board of directors changed dramatically in 1976 (seven new members), in 1979 (eight new members), and in 1980 (five new members). In all 34 different persons served as directors during the nine-year period and five held the post of chairman. A similar pattern is evident at the managerial level. Only two of the 1972 management team (which expanded from nine to twelve persons during this period) still held their positions in 1980. Overall 25 different persons filled these positions. The greatest shift at this level also occurred in 1977 when there was a major change in the various managerial positions and three new administrators joined the company, and in 1980 when five new persons were appointed. Conditions at Karabük, which I shall discuss in detail in Chapter 6, will illustrate just how these and other managerial shortcomings negatively affected the operation of an iron and steel plant and hindered the achievement of technological mastery.

The blatant political interference which characterized this period affected ERDEMIR adversely in a second way – the number of employees rose sharply. Here too the NSP actively sought to find employment for its supporters. Its endeavors were quite successful; the total number of workers more than doubled in the seventies, rising from about 4,100 in 1971 to almost 8,500 in 1978, some of whom were involved in construction. The growth of the labor force during this period is shown in Table 5.3.[50]

Table 5.3 Growth of ERDEMIR workforce 1972–78

	1972	1973	1974	1975	1977	1978
Workers	3,210	3,653	5,020	5,790	5,776	6,120
Professionals	1,322	1,473	1,781	1,931	1,952	2,344
Total	4,532	5,126	6,801	7,721	7,728	8,481

External political developments influenced the plant in yet a third way. During these years, the trade union movement grew in strength and became an important political force. Membership in unions rose from about 300,000 in 1963 to over 2 million in 1970 and reached 5,700,000 in 1980. These workers, however, were not united; the labor movement reflected the political cleavages within the society.

There were two main confederations, Türk-İş, a centrist organization with 1.9 million members, affiliated with the AFL-CIO and DISK, a socialist grouping with ties to the RPP and left-wing groups and a membership of 1.6 million. Two smaller confederations were affiliated with right-wing groups, MISK (290,000 members) to the National Action Party, HAK-İŞ with 68,000 workers to the National Salvation Party.[51] Workers enrolled in the union that reflected their political orientation and conflict between different groups was commonplace. As a consequence labor relations deteriorated and clashes, strikes and lockouts often took place, especially in the late seventies. Beginning in May 1977 a long and difficult strike and lockout paralyzed the plant and, almost as soon as that had been resolved, a conflict arose over which union was authorized to negotiate a new Collective Labor Agreement.[52]

All these factors caused production to fall to low levels. Although ERDEMIR's capacity was increasing as a result of the expansions (reaching 1. 5 million tons in 1978), actual production never came close to this figure, falling from 847,000 tons in 1976 to 623,000 tons in 1977 before rising again to 671,000 tons in 1978 and 875,000 tons in 1979.[53] Concomittantly, productivity, which had been rising, also decreased. Whereas in 1975 23 man-hours were required to produce a ton of flat products (in the USA it normally took 8.66 man-hours to produce one ton of steel), by 1978 the figure stood at 20.43, but in 1979 it climbed to 22.47.[54] Low productivity and high raw material costs translated into high production costs. According to estimates by the National Productivity Center that were made available to the author, casting costs were 79 per cent and rolling costs 78 per cent higher than the optimal figure.

As conditions in the plant deteriorated, so did its financial situation. On 14 March 1977 Ereğli requested that the principal and the interest on lira loans, totalling TL 800 million, which were due to start 1 April 1977 and 30 June 1977 be deferred for three additional years. AID noted that it had to follow the lead of the Turkish government in acceding to these deferrals. If it did not do so, the company would face cash shortages, difficulties with the expansion and further problems for the company's operations, and the possibility of eventual repayment would be more remote than ever.

This restructuring did not resolve the fundamental problems and ERDEMIR's financial situation remained quite precarious. It still possessed heavy medium- and long-term debt obligations, its debt-equity ratio in 1980 remained at 4 : 1, and still more financial reorganizations would be required to ensure its financial viability. And new studies would be required since the changes in Turkey's financial position rendered all the analyses and projections that had been so painstakingly carried out by UEC and the IBRD consultants and Staff concerning ERDEMIR's financial and commercial situation of little – if any – relevance.

CONCLUSION

The 'hiding hand' did come to ERDEMIR's rescue. After great efforts by AID and the other parties, the plant was operating profitably. But rescuing a severely flawed project is a difficult and expensive matter and ERDEMIR continued to teeter on the edge of bankruptcy. And, to the dismay of the World Bank, sophisticated and detailed studies, even with innumerable questionable assumptions, demonstrated that not even a massive expansion could resolve the problems caused by its original lack of equity. But these studies did not affect the World Bank's decision to support a major expansion, for its President was eager to strengthen the private sector in Turkey and to involve the Bank more heavily than had been the case for some time in that country's economic development efforts. All the detailed, rational-comprehensive analyses by its own experts and outside consultants were used to validate a decision that had been taken on the basis of political factors. Once again politics, as manifested in the ways in which decisions were reached within and among organizations, were dominant. In implementing its decision, the Bank behaved according to the organizational process model. As the controversy surrounding the pollution problem indicates, its actions reflected institutional norms.

As had been the case in all the other projects, managerial issues did not receive the attention they required even though these were especially critical at this time, since, unlike the other technology transfers that had preceded it, this major expansion was handled not by outside experts but by ERDEMIR itself. Unfortunately ERDEMIR lacked the requisite knowledge and personnel and the technology transfer process did not proceed smoothly. Now more than just knowing how to operate the plant was required, new technologies had to be integrated into the existing system but the managerial and labor force did not possess the necessary knowledge to enable them to do so.

These developments also draw attention once again to the role of the environment in unexpected events (most notably the increase in energy prices in 1973) over which none of the actors enjoyed any control and decisions taken by the Turkish government (the decision to allocate resources to ISDEMIR, for example) were clearly influential. This decision further underlines the importance of the political variables, particularly the functioning of the political system, for all the governments continued to satisfice. None was ever willing to make the necessary investments in infrastructure, with damaging consequences for the plant's operation. Its policies affected ERDEMIR's functioning in many other ways, particularly, as I have stressed, its management and labor force and hence its ability to master the technologies. As a result, despite the efforts of Koppers, UEC, AID and the IBRD, the attempt to create an effective and efficient plant foundered and the Bank found itself confronted with a most difficult situation which it could influence only to a limited extent.

After a decade and a half and the expenditure of hundreds of millions of dollars and Turkish liras, the involvement of several major international steel companies, and the preparation of innumerable studies, ERDEMIR remained a troubled enterprise. By almost any indicator it had failed to achieve acceptable levels of productivity and quality and its financial situation remained precarious. Yet, despite its checkered history and numerous deficiencies, ERDEMIR was considered by many to be Turkey's best iron and steel complex. How right were they? How did it compare to Karabük, which was being modernized in this period, and to ISDEMIR, the brand new plant, built with Soviet assistance? In Chapter 6 I shall answer these questions by analyzing these projects and by carrying out a comparative analysis of the level of technological mastery achieved by each plant.

6 ISDEMIR, SIDEMIR, Karabük: Projects and Comparative Perspectives

Steel, More Steel, Ever More Steel . . .

INTRODUCTION

While ERDEMIR was undergoing its travails, several other ambitious projects designed to provide a massive expansion in Turkey's iron and steel capacity were implemented. The third iron and steel plant (ISDEMIR) came on stream, work began on a fourth plant, SIDEMIR, and a massive modernization program was launched at Karabük. None of these would serve as a textbook example of how to design and implement a technological project or how to achieve technological mastery.

THE ISDEMIR PROJECT

Work on a third steel plant began in the early sixties when studies for the Second Five Year plan made it clear that the capacity of Karabük and ERDEMIR would not suffice, especially after 1968, to meet the country's needs, especially for the kinds of items being produced at Karabük. If a new plant were not built, dependence on imports would rise dramatically. The project was endorsed by the SPO and enthusiastically accepted by Prime Minister Demirel who soon learnt that the only country with any interest in the project was the USSR which wished to establish friendlier relations with Turkey. Wide-ranging feasibility studies were initiated, mainly by the John Miles Co. Ltd with which the Turkish government had signed a five-year contract on 7 March 1967 for consulting services. Thus the ISDEMIR project was born. It was attached to the Turkish Iron and Steel Works

General Directorate and placed under the control of the Ministry of Science and Technology.[1]

The technical agreement that was signed with the USSR on 10 October 1969 provided for a plant to produce one million tons of melted steel. It would consist of two blast furnaces, each with a capacity of 550,000 tons per year, a coke plant of 69 ovens with a capacity of one million tons per year, three sinter machines, each capable of producing 1,827,000 tons. The steel shop would have two 130 LD converters. One of these would be in reserve so that production could continue when repairs were needed. The plant would employ a continuous caster, a new technology which turns melted steel directly into blooms. Three rolling mills would produce 930,000 tons of blooms, light profiles, rounds and wire rods.

The plant was to be constructed in 58 months, a rather leisurely pace by Western standards, but one that was consonant with Russian practice. Impatient for the new plan to begin operation as rapidly as possible, Turkish officials applied pressure for a shorter construction period and secured a new agreement, signed in Moscow in 1970, that reduced the time slightly, to 52 months. The goal was never met; the plant came on stream only after long delays and even then had great difficulty in meeting any of its production targets, for reasons that I shall analyze below.

The construction delays were attributable, in part, to the decision to enlarge the project. Almost as soon as construction began, Turkish experts decided that this plant had been designed on too small a scale and that it contained imbalances between its various units. Accordingly, negotiations were reopened with the USSR and a new agreement was signed on 28 September 1972. Guaranteed capacity would be boosted to two million tons through the addition of two coke batteries, a third blast furnace, a third LD converter and ancillary equipment, and a new rolling mill.

This revision was to be but one of many. Altogether, the original project was modified seven times and each change escalated the price. Ultimately it cost TL 14 billion (40 per cent of which was covered by external credits), 300 per cent more than the original estimate.[2] The financial implications of each revision is shown in Table 6.1.

This brief historical sketch suggests that at least some of the mistakes of the past were repeated. The degree to which this was the case will become apparent as I examine how the design, impact and management variables were handled.

Table 6.1 Cost escalation of ISDEMIR

Date	Cost (TL million)
1966–73	4,692
1974	6,492
1975	7,986
28 February 1976	8,773
31 December 1976	9,088
1977	12,181
1977	13,952

Source: Çelebi, op. cit., p. 73.

THE DESIGN ISSUES

The question of where to locate the plant received detailed attention and a good site was ultimately chosen. The decision to locate the plant at Iskenderun was not reached easily, however, for there was strong pressure to build it at Sivas (a town in East Turkey located near the country's major iron ore deposits), a site that was considered by most experts as being, at best, on a par with Karabük because of its inland location and harsh winter climate.

The John Miles Company examined twelve different sites, including Sivas, using such criteria as physical conditions, transportation facilities, seismological conditions, local industry and costs of production. It concluded that the best site was Iskenderun followed by Samsun and Mersin respectively. Each of these was located on the coast and had a good harbor. The estimated manufacturing costs based on the use of coal from the Zonguldak field and domestic iron ore at each of these sites are shown in Table 6.2.

Table 6.2 Estimated manufacturing cost for various sites (TL 000)

Site	Coke	Molten iron	Molten steel	Billets
Iskenderun	290	508	605	727
Samsun	262	515	608	731
Mersin	268	514	609	732
Sivas	259	515	617	740

Sourve: John Miles Company Ltd, *Studies for the Third Turkish Steel Works* (Croydon, England, 1967, 6 vols), Vol. 1, 'Market Review and Recommended Market Capacity', Table III, p, 87.

Although these calculations suggest that the costs of production at Sivas would be only slightly higher than elsewhere, the situation changes dramatically if the assumption about total reliance on local iron ore (which, as has been noted in the discussion of the other projects, represented a major limiting factor on production and productivity) is relaxed. Now the costs of production at Sivas increase dramatically, while those at Iskenderun drop equally sharply. The cost of manufacturing billets at Sivas becomes TL 775,000, at Iskenderun TL 710,000. Furthermore, if estimates also take into account the use of imported coal, the costs for Sivas become extremely high.

Neither the John Miles Company nor the SPO felt that the plant should be located at Sivas. The SPO, however, did not favor Iskenderun because of its distance from markets and because rich agricultural land would be lost to production. The other two coastal locations also had drawbacks. Samsun lacked enough space, and since it and Mersin were already industrial centers, the Minister of Industry, Mehmet Turgut, decided to locate the plant at Iskenderun in order to create another growth pole for industry. I shall discuss Sivas in more detail below since it re-emerged as the site of the country's projected fourth iron and steel works, SIDEMIR.

Another important design decision, size, obviously did replicate the errors of the past. As noted above, the original decision called for a small plant to be built, one with a capacity of only one million tons. Why should this have been the case, particularly after the lesson of Karabük had been reinforced by the experience of ERDEMIR? This question has been addressed by a Turkish scholar who has suggested three principal reasons.[3] The first, and most important, involves the estimates and evaluations of demand that were made. According to this analysis, the John Miles Company had estimated, in 1967, that the total demand for iron and steel products in Turkey would reach 3.4 million tons in 1977 and 5.8 million tons in 1982. These estimates were challenged by a Turkish firm which concluded that demand would be 4.6 and 8.16 million tons.[4] These figures came to be accepted and it was decided that the plant had to be enlarged. Second, the size of the plant was based on the use of local raw materials which were relatively scarce. Subsequently, the SPO concluded that it was preferable to import raw materials rather than finished iron and steel products. A decision to import the entire supply of coking coal and part of the iron ore supply eliminated the limits imposed by raw material shortages. Third, the amount of financing provided by the USSR enabled Turkey to build only a relatively small plant.

While these factors did play a role, the actual situation was somewhat more complex. First, the demand estimates were quite elaborate and sophisticated. The USSR had produced, to everyone's consternation, a multi-volume report which called for a plant that would produce heavy sections, the demand for which, according to the John Miles Company's estimates, was quite limited (67,000 tons in 1972, 100,000 tons in 1977). After lengthy negotiations, the Russians agreed to build a plant that would produce non-flat products, the kind that were most needed. In its study the John Miles Company estimated the demand for these products and then calculated what portion Karabük could produce. The difference between the two figures was to be the capacity of the new plant. Essentially this amounted to 690,000 tons in 1972, 1.2 million tons in 1977. Accordingly the plant's size was fixed at 1 million tons.[5]

The role of raw material considerations is less clear, though quality was at least as much an issue as quantity. The John Miles Company, after detailed studies,[6] concluded that coal was not a problem as far as quantity was concerned: there were adequate reserves at Zonguldak (204 million tons of proved reserves, plus 277 million tons of probable reserves and 850 million tons of possible reserves) but the high ash content (13.2 per cent) would create difficulties. The iron ore situation, however, was more problematic. Official Turkish estimates claimed a total of 175.9 million tons of proven reserves and over 200 million tons of possible reserves. John Miles's estimates were only about half these figures; moreover, it concluded that only a small percentage of the proven reserves could be used, 11.8 million tons. How these studies affected the size decision is not clear for the agreement to increase capacity was reached in September 1972 and the decision to utilize imported raw materials was not taken until May 1973.[7]

On the other hand, there is little doubt that the plant's size was profoundly influenced by the amount of financing that the USSR was willing to provide. As had happened before, the Turkish government would accept almost any kind of plant. And, as had also occurred in the past, the available resources imposed parameters that determined many aspects of the plant's design.

These choices have been criticized on various grounds. Some of the technologies, the sinter plant and particularly the continuous caster, proved to be major bottlenecks, as will be discussed below. And a

British expert who is familiar with the plant has argued that, as was usually the case with Russian projects, it was overdesigned in order to ensure that the various units met the guaranteed production figures. The idea, for example, of holding one LD converter in reserve, was a sensible one if poor refractories and a small number of heats were involved. In the past, a lining had to be replaced every six days after 200 heats; if the work schedule calls for only ten heats a day, the lining has to be replaced even more frequently. In modern mills, however, 1,000 heats are usually achieved with good refractories.

THE IMPACT ISSUES

Past patterns also influenced the way that the impacts were analyzed. The driving force behind the plant was the country's need for steel. Its economic benefits were essentially taken for granted and all other costs and benefits – environmental, social, cultural – were neglected. The plant's rationale essentially rested on the traditional pillars of employment generation, import substitution and foreign exchange savings: (1) the country's iron and steel needs would be met domestically using local raw materials; (2) ancillary industries that are based on iron and steel would be stimulated; (3) the plant would promote production by assembly and heavy machinery plants which rely on iron and steel; (4) it will meet the country's domestic demand for iron and steel and eliminate the need for imports thus saving an estimated $186,000,000 in foreign exchange (930,000 tons at $200 per ton); (5) considerable employment will be generated in the plant and in new ancillary industries. At 2 million ton capacity the plant would employ 13,437 workers.[8]

The British consultants did provide more sophisticated analyses in their 1967 report. They carried out an economic feasibility study based on estimates of costs, sales and the like. Their analysis began with estimates of the costs of inputs (ore, TL 104 per ton, coal, TL 206 per ton, limestone, TL 25 per ton, manganese, TL 25 per ton, electric power, TL 0.015 kWh) and of labor (at the union rate of TL 6 per ton). On the basis of these estimates they calculated the costs of production, the sales price, the value of sales for each item and, on the basis of these assumptions, calculated that the enterprise would earn between TL 230 and 315 million in 1978, depending on whether import duties had to be paid and the level of equity involved.

THE MANAGEMENT ISSUES

There is little evidence that this important dimension received any particular attention apart from the decision to use local companies to perform all the construction and assembly work. That it was almost totally neglected is suggested by what happened once the project was underway and administrative and other problems began to plague it.

IMPLEMENTATION AND OPERATION

The project was one of the largest ever built in Turkey and probably the largest ever built by local contractors. At its peak 673 technicians and 14,900 workers were working on it.

As I noted above, the scheduled completion dates proved to be a fantasy. The project encountered one difficulty after another and long delays became the norm; altogether nine years elapsed between the implementation of the project and its conclusion instead of the 52 months that had been agreed upon. Construction began in 1970; the first unit, the No. 1 blast furnace, began operating in April 1975, the No. 1 coke ovens in October, the second battery of coke ovens, the steel shop and the rolling mills in 1977 and 1978, and the second blast furnace in 1979.[9] According to the official history, several factors caused these delays. First, most of the equipment which came from abroad suffered import delays. Secondly, there was a shortage of technical elements and skilled workers. Thirdly, numerous administrative difficulties were encountered.[10] Although all these factors played a role, and other can be added, the basic cause lies with the 'administrative difficulties'. Clearly the planning process was not rigorous enough and when time came for actual construction to begin, even a highly qualified team would have encountered numerous problems. But since managerial and manpower issues had been slighted, the personnel who were placed in charge of this ambitious project lacked the necessary experience and expertise and could not meet the challenge which they faced. Besides the low quality of the administrators, another factor was involved – they lacked any incentive to meet the deadlines. There were no penalties for falling behind schedule and, since the construction industry was in recession thus reducing the demand for the steel products to be produced by the plant, many decision-makers were indifferent to the construction schedules. The combination of weak administration and a lackadaisical attitude towards goal achievement continued to represent serious handicaps to the functioning of the plant after units became operational.

These shortcomings were aggravated by the instrusion of political factors. In preparation for the plant, a training program was established according to which personnel would receive training in the USSR for six months. But, when the government fell and a new coalition was formed, the NSP insisted on having its own men, who were not qualified, hired by the plant.[11] Thus, 'in the early days, when putting the plant into operation . . . untrained persons were employed.'[12] The results for the plant were, of course, devastating. The situation was even worse than might have been expected since the plant found itself employing a much greater number of personnel than it needed. In the mill producing cold rolled products, for example, about 4,000 persons were doing work that was normally carried out by 640 operators. Altogether about 17,000 persons were employed at the plant, of whom 1,600 were administrators and engineers.[13] Of this total as many as 7000 were surplus but they could not be dismissed, because of governmental concerns about the country's high unemployment rate.

A leading member of the NSP who was directly involved in iron and steel policy in the late seventies acknowledged to the author that ISDEMIR was seriously overstaffed but argued that this represented a deliberate decision to use ISDEMIR as a training ground for the personnel that would be required for the fourth steel plant (SIDEMIR) that was being planned at the time. Although questions of manpower need forethought, if this was indeed the reason why ISDEMIR employed so many unqualified workers, one must raise some basic questions about the quality of a decision process that would result in lowered production, heavy costs and no systematic training. In any event, there is no doubt that labor productivity at ISDEMIR was extremely low because of the swollen labor force and its poor quality or that labor costs accounted for a high percentage of all expenses, 42 per cent in 1980.[14] There is general agreement that the labor force should have been reduced and that workers needed 'training, upgrading, updating, higher productivity'.[15]

The observation that training and upgrading was required applied to all levels, including the managerial. ISDEMIR suffered to an even greater degree from all the administrative shortcomings prevailing at ERDEMIR that were discussed in Chapter 5. These also plagued Karabük since both plants were state enterprises, run and administered by the Turkish Iron and Steel Works. To avoid repetition, I shall therefore discuss this topic in detail in the context of Karabük's operations. In brief, few qualified administrators were to be found at ISDEMIR which experienced a rapid turnover of senior staff because limited incentives encouraged persons to leave for more desirable positions, usually in the private sector, as soon as they acquired skills. The consequences of this state of affairs for the achievement of mastery of the technology do not require elaboration.

The plant's productivity was also adversely affected by several other factors, notably the availability of raw materials. Zonguldak was expected to ship 1.6 million tons of coal yearly but the State Coal Works proved unable to meet its obligations. Similar problems arose with iron ore which was supposed to be of two types – 1.8 million tons with an iron content of 56.65 per cent and a sulfur content of 1.21 per cent, and another 0.2 million tons with an iron content of 60 per cent and sulfur content of 0.05 per cent. Domestic sources could not supply these amounts and imports became inevitable. Thus ISDE-MIR gained access to high quality raw materials but, as we shall see below when I compare its performance to that of the other plants, this powerful advantage did not yield the results that might have been anticipated.

Whether the inputs were domestic or imported, good transportation facilities were essential but these proved once again to be a bottleneck. As in the case of ERDEMIR, the infrastructural requirements were neglected but in this case the problem was not due to a lack of awareness or a concern with minimizing costs. Infrastructural facilities were included in the plan and even emphasized by the SPO, but it proved a difficult matter to coordinate the activities of autonomous agencies and ministers who, though responsible for implementing the particular projects, sometimes accorded them a low priority or amended them in unexpected ways. As a result, the railroad system, despite commitments, once again proved unable to meet its delivery schedules, and some new facilities proved to be inadequate. A new pier, for example, was built too small to permit large iron-ore carriers to draw alongside. After much effort, it was enlarged, a decision that proved highly profitable when the Iran–Iraq war erupted and the tonnage of goods transported via Iskenderun rose sharply.

Some of the equipment that was installed in the plant also presented difficulties, especially the continuous caster, a machine which stands at the heart of the steel-making process. This piece of machinery proved to be of inferior design and could not be made to work properly, not even by a team of Russian experts who came from Leningrad University in 1979 to study the problem. Turkish steel men have advanced various explanations for this phenomenon, the most common being that the USSR had been experimenting with a new type of continuous casting technology, one that was vertical rather than radial, and decided to use Iskenderun as a pilot project. When it because obvious that the technology was a failure, the Russians abandoned the design.

As a result of all these difficulties, ISDEMIR was, in the late seventies and early eighties, a very uneconomic plant. It produced at only a small percentage of its rated capacity and productivity levels were extremely low. Blast furnace operations reached 44 per cent of capacity in 1978, 47 per cent in 1981 and 57 per cent in 1982, steel production 34.2 per cent, 34 per cent and 42 per cent, and the rolling mills 40 per cent, 43 per cent and 50 per cent.[16]

Active efforts were put in hand to remedy these problems, notably an expansion designed to enable ISDEMIR to produce two million tons of finished products. This project eliminated some of the bottlenecks and improved the functioning of the plant in other ways. Yet the expansion has not been designed in such a way as to take full advantage of the country's technological capabilities or to strengthen them. Experts from Karabük and elsewhere did play a role in assembly and construction but no consideration was given to the possibility that Turkish manufacturers might bid on equipment, as had been the case for ERDEMIR's expansion. For the first time in the plant's history, however, attention was being paid to pollution problems because the increasing air pollution adversely affected the quality of life of the technical people and managers who live nearby.

More than new facilities will be required to turn Iskenderun into a productive plant. As I have already noted, it suffers from numerous administrative and managerial deficiencies common to all State Economic Enterprises. ISDEMIR, however, possessed a unique weakness. Unlike Karabük, the organization had become accustomed to failure. Low productivity had become an accepted norm at all levels and no dramatic changes could be anticipated until managers and the workforce accepted the idea that they were capable of operating and maintaining a modern plant efficiently and effectively and acquire the necessary skills to do so.[17]

Whether this expansion will be the last of the revisions remains to be seen. Preliminary plans have been drawn up to raise capacity to four million tons or more in order to achieve economies of scale but the feasibility of such an expansion is questionable because of the manner in which the original plant was conceived and constructed. In the late seventies a team of Russian experts came to analyze the possibility of expanding ISDEMIR to six million tons.[18] They limited themselves to a detailed consideration of the technical aspects and did not consider any financial, commercial or economic factors because 'the customer provides the economic part'.[19] Their conclusions were quite pessimistic. Expansion to 2.5 million tons could be achieved quite easily; an increase to 2.8 million tons would be feasible though that would involve major changes in numerous auxiliary departments. Further growth would be difficult and expensive. An increase to 3.12 million tons would require extensive reconstruction of various systems within the plant.[20] Clearly even the numerous amendments in the design of the plant did not produce one that can easily be expanded in the future.

THE SIDEMIR PROJECT

The Fourth Five Year Plan had called, like the Third Plan, for the addition of another 10 million tons to the country's capacity. Unlike the previous Plan, however two plants rather than one were to be built. The larger, of eight million ton capacity, never moved beyond the concept stage; the other, of only two million tons, was to be located at Sivas, a provincial center in Eastern Turkey. This remarkable site (every modern steel plant is built on a coast in order to take advantage of water transportation) was justified in the Plan on the grounds that it was close to the iron ore deposits and to thermal and hydro-electric power sources. Its other supposed advantages were its location on major north-south and east-west rail and highway lines. The plant was expected to promote the region's development by creating jobs and by stimulating the growth of satellite industries and of construction and science activities. Hence the plant would contribute to a reduction in the existing divide between the developed western part of the country and the underdeveloped eastern part and would lessen or even reverse the outmigration which characterized the region.[21]

These arguments are not particularly persuasive if one considers the costs that are involved in achieving these potential benefits. Although it is true that the area is in need of development, an ron and steel plant is a poor choice to stimulate regional growth, being highly capital intensive and not greatly catalytic in terms of stimulating the growth of other industry. I shall return to this topic in Chapter 7. Most importantly, it is difficult to envisage how any iron and steel plant located there could produce goods competitively, particularly if imported coal and iron ore have to be utilized. Though all the designs were based on the use of local iron ore, the shortage of high quality ore and the limited ability of the Zonguldak coak fields to meet existing demands made it very likely that assumptions about the use of domestic raw materials would have to be revised, as happened so often in the case of the other integrated plants. Under these conditions, the costs of production at Sivas would (as noted in the discussion of the ISDEMIR plant) become much higher.

Although it is true that it is extremely difficult to find a good site for an iron and steel plant in Turkey because of the inadequacy of the country's antiquated rail network, that weakness is even more relevant for an inland site than for one on the coast because any steel plant consumes huge amounts of raw materials and produces a large tonnage of goods, all of which have to be transported to and from the plant. SIDEMIR was expected, ultimately, to produce six million tons of finished products. A plant of such a size would transport 12 to 15 million tons of goods, a burden that the existing road and rail network could handle only with the greatest difficulty. Moreover, the extremely harsh climatic conditions – the average temperature in winter is 8°C, the minimum −32°C – would require additional investments in heated sheds and other special facilities. Even then, problems would probably arise in handling raw materials, in the water supply and in numerous other areas.

Under such circumstances it is hard to explain the continuing viability of the Sivas site apart from quite narrow political considerations. Many parties competed for the region's vote; building a steel plant there would be enormously popular.[22] The local populace lobbied strongly for the project. Their passion stemmed from two basic factors: the area was heir to a proud tradition of working iron and many believed that the project would stimulate the area's economic growth. A great deal of political pressure was generated in favor of the project. According to one story, when Prime Minister Demirel, on a visit to Sivas, announced that the project had to be deferred owing to lack of funds, the inhabitants threw their gold bracelets and other jewelry under his car to symbolize their commitment to the plant. Certainly, their parliamentary representatives

were very active and generated a tremendous amount of political
pressure for many years; the idea of locating an iron and steel plant
there was already so powerful by the mid sixties that, as we have
seen, the third plant was sited at Iskenderun only after considerable
debate, even though extensive studies had demonstrated the many
drawbacks of the Sivas site.

SIDEMIR was conceived in order to fill the need for flat products
which was being only partially met by ERDEMIR. The need to
increase their production seemed to the planners to be inescapable
since they estimated that the shortfall would more than triple from
1.56 million tons in 1977 to about 5 million tons by 1987. The SPO's
estimates were quite similar to those developed by John Miles and
ERDEMIR who calculated that the gap would increase from 1.5
million tons to 4.8 million tons and from 1.7 to 4.75 million tons
respectively.[23] ERDEMIR, of course, argued for expansion and
against building an entirely new plant. Its proposed Stage III
expansion would accommodate the demand but this project (whose
practicality is debatable as we shall see in Chapter 7) lost out to the
appeal of a new plant.

SIDEMIR was to have a capacity of 1.5 million tons; this was
quickly revised and by 1977 its capacity was increased to two million
tons. This would still not meet the projected demand but, given the
nature of the ore supply, expansion beyond two million tons was
judged feasible only if a pipeline were built to carry ore concentrates
to the plant. Such a project, however, would be expensive and would
raise the costs of production to astronomical levels. Accordingly, the
plant's size was limited to about two million tons.

The John Miles company prepared two designs, one for a plant that
would turn out only hot rolled products, the other for one that would
also produce cold rolled goods. The former would produce 1.4
million tons in 1983, 2.1 million tons in 1987, the latter 1.5 million
tons and 2.4 million tons respectively. A hot rolling plant would cost
$720 million plus TL 6 billion in local currency; one that also turned
out cold rolled goods, $770 million plus TL 6.6 billion. The additional
cost involved in building a plant that would produce both sorts of
steel products was, obviously, quite small but profitability would be
adversely affected. By 1998, with all loans repaid, the hot rolling
plant would earn TL 3,314.4 million as compared to TL 2,854.6
million for the other scheme.[24]

These plans were scrutinized closely by Turkish officials who called
in new consultants for additional studies because the greatest short-

ιge was now deemed to be for non-flat products. Accordingly Kaiser Engineering, in cooperation with a Turkish engineering firm, proposed building a very different kind of plant.[25] This project would be implemented in stages, the first of which would cost $1.72 billion for capital equipment plus another $192 million for financing costs, considerably more than had been projected by John Miles and Co. for its plant. In its first stage the plant would produce 802,000 tons of bars, rods and light sections, and 447,000 tons of heavy bars and medium sections for a total output of 1.25 million tons. The various units were geared to that tonnage in the following manner: coke ovens 684,700 tons; blast furnaces, 1.4 million tons; molten iron, BOF shop, 1,428,000 tons of molten steel; continuous billet caster, 1,350,000 tons; rolling mills 250,000 tons. Manufacturing costs were estimated as in Table 6.3.

Table 6.3 Estimated manufacturing costs, SIDEMIR

	TL/ton	$/ton
Bars and rods	5,893.35	253.73
Bars and sections	6,049.59	241.98

Source: Feasibility Report for SIDEMIR Iron and Steel Works prepared for TDÇI by Kaiser Engineering and Ayyildiz Engineering, February 1979, Vol. 1, p. 14.

The plant was designed to use the nearby iron ore deposits but this ore contains less than 14 per cent iron and requires benefication. TDÇI would build the necessary plant to produce iron pellets with an iron content of 69 per cent. To ensure that the alkali and titania content would be within desirable limits, this ore would be blended with ore from another source. Lignite, not coal, would be utilized because 'quality coal and especially coking quality coal are in short supply in Turkey and are already allocated to other plants . . .'[26] The implications of this recommendation for the plant's operation would, of course, be significant but these were never explored in any detail.

The environmental problems, were accorded equally limited attention, a mere $2^{1}/_{2}$ pages being devoted to this topic. Essentially pollution issues were treated in a way that would satisfy donor requirements. The report simply stated: 'Although no air pollution or waste water criteria have been established for the Sivas region, pollution control and abatement equipment will be provided to protect the local environment'[27]

Like most consulting firms, Kaiser wished to please its client but found that to do so in this case was no easy matter. It began by spelling out the conditions upon which the subsequent estimates were based, conditions relating primarily to the creation of an appropriate transportation network and the provision of an adequate and timely supply of inputs. It then analyzed four sites near the town and selected Yilzeli.

At least one other critical assumption, one that is not spelled out in the study, was required to produce cost and other estimates that sounded reasonable. It involved the level of production to be attained by the plant. When discussing the ERDEMIR project, I pointed out that it had been expected to reach 100 per cent of capacity within three years, an assumption that had been subsequently questioned and had, of course, proven to be invalid. Nevertheless, SIDEMIR was expected to perform at similar levels; it was scheduled to reach 100 per cent of capacity by 1987. Any prudent planner would wonder about projections based on such an assumption, especially in light of the severe climatic conditions and the history of the other plants.

The financing arrangements were also eerily reminiscent of the original ERDEMIR project; about half of the total cost, $1 billion, would come from a foreign loan; the remainder would be provided domestically, mainly in the form of an 'equity contribution'. The amount of cash involved would be a mere TL 84.2 million. Given such a financial structure, it should not be surprising that the analysis of the debt service ability revealed that the debt burden would be a significant one; it would be retired in a 'minimum of fifteen years'. The other calculations (even with all the built-in assumptions) also failed to demonstrate that the project is financially attractive. The return on investment (ROI) turned out to be only 8.81 per cent, the return on equity figure (ROE) a mere 6.09 per cent. The other benefits cited in the study were that 3,400 jobs would be created in the region and $9.6 billion in foreign currency would be saved.

Clearly many questions can be raised about the project's feasibility. The report's assumptions are questionable and, even if one accepts them, the project is not a particularly attractive one given its rather poor financial prospects. Since those plans were drawn up, however, the political scene in Turkey has changed dramatically and the SIDEMIR project, which has been placed on hold, may never be implemented.

THE KARABÜK EXPANSION

The Third Five Year Plan had also called for huge new investments at Karabük and, beginning in the early seventies, a third major expansion estimated to cost over TL 2.6 billion was launched. The first project, initiated in 1972, called for an expansion of blast furnace capacity to 900,000 tons by improving the quality of the charge through the modernization of the sinter plant, new material handling facilities and improved preparation of iron ore. These changes were badly needed for the three blast furnaces were quite antiquated. Fatma had started operation in 1939, Zeynep in 1950 and Ulku in 1962. The capacity of the first two is quite small, only 300–400 tons per day and their air temperatures are low, 750°C. Ulku's capacity is 900–1,000 tons and it can achieve air temperatures up to 850°C.

Foreign firms were heavily involved in all these activities but Karabük itself and some Turkish engineering firms also participated. They carried out the preliminary studies and defined the contract specifications on which bids were to be submitted for the sinter plant modernization and other projects, and also manufactured some of the components in the plant's steel construction shop. Most of these projects fell well behind schedule and many still had not begun production by the early eighties, owing partly to a lack of foreign exchange, partly to the priority accorded to ISDEMIR which caused resources that were scheduled to be spent at Karabük to be made available to the new plant instead, and partly to managerial weaknesses, a problem to which I shall return below.

A second set of projects, formally approved in 1974, were designed to increase the capacity of the steel shop and the rolling mills through improvements in the continuous casting and other facilities. Steel shop capacity would rise to 950,000 tons a year; the goal for finished and semi-finished goods was 850,000 tons a year. In the course of preparing the detailed specifications, however, it became apparent, partly as a result of studies by the State Planning Organization, that major amendments were required if domestic demand patterns and technological developments were to be accommodated. Accordingly important changes were inaugurated to permit a different product mix to be produced. Construction steel capacity was to be increased from the projected 600,000 tons to one million tons with an emphasis on high resistance and quality steel and on meeting all the country's rail needs. The existing SM furnaces which had exhausted their productive life would be replaced by two 100/115-ton LD converters capable of producing one million tons of steel year. New rolling mill equipment and oxygen plant were to produce 275,000 tons of heavy profiles, 121,500 tons of light profiles, 345,000 tons of rounds and 107,200 tons of blooms, a total of about 850,000 tons. These goals were never realized; production in the late seventies was only a fraction of the planned targets and actually declined as Table 6.4 demonstrates.

Table 6.4 Karabük capacity and production

Unit	Capacity	1978 production	1979 production
Coke ovens	960	60%	69%
Blast furnace	600	95%	85%
Steel shop	600	100%	92%
Rolling mills	568.7	88%	85%

Source: Çelebi, op. cit., p. 57.

The Karabük management attributed these developments to the inadequacy of the inputs that were available to the plant. As I have pointed out, ERDEMIR and ISDEMIR suffered from similar problems. Coal shipments, for example, ran between 88 per cent and 97 per cent of planned deliveries from 1974 to 1977, owing to the inability of the State Coal Works to provide adequate supplies and of the railroad system to transport, in a timely fashion, what was available. As a result, the charge in the coke ovens was reduced to the lowest possible limit and the time lengthened as much as possible, with adverse consequences for coke production and for the operation of the blast furnaces.[28] Iron ore was equally scarce. A strike at Divriği so limited supplies in late 1977 that very low quality materials had to be used. The consequenced were serious; output fell 30 per cent in the steel shop, productivity as measures by energy use, the time required to repair the furnaces, etc., fell by 23 per cent. Another important consequence was the increase in the sulfur content of the hot metal which adversely affected the quality of the steel that was produced. Inadequate shipments of tar from both Iskenderun and ERDEMIR further impacted on production in the steel shop. Fuel oil and coke gas were also in short supply, and in order to maintain production, various technological innovations were undertaken, with consequences that will be discussed below. All these problems were aggravated by the shortage of foreign exchange which made it impossible to complete the investment planned for the 1972–80 period on time; particularly adversely affected were the projects designed to improve blast furnace performance.[29]

Although the shortage of inputs undoubtedly contributed greatly to the problems of productivity and quality that afflict the plant, other factors, especially the level of technological capability that had been built up over the years, the age of the equipment, and the quality of the management must also be taken into account. The expansion had included several projects to upgrade the capabilities of the managerial and technical staff. One project, for example, called for managers and technicians to study and implement recent technological innovations in such areas as the use of high temperatures, refractories and oxygen so as to increase blast furnace performance. But, despite such efforts, the plant continued to be severely handicapped by a lack of mastery over its technologies. How mastery affects operations is highlighted in the following consideration of the condition and functioning of each of the major elements of the plant in the early eighties.[30]

Coke plant

Many of its components were not working satisfactorily because of poor maintenance and administrative practices. The coke crushing plant, for example, lay idle for four years even though numerous foreign experts had urged that it be made operational in order to achieve improvements in the coke rate and hot metal production.[31] Moreover, attempts to solve problems were not based on a thorough knowledge of the technologies and often created additional difficulties. Thus when the seals on the coke oven doors began to deteriorate causing leakage and the danger of fires, the problem was solved by lowering the oven pressure. As a result, the condition of the coke ovens deteriorated even more because this practice allowed large amounts of air to leak into the ovens. This had extremely dangerous and costly consequences, including the possibility of an explosion, further damage to the ovens, increased ash content, and loss of coke oven gas valued at between $4 and $6 million per year.

Production was also significantly affected by the age of the equipment, especially of the second battery of coke ovens which came on stream in 1952 and should have been retired after twenty-five years of service. A new battery was considered by the SPO to be an 'important project' but by early 1983 no attempt had yet been made to obtain the necessary financing.[32]

Sinter plant

Here too maintenance was a major headache: 'the maintenance department is unable or unwilling to perform the required maintenance'.[33] This state of affairs can be traced back to inadequate administrative and control procedures. Better planning and scheduling would have reduced the time spent and improved its quality. Better control practices such as taking more frequent samples and running more tests would have improved the sinter characteristics. And, if the flux had been added at the plant instead of at the blast furnace as is now the case, the coke rate would have been reduced, sinter strength increased, and the iron oxide content reduced. By upgrading various elements, particularly the presently inadequate process control instrumentation, improving maintenance (better planning and scheduling would reduce the time involved), sinter production can be increased to 870,000 tons per year as compared to the goal of 630,000 tons. By replacing the antiquated machine with a modern one, production would increase by another 890,000 tons, an amount which is essential since the projected improvements in sinter production will supply only 36 per cent of the requirements.

Blast furnace

The two ancient blast furnaces cannot be modernized. Blast furnace technologies have evolved greatly since their construction and today they are practically museum pieces. Moreover, there is no space available for ancillary projects that would improve the quality of the inputs, a vital prerequisite to increased production. The sinter has too high an acid content, is too large and contains excess fines. The coke possesses a high ash content (which leads to the introduction of such undesirable elements as alkali, alumina and excess gangue), and is of low strength and large particle size. The high ash content 'is probably the single most important factor affecting hot metal production and coke rate.'[34] Although this problem has plagued Karabük (and the other plants) for years (the rate has traditionally run well above the world average of 8–10 per cent), the quality of the coking coal available to the plant, from the late seventies onwards, deteriorated greatly – the ash content climbed from 17.5 per cent to 23.4 per cent in 1982. A 1 per cent increase in ash content causes a 2.8 per cent decrease in the productivity of the furnace and the amount of coke required to produce one ton of hot metal increases by 20 to 30 kg.[35]

Hence, production of iron declined from 1,710 tons per day to 1,440 tons per day and coke consumption rose from 889 kg per MTHM to 998 kg.[36]

These problems are aggravated by the same weaknesses as elsewhere: poor control, management and maintenance. There is a shortage of instrumentation and much of the available equipment is out of order. And some of the technologies which have been produced locally, such as the hot blast valves, are of poor design and quality, another indicator of the limited mastery that had been achieved. Because of such practices 'the operational results are poor when compared to hot metal quality and cost.'[37] The situation will improve when the planned improvements are implemented for 'The blast furnace plant will no longer be the plant bottleneck'[38] but, even with better operational practices, problems will always remain because of the antiquated equipment.

Steel production

This part of the plant possesses good equipment but administrative practices hamper productivity and quality. Managerial weaknesses are evident in several ways. The time taken to rebuild a furnace is very high (25 days instead of 16) because of poor planning and lack of coordination between different units. Moreover various technological innovations that were implemented in most steel production countries over three decades ago have never been adopted – some facilities such as slag pots, for example, though abandoned elsewhere, are still in use and various physical modifications to the blast furnace remain to be carried out. Such technological changes would result in major savings.

Production, which reached a high of over 640,000 tons in 1974, fell to 558,000 tons in 1981 owing to increased sulfur levels in the hot metal. Moreover, the present quality is too low to make the product exportable. Reducing sulfur levels would lead to increases in quality and productivity. Although some short-term measures can be taken to improve the situation, an expensive desulfurization plant is required to deal with the increase in production of hot metal which is foreseen by the modernization program, and an oxygen plant would also be useful. Heat times run 250 per cent longer than in the USA owing, in large part, to the poor quality of the flux (dolomite) which is available and to the ways in which various activities are carried out.

Better scrap handling procedures would reduce costs and increase production. Quality can be upgraded through various measures such as the use of improved mold designs, the installation of mold cooling sprays and reducing transit times. No inventory system for inputs exists to deal with unexpected delays. Furnace doors are poorly maintained and no records are kept.

Rolling mills

A lack of technological mastery has aggravated the problems which result from poor practice and obsolete equipment. Because of a mixed gas shortage, the soaking pits were modified to burn fuel oil as well. It was soon discovered that burning a mixture of the two fuels would increase productivity, a highly welcome event since this area represented a major bottleneck in the plant's operations. This innovation yielded unexpected adverse consequences, however – consequences which were ignored but which require that the practice be abandoned. Once again the costs of an innovation outweighed the benefits that were achieved because the decision-makers did not understand the technology deeply enough to recognize that its introduction would yield damaging results.

The shortage of fuel has also created significant delays in the operation of the continuous mill, a problem that can apparently be resolved by converting its furnace to burn fuel oil. If this were done and if its delivery speed – which stands at 5,000 feet per minute, 25 per cent of what modern mills achieve – were increased, its capacity would rise greatly and it could also turn out those items which are presently being produced by two obsolete pieces of equipment, the 28 inch and the 12 inch mill. The 16 inch mill, another obsolete machine, produces items which cannot be transferred.

Administration

All the control, maintenance and supervisory shortcomings that are evident throughout the plant ultimately stem from poor management. The available laboratory equipment, for example, is adequate but since each unit is an autonomous entity, there is no attempt to check, in a coordinated manner, quality at each stage of the production process. Moreover, qualified metallurgists are assigned to posts that do not require their skills. Little cost analysis is carried out and what data is generated is submitted months late. Yet management has never attempted to identify the reasons for this situation or to remedy it. As a result critical information dealing with costs and finances is seldom available when needed though timely, detailed and accurate data is a prerequisite to effective and efficient operation. Changes in financial and commercial administration will be required to ensure that such information is produced and utilized.

Administrative deficiencies, however, go well beyond the absence of an effective management information system; they begin with the organizational structure itself. Power is highly centralized; the plant manager has overall responsibility for the operation of the plant. He carries a heavy burden but there is no assistant plant manager to assist him with the daily routine. Hence, not only is he overloaded with details that could and should be taken care of by assistants so that he has little time for strategic planning, but when he is absent, as is often the case for he frequently has to go to Ankara, no one can act on his behalf. Thus the general manager is overburdened with detail. Moreover, he has traditionally been a political appointee whose tenure has often coincided with the length of time that a particular government has stayed in power. As in ERDEMIR, the turnover in this and other important positions was quite high in the seventies when weak coalition governments were the norm. Adding to the instability is the fact that Karabük has essentially functioned as a training school. Many of its most able managers spend a few years there and move on to the private sector or to other positions with more attractive salary structures, fringe benefits and location.

These managerial shortcomings are aggravated by the division between the managerial and the technical staff. Many engineers have a white collar mentality and tend to prefer not to get their hands dirty, an orientation that is reinforced by the emphasis upon recording-keeping rather than problem-solving. The existing tendency is to maintain existing practice and to discourage initiative. As a result, rather than seeking to resolve problems, lower level employees prefer simply to wait and record what is happening. This has often meant that minor operating problems are not resolved and that they cumulate into major disasters.[39]

Moreover, only persons who attended a university are deemed worthy of being considered members of the management team even though the foremen who have been with the plant for many years are the key personnel. Most of them have settled contentedly in Karabük and have lived there for years, many moonlighting in one of the little rolling mills which have sprung up in the town. They are technologically quite sophisticated and can apply their knowledge if they are permitted to do so but, because they actually work with machinery, they possess inferior status, receive lower remuneration, and are seldom accorded an opportunity to do more than follow orders. Treating them as a separate class (a practice which, as I noted in Chapter 2 was condemned by Western experts in the forties) adversely affects efficiency and productivity. The consultants attacked this practice in language reminiscent of earlier criticisms:[40]

> It is of paramount importance that both groups be combined into a single, unified group . . . rewarded in relation to responsibilities and individual performance . . . Deferring action on this change will continue to erode the productive capability of the Karabük Works through loss of many competent people to enterprises in the private sector plus de-motivation of those remaining from the present illogical system with its inequitable compensation policy.

Thirdly, communication within departments and between levels within the plant is quite poor. This situation creates numerous problems for the needs of the operating units are often not met and coordination is difficult to achieve. Finally the consultants noted that the plant was significantly overmanned.[41]

Personnel problems are accentuated by the lack of modern personnel practices. Promotions are not based on explicit criteria since there is, at present, no evaluation system to determine and reward individual ability. Such a system would permit promotion on the basis of merit and would solve the problem of low morale and high turnover among capable young engineers, many of whom hold positions that are not especially challenging but which are essential to the effective running of the plant.

Nor is managerial effectiveness assessed in any rigorous manner. At present only one indicator is used to measure productivity, and even this objective is poorly defined because it is established by the SPO on the basis of theoretical capacity and does not take into account such factors as the quality and quantity of raw materials that are available, the condition of the equipment, or capital spending plans. The General Directorate, in consultation with the management, should establish realistic objectives that incorporate, in addition to productivity, profitability and cost factors. Managers at all levels should be held accountable for meeting these objectives as well.

Under these conditions, it should not be surprising that quality remains a major shortcoming or that it is difficult to improve the plant's performance, or that Karabük's level of technological mastery is sufficient only to keep the plant running. The key to improvement lies with better managerial and operational procedures as is evidenced by the results that were achieved by a consultant who focused on existing practices. In his report he stated: 'Utilizing facility programs now underway and only minor additional facility changes, methods and procedures were developed which should result in increased new steel production of approximately 99.000 tons per year and operating cost savings of $4.5 million per year.'[42]

Further improvements are obviously feasible. The problem has been studied in great detail by numerous Turkish and foreign experts and a recent four-year study sponsored by Unido culminated in a five volume report with detailed recommendations for improving the situation. These include (1) more extensive quality control processes and procedures, (2) extended and improved sampling methods, (3) improved data systems, including computerization, (4) new organizational structure with manning and qualification level specifications, (5) better laboratory facilities, (6) the purchase of about $5 million worth of new equipment.[43] A subsequent study strongly endorsed all these points and added a recommendation for the establishment of a training program that would emphasize several basic areas including English language proficiency (in order to keep up with technological developments in one's field), modern management methods, computers and safety (at present a largely neglected area).[44] Implementing these projects would undoubtedly be useful but the degree of improvement that can be achieved will depend upon the ability to change the plant's operational culture from passivity to innovativeness. To do so will be no simple matter – the cleavage between the managers and the technicians, for example, has characterized the plant since its inception and reflects broader societal values.

COMPARATIVE PERSPECTIVES

Despite all its shortcomings, Karabük has achieved a level of technological mastery that permits it to function quite well in comparison to the other plants. Its managerial and labor deficiencies are common to all State Economic Enterprises and exist, as I have noted, to an even greater degree at ISDEMIR. ERDEMIR, on the other hand, because of its private-sector orientation which, though eroded during the seventies, was still able to maintain a relatively stable and strongly motivated managerial team and workforce that has enabled it to operate at a profit.

The levels of mastery achieved by each of the three plants can be measured by several indicators. Table 6.5 indicates the extent to which each plant's major components achieves its potential capacity.

Clearly, all three plants were operating below capacity at each stage of the manufacturing process. Karabük's performance was

Table 6.5 Capacity utilization of Turkish plants

	1977	1978	1979	1980	1981
Coke ovens:					
Karabük	73.4	72.1	66.9	66.7	66.8
ISDEMIR	39.4	48.8	68.2	56.6	51.2
ERDEMIR[1]	26.0	60.0	44.0	42.0	
Blast furnaces:					
Karabük	106.1	88.3	84.6	91.7	91.0
ISDEMIR	39.3	45.4	63.0	55.4	47.1
ERDEMIR		30.0	77.5	56.0	55.0
Steel production:					
Karabük	100.2	99.6	97.0	94.1	93.1
ISDEMIR	17.7	37.1	43.5	42.0	37.4
ERDEMIR		63.3	94.5	65.0	63.0
Rolling mills:					
Karabük	106.3	99.2	96.9	92.8	90.4
ISDEMIR	10.3	40.9	38.9	46.2	32.4
ERDEMIR[2]		44.0	44.6		

1. ERDEMIR's poor performance in 1980 and 1981 can be attributed to its reduced need for coke since only one of its two blast furnaces was operating in these years.
2. ERDEMIR has a large idle capacity because its combination mill has a capacity of 550,000 tons a year while its semi-continuous mill has a capacity of two million tons a year.[45]

Sources: Karabük and ISDEMIR data are from Devlet Planlama Teşkilatī, *Demir-Çelik Özel Ihtisas Komisyonu Raporu, Son Taslak* (Ankara: DPT, February 1983), pp. 48, 53: the ERDEMIR data for 1978 and 1979 are from Çelebi, op. cit., p. 62; the 1981 and 1982 figures are calculated from data in S. Tan, *Demir-Çelik Sanayiinde Verimlilik* (Ankara: Milli Prodüktivite Merkezi, 1983).

extremely good though it declined over time. ERDEMIR ranked second and ISDEMIR struggled to achieve a respectable level.

More precise insights into the extent to which each of the plants has achieved mastery over its technologies is provided by a detailed consideration of the situation at each stage. Data on both the overall problems and on productivity levels at each plant according to different criteria are available. The former were defined in the early seventies by a team at the Marmara Research Institute which carried out an extensive and sophisticated study of the sector's needs in order to develop a coherent policy that would reduce the existing technological gap and improve the sector's performance.[46] It identified the industry's major problems (which by now should be quite familiar to the reader) and prioritized research projects for each phase of the production process, beginning with raw material gathering and preparation. It called for detailed studies of the country's iron ore and coal deposits, for studies on how to increase productivity and efficiency in mining practices and transportation networks, and for establishing priorities for the Zonguldak mines (coking coal should be reserved for the industry and not shipped to electric power plants). The need for such projects is readily apparent from a consideration of the coke oven situation given in Table 6.6.

Although none of the plants were operating at satisfactory levels, the differences between them are quite startling. Karabük ranks first

Table 6.6 Coke oven productivity of Turkish plants (1980–81)

	ISDEMIR	Karabük	ERDEMIR
Raw material usage (ton coke/ton coal)	77%	77%	62%
Energy usage (× 10 ton coke/kcal)	1.25%	1.15%	0.95%
Manpower productivity (ton/man hour)	0.35%	0.70%	1.0%
Capacity use (ton produced/theoretical capacity)	50%	70%	50%
Coke ovens usage (charge/potential charge)	47.5%	62.5%	55%

Source: Tan, op. cit., Graphs 26–31, pp. 141–6.

on every measure except manpower productivity; ERDEMIR ranks first only on that measure. The quality of ERDEMIR's performance is evidenced by an international comparison: in the USA the figure is 0.91 ton per man hour;[47] Karabük achieves 77 per cent of that level and ISDEMIR manages slightly more than a third. ERDEMIR's special status, which has permitted it to train and retain qualified personnel, is largely responsible for its superior performance. Its low productivity in regards to coke usage and energy is due to the quality of the coal available to it. Karabük uses good coal from Zonguldak, ISDEMIR imports high-quality coking coal from the USA but ERDEMIR has to blend high-quality imported US coal with semi coking coal from the Armutcuk-Amasra mines. In addition to good inputs, ISDEMIR benefits from its modern technology, but these advantages are offset by all the managerial and labor difficulties discussed above.

At the blast furnace stage, shortcomings to be remedied included low productivity, high costs, unnecessary coal consumption and inefficient use of by-products. Proposed research projects ranged from studies on new systems to the development of mathematical models for better control and planning. The situation at each plant is as given in Table 6.7.

Here too ERDEMIR leads in manpower productivity, followed quite closely by Karabük; ISDEMIR trails dismally. Even ERDE-MIR's performance, however, falls well below international standards. In the USA 0.96 tons are produced per man-hour, ERDEMIR achieves 72 per cent of this level, Karabük and ISDEMIR 65 per cent and 22 per cent respectively. All three plants achieve roughly the same levels in terms of raw material usage, a low 35 to 40 per cent. This is due to the poor quality of the iron ore (some improvement will occur when the ore pelletization plant now being constructed at Divriği is completed) and to the low percentage of sinter in the charge at all three plants, a percentage well below the accepted level of 70 to 80 per cent; ISDEMIR which utilizes the most sinter reaches about two-thirds of this figure, [48] the others only about one-third.

Steel production practices were also in need of improvement. The team's analysis revealed problems in regard to decision-making (research reports do not reach managers in time so that they are unable to incorporate the findings into production strategies), inadequate energy and oxygen supplies, and limited storage facilities. The specific projects were designed to achieve a better understanding of new technological developments and to produce cheaper and higher quality goods, including improvements in the production of refracto-

Table 6.7 Blast furnace productivity of Turkish plants (1980–81)

	ISDEMIR	Karabük	ERDEMIR
Raw material usage (ton liquid metal/ton coal)	40%	35%	37%
% of sinter in charge	52%	32%	34%
Sinter energy productivity (ton liquid metal/10)	0.8	1.3%	0.95
Coke consumption (ton liquid metal/ton coke consumption)	1.0	1.0	1.2
Manpower productivity (ton liquid metal/man hour)	0.21	0.625	0.69
Productivity according to blast furnace diameter (ton liquid metal/m diameter)	450	525	475
Productivity according to blast furnace size (ton liquid metal/size)	40	28.5	17.5

Source: Tan, op. cit., Graphs 33–40, pp. 156–63.

ries, research on how to reduce the high sulfur content (40 per cent above the norm), to eliminate unnecessary coal consumption, the development of new cooling systems, and strategies to increase the heat levels and new control techniques. The situation at each plant is given in Table 6.8.

Once again ERDEMIR ranks first in manpower productivity though the difference with Karabük, when allowance is made for the different steel-making technologies used at the two plants is quite small, about 20 per cent. Productivity measured by the molten steel/input ratio is about the same at the three mills. Energy use is very poor at Iskenderun, especially in the light of the modern equipment at the plant. And even with a high charge to molten metal ratio ISDEMIR still achieves low productivity. These results are due to poor labor and managerial inadequacies. Karabük's performance is very good given its lack of continuous casting machinery and its low productivity Siemens Martin furnaces. ERDEMIR uses energy efficiently.

Table 6.8 Steel shop productivity of Turkish plants (1980–81)

	ISDEMIR	Karabük	ERDEMIR
Raw material usage (ton/ton)	0.78	0.77	0.80
Continuous casting ratio (ton/ton)	0.97	—	0.35
Energy productivity (10 ton/kcal)	1.0	0.6	3.2
Molten metal ratio (ton/charge)	0.82	0.59	0.67
Manpower productivity (ton/man hour):			
Direct	0.1	0.3	0.7
Direct (adjusted for technology used)	0.1	0.5	0.6
Total	0.1	0.35	0.75
Total (adjusted for technology used)	0.1	0.5	0.6
Plant productivity (period worked/total period)	0.40	0.58	0.48
Cast tonnage ratio (ton/ton)	0.85	1.0	0.96

Source: Tan, op. cit., Charts 41–50, pp. 168–77.

Finally we come to the rolling mills whose operations are marked by weaknesses in many areas: (1) poor implementation of needed planning and design strategies, (2) inadequate coordination, (3) lack of energy, (4) low quality inputs, (5) technical difficulties, (6) maintenance problems and (7) inadequate quality control measures. These were caused by poor administrative practices, an unskilled, undisciplined, politicized workforce, political interference, and a lack of qualified managers. How these are reflected in the plants' performances is indicated in Table 6.9.

Labor productivity is again very low at ISDEMIR because of the size and nature of its workforce. Performance at the other plants is quite similar, a noteworthy result given ERDEMIR's personnel and managerial advantages. Karabük's performance is also noteworthy in regard to energy where, despite antiquated facilities, its results are

Table 6.9 Rolling mills productivity of Turkish plants (1980–81)

	ISDEMIR	Karabük	ERDEMIR
Raw material productivity (ton/ton, adjusted for technology)	1.10	1.0	1.05
Energy productivity (ton/kcal)	0.15	0.3	0.2
Manpower productivity (ton/man-hour):			
Direct	2.5	6.0	5.5
Direct (adjusted for technology)	0.01	0.02	0.025
Total	1.5	5.0	4.0
Total (adjusted for technology)	0.01	0.02	0.02
Facility productivity	0.30	0.67	0.62

Source: Tables 53–60,pp. 185–92.

superior to those of the other two plants. These facilities are responsible for its weak performance in terms of raw material usage. ISDEMIR achieves a high level because of its equipment; ERDE-MIR, which also has good equipment, does not rate well on this indicator.

It is evident from these figures that the ISDEMIR plant, despite its modern Soviet technologies, operates at a very low level as measured by practically any indicator. Its poor performance stems from problems with its sinter plant, and, even worse, its continuous caster which stands at the core of the steel-making process. More fundamentally, its operations are severely handicapped by the limited understanding of the technologies that its personnel have achieved. Its low level of technological mastery (on the scale that I introduced in Chapter 1, ISDEMIR ranks at the lowest level, the 'implantation' stage) is due to several factors including sectoral and other policies that I shall discuss in Chapter 8. These policies have created a situation which would not permit any organization to become effective and efficient, certainly not one with ISDEMIR's shortcomings.

Manpower issues have been consistently neglected at the plant; its workforce is too large, its quality too low. Administration too suffers from numerous deficiencies; managers are poorly trained and motivated, there is a high turnover, and policies and techniques are quite traditional. The result is poor coordination, planning, communication and implementation. Particularly affected is the entire area of maintenance which is largely neglected. Moreover, the problems of the plant are so large that everyone connected with it has assumed a fatalistic orientation which further limits the efficacy of attempts to improve the situation.

Many of these problems are also characteristic of Karabük for both plants are part of the Turkish Iron and Steel Works Directorate and are subject to the same policies. In fact the latter tends to be discriminated against when resources of all kinds such as foreign exchange and raw materials are allocated. Despite such handicaps, however, the difference in the performance of the two plants is quite clear, a remarkable situation since Karabük also labors with obsolete equipment (especially the coke ovens and some of its rolling mills) and a poor location.

The explanation for the difference between the two plants lies in the differing levels of technological mastery that each has achieved. Here the time factor must be introduced. Whereas ISDEMIR is a relatively new plant, Karabük has, over the years, built up a cadre of skilled workers, especially at the foremen level, who have acquired the know-how to achieve the quite impressive results noted above, results that could be enhanced with better management. As discussed earlier, the organizational structure and culture are not appropriate for a modern tchnological enterprise; serious shortcomings have been identified at Karabük in such areas as information management, communication, analysis, control and coordination, but the plant does operate well. Over the years its workers and managers have learnt by doing. In terms of the levels of technological mastery, it probably has reached the 'assimilation' stage, though its maintenance is below par.

ERDEMIR's situation is very different because it was organized as a private-sector enterprise with great autonomy; its management could essentially establish its own policies in many critical areas such as personnel, unhampered by pressures from the state. Hence it set its own price and salary levels. Moreover, decisions could be taken relatively quickly and easily since they only had to be approved by the board of directors whereas in the state enterprises, decisions had to go from the plant to the TDÇI to the High Planning Commission. As a result, ERDEMIR's management is stronger than that in the other plants. There has been a high level of continuity, data gathering and analysis is more sophisticated and current than elsewhere, and communication patterns are more effective. Morale is high and turnover at all levels low. Furthermore, its technologies are modern ones and it has had an organic link for many years to external expertise. What is surprising, given such conditions, is that the level of mastery is not higher, that the plant does not perform at higher levels.

Some of its shortcomings are due to the plant's history. Its transportation problems need attention, the numerous expansions have created imbalances of various sorts, some of its units such as one of its blast furnaces should be modernized, and a second sinter plant is needed. Most of its weaknesses, however, can be traced to the limited level of mastery that has been achieved. What maintenance is done is generally of poor quality and little preventive work of any sort is carried out. There are also problems in planning and scheduling projects of various kinds. The plant, for example, is out of commission for about 45 per cent of the time instead of the usual 10 per cent.[49] In addition, some operating practices, especially in the area of in-plant transportation, should be improved. As the productivity figures suggest, the existing sinter plant is not effectively utilized. Its coke consumption is also extremely high and blast furnace performance could be improved with better operating practices. Hence, ERDEMIR can best be placed in the 'assimilation' stage of technological mastery. The plant operates at reasonable levels but it has not reached the 'competitive' level for its products fall below international standards in terms of price, productivity and quality.

With these levels of mastery, the industry was ill equipped to deal with a significant and unexpected external development. As I noted in Chapter 2, the late seventies and early eighties were a difficult period for the iron and steel industry everywhere as new producers entered the market, creating great excess capacity. Many producers engaged in dumping and prices were pushed down to very low levels as governments sought to protect their industries.[50] The consequences for the Turkish plants were disastrous. They were simply unable to compete in this environment and reached a state of crisis the magnitude of which becomes evident when their financial condition is considered. Data on profits and losses are available for ERDEMIR and for Karabük and ISDEMIR combined (the Turkish Iron and Steel Works (TDÇI)). As is evident from Table 6.10, ERDEMIR was earning large sums, a total of TL 9.2 billion between 1977 and 1982, while TDÇI was losing even larger amounts, TL 18.5 billion.

ERDEMIR's profitability can be attributed only partly to its level of technological mastery. More important is the monopoly that it enjoys. No private sector firm produces flat steel; the mini steel

Table 6.10 Profitability of Turkish plants (TL million)

	1977	1978	1979	1980	1981	1982	1983 (5 months)
TDÇI:							
Amount	(1,917)	(2,977)	1,654	2,074	(9,211)	(8,000)	
Profit-loss ratio	(7.3)	(21.5)	14.2	8.1	(11.6)	(5.6)	
ERDEMIR:							
Amount	497	747	1,144	3,298	687	3,084	8,000
Profit-loss ratio	29.9	23.7	29.5	24.0	16.7	20.9	

Source: Rapor. Tables 11 and 19, pp. 30, 35–6.

plants, with their higher productivity rates, compete with Karabük and ISDEMIR. Hence ERDEMIR can essentially sell everything it is able to produce without much attention to considerations of quality or even price.

Even under these conditions, Karabük apparently outperforms ISDEMIR. Although detailed information on the financial situation of the two plants is hard to come by, it is known that ISDEMIR has consistently lost money: in 1980 TL 6,754 million, in 1981 an estimated TL 7,000 million.[51] It appears therefore that Karabük earned a profit of about TL 9 million in 1980 and lost TL 2,211 million in 1981. In any case, TDÇI confronted a very serious financial problem: its costs increased by 125 per cent between 1980 and 1982 while it was able to raise its prices by only 56 per cent.[52]

CONCLUSION

The condition of Turkey's iron and steel sector in the late 1970s was clearly not a healthy one and serious questions were being raised about the implications of this situation for the industry's future and for economic development in general. However, important political and economic changes have taken place in Turkey in recent years. These have affected the iron and steel industry in many ways, including the decision not to proceed with the SIDEMIR plant whose rationale, as I demonstrated, was based on feasibility studies which, even with significant doubtful assumptions, showed the project to be a marginal one at best. Such results have hitherto seldom prevented the realization of a project; this decision represents a profound shift in the values and objectives of Turkish policy-makers. The nature of these changes, their implications and the lessons that emerge from the Turkish case are among the topics to be discussed in the next and concluding chapter.

7 Projects and Politics
Towards Rational Decision-Making

INTRODUCTION

Turkey's determined efforts to forge modernity by building up the iron and steel industry date back over fifty years but Ataturk's vision has only partially been realized. Turkey has emerged as a major Third World producer but each of its integrated plants, Karabük, ERDEMIR and ISDEMIR, were typical technology transfer projects – they encountered numerous problems which have been only partially resolved. And, though one can discern differences in the levels of mastery achieved, none could operate its technologies at internationally accepted levels of productivity and quality.

As a result, the industry's contribution to the achievement of national goals has been limited. Rather than serving as a forge for development by generating a surplus and by providing other sectors with products at a quality and price that would stimulate their growth, it probably inhibited the country's industrial progress.[1] Moreover, one of the fundamental rationales for the development of the industry was to enhance the country's security and independence, by permitting it to become self-sufficient in this basic commodity. Yet this goal was never realized. Turkey remains highly dependent on foreign actors in many ways – for their technologies, for their skills, for their financing, and, to some extent, for their raw materials. Nor has the functioning of the economy, of which the industry is such an important component, advanced the country's democratic development. At least two military interventions, the one in 1960 and the one in 1980, can be attributed, at least partially, to deteriorating economic conditions.

Should one conclude, therefore, that Turkey's development would have been furthered if it had not striven so enthusiastically to establish an iron and steel industry at practically any cost? To answer such a question is no easy matter for there is no way of knowing how

189

much foreign aid might have been available for an alternative strategy, how the capital that was invested in iron and steel would have been spent or what pattern of development would have resulted – even though studies (which I discussed in Chapter 2) have shown that an alternative strategy would theoretically have yielded better results. What is beyond question, however, is that the selected strategy was not implemented in an optimal manner, that its consequences were not especially positive, with important consequences for Turkey's economy and polity.

Why was this the case? Why did the technology transfer process not yield better outcomes? These are fundamental questions for substantive and theoretical reasons. If the defects stemmed from factors that were rooted in the specifics of the sector, then an alternative strategy would have been far more productive. If, on the other hand, the factors are endemic to Turkey or are part of any large technology transfer project, then problems would have arisen, and may continue to arise, regardless of the sectoral emphasis which the state pursues, with negative consequences for its development. Since Turkey, like many other countries, continues to strive for more rapid growth through major projects in many areas (the value of its technology transfer projects stood at over $25 billion in the late seventies) such findings can have obvious policy relevance. Moreover, the Turkish iron and steel industry, whatever its deficiencies, remains a major industrial sector in which additional investments will inevitably be made.

Nor can one overlook the more general contribution that might result from a better understanding of the factors that limited the projects' outcomes for the issues transcend the Turkish case. As I stressed in Chapter 1, project failure is a widespread phenomenon, one that occurs frequently in advanced as well as developing countries. The costs of such failures are a burden for rich countries such as the USA, the UK and Sweden where numerous projects are known to have suffered huge cost overruns and other problems of various kinds,[2] but they are often crippling to developing countries which are struggling to develop with limited resources. Accordingly, improved understanding of the reasons why projects so often yield sub-optimal outcomes can contribute to the development of both theory and practice. It can lead to improvements in the technology transfer process, facilitate the efforts by Third World states to raise the standard of living of their populations and help narrow the gap between rich and poor nations. It is with such considerations in mind that I now return to the analytical framework that I elaborated in Chapter 1. First, I shall analyze the decisions that were made in regards to the design, impact and management dimensions that I have utilized throughout and then I shall consider the role that specific variables played in shaping the decisions. Subsequently I shall discuss the dramatic changes that have occurred since 1980 and draw general conclusions concerning politics, technology and development.

THE QUALITY OF THE TECHNOLOGICAL DECISIONS

To begin with, it is clear that the technology transfer process did not produce positive outcomes on either of the two output dimensions that I identified – the quality of the project and the acquisition of technological mastery. The development of the iron and steel industry indicates clearly that a successful transfer must take both of these into account. Each is a necessary but not a sufficient condition. If a project is to meet its goals and achieve its full potential, it must be well designed and implemented and the recipient must achieve an appropriate level of technological mastery. In every case analyzed above, problems of design and implementation have been aggravated by a limited technological capability. The decisions that were made and the ways in which they were implemented created this situation.

The design dimension

The first component of the design dimension, location, was always analyzed systematically and, as prudent project planning suggests, various sites were considered. But the process of choice and implementation differed in several significant ways from textbook practice. First, the criteria that were utilized were not comprehensive enough – future developments and the plant's potential for regional development were never accorded proper attention as I shall demonstrate below. Moreover, political factors ranging from national security in the case of Karabük to electoral ones for the aborted SIDEMIR project were often primary.

Second, even when a good site was chosen (ERDEMIR, ISDE-MIR), its potential was never fully realized because of political decisions: no government ever made the investments that would optimize the advantages of a site. ERDEMIR's coastal location, for example, has never been exploited fully. Its harbor was developed, at the time of the original construction, to accommodate vessels up to 35,000 tons but in the early eighties the company had only four 5,000 ton vessels to haul the coal and iron ore. Plans are now being implemented to deepen the harbor to handle 60,000 ton vessels but an efficient operation would involve modern ore carriers with a capacity of 200–250,000 tons. In addition, little of its production is shipped by boat, although Istanbul, a major market, is only 240 km by sea. Nor was adequate attention paid to the road and rail systems. The country's road system is overburdened and its rail system antiquated but these inadequacies were never taken into account and the kinds of investments that might have ameliorated the situation were never undertaken. In the case of ERDEMIR, for example, the Turkish government's decision not to build the connecting link of the railroad between Ereğli and the major Zonguldak–Ankara route, because of its cost, severely constrained the shipment of outputs and inputs. Particularly affected is the movement of goods to the interior of Turkey for ERDEMIR has to rely heavily on road haulage but its connections to the rest of the country are of poor quality. It is essentially served by one highway which runs for a distance of about 40 miles to one of the most traveled roads in Turkey, the one linking Istanbul to Ankara. High transportation costs are a continuing burden under which ERDEMIR labors, and an expansion (one that would double capacity to four million tons has been studied in detail) would further aggravate this situation. Similar problems characterize the transportation situation at every plant.

These findings are consonant with those of Turkish experts who have analyzed the reasons for the industry's poor performance. They concluded that the design process was seriously flawed because inadequate attention was paid to the nature and quality of the inputs and to the infrastructural requirements, especially transportation. As a result, the plants have had to struggle with poor quality coal and iron ore that is often not available in scheduled quantities yet whose costs are very high. Nor was the role that the plants could play in regional development analyzed adequately so that their potential has never been fully realized.[3]

The failure to recognize a plant's role in stimulating regional growth or to anticipate future developments led to the selection of sites that were not large enough to permit expansion or to accommodate ancillary industries and to poor use of the available space. Karabük was sited in a small valley and there is simply no room left to build new facilities. At ERDEMIR the remaining space is so limited that an expansion would require extensive and expensive land reclamation, filling in 700,000 square meters with approximately 7 million cubic meters of dirt. Moreover, only a limited amount of water is available at Ereğli and additional reservoir capacity cannot be provided easily or cheaply because the Guluc river lacks good dam sites. A consulting firm labeled the extensive works that would be required to supply the necessary water 'a monumental but not impossible task'.[4] The understatement is obvious and one knowledgeable observer has suggested that a more appropriate phrase would read 'a monumentally insane but not impossible task'!

Nor is it possible to establish the ancillary industries that could have stimulated regional development. While steel mills are not the most powerful catalysts of regional development (despite the claims of the proponents of the SIDEMIR project) two types of industrial projects – steel consuming and satellite plants – are symbiotically related. The first tend to locate near their market because the cost of transporting their products is higher than the cost of transporting their inputs. Thus transportation becomes a key factor and even if land were available, it is not likely that many businesses of this type would locate at Ereğli, Iskenderun or at Sivas. In fact few secondary and tertiary industries have settled in Ereğli. Rather, because of their market orientation, they established themselves in the urban centers, notably Istanbul, from whence come most of the various manufactured products that the plants utilize. The second type of ancillary industry, satellite plants, have different cost structures, for they either supply raw materials for use in the mill or process waste materials. These, especially fertilizer and cement plants, seek to minimize transportation and handling expenses by locating close to the works. Originally, ERDEMIR's by-products were to be the basis of new factories but ERDEMIR was laid out in such a way that the most desirable space for such factories, the land next to the plant, has been utilized for housing and community facilities.[5] Now these plans can never be implemented because of the limited water supply and the lack of available space. In short, apart from generating employment (today over half of the active population, about 13,000 persons, have some kind of working relationship with the plant) ERDEMIR has contributed little to the local economy and its potential has probably been dissipated.

The short-term horizons that dominated the design process are particularly evident where decisions concerning size are concerned.

The technological dynamics of the industry that made only mini mills or very large plants economic were ignored. When ERDEMIR was being designed, a normal sized mill possessed a million ton capacity but such a project would have cost between $600 and $700 million, three times the amount of financing that the USA was willing to provide. And, by the time that ISDEMIR was planned, modern integrated plants were at least two million ton capacity. Yet the original plans called for a plant half that size; only after extensive and strenuous interventions by Turkish experts did the government embark upon what turned out to be a stream of expansions. By the time of the Third Five Year Plan, the size problem was understood but even then political factors intruded and the Fourth Five Year Plan called for building two plants, one of which would be the relatively small (two million ton) SIDEMIR project.

The willingness to build a small plant at minimum cost determined the technological choices that were made. Experts studied these at length in order to decide the most desirable combination of technologies but imbalances were inevitable because certain units could not be cut back. Numerous examples of this phenomenon are evident in the Karabük plant as well as at ISDEMIR and ERDEMIR. Such deficiencies have important economic implications. Turkish experts who have analyzed the functioning of the plants have concluded that none of them could operate economically because of these factors – each was designed on too small a scale and its operation was constrained by serious bottlenecks and imbalances. Moreover, efforts to remedy this situation through expansion to a point where a plant could take advantage of the economies of scale that technologies make possible and streamlining its operations has proven to be extremely costly.[6] As a result Turkey's investment per ton of steel remains extremely high by international standards, $450 per ton at ERDEMIR and $630 per ton at ISDEMIR.[7]

The impact dimension

The analysis of impacts should determine the size of a project, whether it is commercially and economically sound, whether its implementation will benefit the society. Such calculations, however, which should be central to any decision to proceed with a project, played a small role in every case. The analyses for Karabük were probably quite limited. The first loan paper for ERDEMIR is a very thin document and little detailed work was done on the project by the

Turkish government although, subsequently, AID and the World
Bank paid considerable attention to calculating the financial soundness of ERDEMIR's various expansions. In the case of ISDEMIR
and SIDEMIR, however, it does not appear that the studies were as
thorough; the USSR explicitly left 'economic considerations' to the
Turkish government and its external consultants.

Although many Turkish experts were familiar with the techniques
and principles of cost–benefit analysis, these were seldom applied to
any project in a rigorous fashion. As one experienced analyst has
noted:[8]

> I have had occasion to see many sector, project, and feasibility
> studies prepared for the Turkish development plans. As in many
> other developing countries, these are often weak and fallible
> building blocks not to be confused with the real thing.

The situation was similar in the private sector. Although entrepreneurs needed detailed feasibility studies to obtain credits, these
studies usually were so deficient that they had to be redone.[9]

All the studies in the iron and steel sector were indeed 'fallible
building blocks' even though all the actors recognized the importance
of analyzing the direct economic impacts of each project. Practically
every study, whether prepared for the World Bank, AID or the
Turkish government, was flawed in one way or another. First, some
vital areas were neglected completely or treated in a cursory fashion.
This was especially true of the management dimension. Second, some
studies (including many that dealt with physical elements that should
be easy to measure such as soil conditions and especially the quantity
and quality of domestic iron ore) were poorly executed. Third, most
if not all studies contained unwarranted assumptions – that the rail
network could transport domestic raw materials cheaply and effectively, that ERDEMIR and SIDEMIR could operate at 100 per cent
productivity within three years, and that Turkish private investors
would participate eagerly in ERDEMIR's financing, to cite but a few.
Fourth, certain data (the value of the TL, for example) often proved
to be valid for only a short time because of unexpected developments.

Every study contained one or more of these shortcomings, though
some differences can be cited between those prepared by the various
actors because the quality of the analyses varied with the norms of the
organization that was responsible for the project. Several reasons can

be advanced to explain why all these studies were so error prone. As I pointed out in Chapter 1, cost-benefit methodologies cannot be applied mechanically. They require more than simple calculations for many difficult questions such as shadow prices, discount rates and trade-offs must be taken into account by the analyst and different values will yield quite different results. In addition, different techniques can be used to calculate various costs and benefits, each of which may – and often do – produce different estimates. And, whatever the technique, information is required, information that may not be available in the form and to the degree of accuracy that is needed. For example, to estimate market demand, data on consumption and imports is required, but when ERDEMIR was planned, only limited data was available in both of these areas.

Other factors, however, deserve serious attention for far more than methodological difficulties are involved. First, as I have noted, many studies produced certain results because those results were required if the project were to be implemented. The studies of iron ore availability illustrate this point well. Building a second major plant could be justified only if certain amounts of quality ore were available. The studies demonstrated that an adequate supply existed. Furthermore, many of the studies were constrained from the outset in one way or another. Many were designed within pre-established parameters that determined the results that would be obtained. Numerous technical studies were carried out to identify the appropriate size of each plant, for example, but these were all geared to the estimated domestic market and to how much financing, usually from external lenders, was available. Hence they all legitimized plants that were uneconomical. And, once the decision on size had been made, the technological choices were, in turn, predetermined. Second, as might be expected, all these projects encountered unexpected events. Often caught by surprise by the Turkish government's decisions (to devalue the currency, to impose new restrictions on imports of raw materials) and even by those of the receiving organization, the experts often had to carry out new analyses.

To understand the reasons for this state of affairs, it is necessary to consider the qualifications and orientations of the analysts and the context in which they work. Some may have lacked the necessary skills to apply a particular methodology correctly or to recognize its shortcomings in dealing with a particular issue, or they may have simply miscalculated. Human beings are fallible and they do make mistakes. More importantly, most were technical specialists whose educational background has prepared them to concentrate on specific technical details and not to go beyond these to value and cultural issues. As a result, they were not particularly sensitive to the role of environmental factors upon a project or trained in cross cultural communications. Few possessed any knowledge of the Turkish scene. While technically proficient, persons with such a background were not likely to anticipate changes in the forces impinging upon Ankara or a recipient organization or be prepared for an 'unexpected' event. Their background also predisposed them to accept parameters that rendered a project vulnerable; their responsibility was to carry out analyses of specific technical details and not question the assumptions that underlay the projects assigned to them by the decision-makers. Moreover, many of the experts shared the values and orientations of those in power and worked hard to help them achieve their goals; they genuinely believed that iron and steel promoted development. Nor can one eliminate self-interest and the pressures, usually implicit, that result when one works for an organization, public or private, that has a vested interest in a particular project or in pleasing the client who has commissioned the study. Whatever the motivations, psychological and other, the willingness of experts and consultants to make assumptions of all kinds or to accept doubtful information as the basis for calculations that would provide desired answers does demonstrate the validity of the perhaps cynical view advanced in Chapter 1 that political power determines whether technical analyses will be used to legitimize or eliminate projects. I shall discuss the implications of these conclusions below for it is obvious that existing practices for analyzing technological transfer projects are problematic and raise fundamental questions about the entire approach.

The difficulties inherent in the analysis of the first-order economic costs and benefits are magnified when one attempts to analyze social, political, cultural and environmental impacts, but few problems arose in these areas because all of these – catalytic potentials, questions of pollution, second- and third-order consequences – were accorded minor attention. Some did become issues, but only because of decisions by external actors. The World Bank, for example, raised the pollution issue at ERDEMIR. It is, of course, true that pollution was not a priority anywhere in the world, even in the USA, until recent decades, and that even the World Bank's efforts were constrained by its organizational processes; it is also true that it has never become a major issue for the Turkish government or for other LDCs who feel that the opportunity costs of investing resources in this area are very high.

The Turkish government accorded an equally low priority to all other impacts and AID largely ignored them. In the case of ERDE-MIR, for example, officials were aware of the changes that would come to Ereğli as a result of the plant's construction, but little was actually done to mitigate what has been called the 'boom town syndrome' as its population – which had increased from 3,628 in 1941 to 8,812 in 1960 – exploded to 18,978 by 1964 and reached 43,325 in 1974. As early as 1962 its water supply and other municipal services did not suffice to deal with the existing in-migration, but not till that year were any plans to deal with the newcomers even formulated.[10] The consequences were only too predictable: problems of inflation and shortages of water, land, housing, education and transportation.

Nor was much attention paid to enhancing ERDEMIR's potential for industrial development. This had been the case of Karabük too. Both it and ERDEMIR are located in Zonguldak province which has been the site of quite extensive economic development but, as one analyst noted: 'In 1962, some 30 years after the first efforts to mobilize local activities, Zonguldak was closer to a region mired in the periphery than one in process of dynamic growth.'[1] The construction of ERDEMIR did not change this state of affairs. Little was done to develop a coherent plan that would link ERDEMIR in a creative and systematic manner to the region's resources and potential.

While one can understand that Ankara might be unwilling to allocate scarce resources to deal with pollution issues or to help a booming muncipality, it is more difficult to understand why so little attention was paid to enhancing ERDEMIR's potential for stimulating the region's growth, though part of the answer is to be found in the country's administrative patterns.

The management dimension

As I have emphasized, management is a critical variable which largely determines the performance of any enterprise. Yet almost every, if not every, study that was carried out ignored fundamental questions of organizational structure, of administrative and managerial systems, of a systematic, long-range program of manpower recruitment and training at all levels.

Some Turkish personnel were sent abroad for training but most learning was expected to take place by doing and by watching foreign experts working alongside. Whatever learning did take place under these conditions was simply too limited in breadth and in depth to permit Turkish counterparts to engaged in creative problem-solving. Knowledge transfer does not take place easily; numerous obstacles (e.g. cultural differences and problems in communication) can be anticipated but little thought was accorded to how these might be overcome.

As a result, Karabük in the seventies still suffered from managerial deficiencies which had been identified in the forties, and ISDEMIR was plagued with administrative weaknesses of all kinds. ERDE-MIR's management, the most effective of all the plants, shared many of the patterns that prevailed at Karabük and ISDEMIR and within the national bureaucracy as a whole, patterns that not only failed to encourage the development of mastery but which actively hindered it. Managers tended to approach their responsibilities in a traditional, authoritarian manner. The structure was centralized, little delegation of authority took place and the culture emphasized subservience. Mid-level administrators were reluctant to make independent decisions or to take initiatives. The emphasis tended to be on rigid control rather than on innovation and improvements in productivity. The hierarchical and centralized system of decision-making meant that the plant's successful operation depended largely on the skills and abilities of one person and that any change at the highest levels of management had immediate and serious repercussions for the operation of the plant. Moreover, those persons who possessed the best technical knowledge were excluded from the decision process, especially at Karabük where the cleavage between the skilled foremen and the administrators was severely criticized in the forties and again in the early eighties and at ISDEMIR. ERDEMIR's organizational culture differed in degree, though not in kind. The interaction between the cultural environment and managerial shortcomings proved detrimental in many ways. An able manager would have achieved a better performance, but for the plants to operate optimally, he would have to generate changes in the culture so as to encourage innovation and creativity.

Only two managerial issues ever became topics of major concern and these arose because of the interests of the foreign donors – the possibility that ERDEMIR's special position as an autonomous enterprise would be eroded and the increased politicization of the plant that took place in the seventies. AID and the World Bank struggled to maintain ERDEMIR's special status and to ensure that its management would be stable and qualified, but these protests proved to be ineffectual and it lost its existing ability to control its own operations. It came to suffer, like the other plants, from frequent personnel changes and the appointment of unqualified persons to high positions. And the number of workers, who also became politicized, increased to a level that greatly exceeded actual needs, with damaging consequences for the sector's operation.

Whether more forceful action by the Bank would have altered the outcome has been debated by some observers but the assumption that ERDEMIR could be isolated from its political environment, particularly given the size of the Turkish government's stake in the corporation is, in my view, quite naive. Even with a different capital structure, the prevailing political atmosphere would probably not have allowed the plant to maintain its special position.

Not surprisingly, therefore, the project implementation stage was trouble free only when foreign contractors were in charge. The project manager for the original construction of ERDEMIR carried out his responsibilities skilfully whereas those who were responsible for the construction of ISDEMIR and for the ERDEMIR expansion did not possess his abilities and never made use of well-known techniques of control and coordination. As a result, ERDEMIR's expansion and ISDEMIR's construction encountered numerous delays and difficulties, though national economic conditions and various organizational requirements were partly responsible. Still, Turkish experts have placed much of the blame for the delays which led to higher than anticipated expenditures upon poor management. Eventually, after great expenses and human efforts, the projects were completed but the transition to the operational phase seldom proceeded smoothly. And since the technologies had not been mastered, each plant began operation under difficult circumstances and was never able to perform at a level that came close to the original expectations.[12]

Turkish planners have concluded that a major reason for this situation lies with the manner in which the plants are administered. All plants suffer from relatively poor operating practices and management methods; the organization and control of work is inadequate as evidenced by poor planning for inputs and spare parts and the low levels of maintenance. Moreover, all plants have been affected by the intrusion of political factors in hiring at all levels. As a result all have lost qualified managers, have often been forced to employ unqualified persons in high level positions, and all suffer from extensive overstaffing while, ironically, all plants simultaneously face a shortage of skilled workers in many areas.[13]

POLITICS AND TECHNOLOGY TRANSFER

These findings specify clearly the poor quality of the decisions that were made in the course of the transfers. What remains unclear is why the technology transfer process operated in the manner that it did and why it has proven so difficult to bring the operation of the plants up to acceptable standards. To answer such questions it is necessary to consider the ways in which the variables that I incorporated in my analytical scheme, particularly the nature of sending and receiving organizations and the role of policies, development strategies and political systems, affected the decision process.

The sending organization

The role and responsibilities of external actors deserves to be emphasized. They should be held accountable for the outcomes for they sponsored each of these projects and foreign experts carried out practically all the studies that were made, studies which validated the decision to build inadequate plants. The possibility of postponing a project until the domestic market grew in size was never taken into account. Nor were export sales ever considered seriously even though one could then justify a large, economical plant. That so little attention was paid to exports is largely attributable to Turkey's traditional emphasis upon an import substitution strategy that was inward oriented. Even so, the other actors did not have to accept such parameters; they could have refused to support the project at that time and offered to fund another. They did not do so because their own interests and objectives (political in the case of governments, economic in the case of corporations) would not be served by challenging the Turkish government's perceptions of its needs. In other words, the project design process (when external financing is involved) is driven by political considerations and its outcome depends upon the kinds of factors that students of international affairs have been concerned with for decades.

The history of ERDEMIR illustrates these points well. Prime Minister Menderes wanted a second iron and steel mill, accorded a high priority to it and then tried to sell the concept to the USA so that he could obtain the resources to implement it. Before long US policy-makers, for ideological and foreign policy reasons, became so enamored of the concept that they wished to see the plant built almost as much as Menderes did. As a result, the USA committed itself to support a mill that was almost totally debt financed and made the large loan, neglecting to obtain any guarantees from the Turkish government. Thus, the decision was essentially a political one; the analyses were expected to specify the technical aspects of the plant. Though more rigorous studies might have revealed that the low capitalization did not make the project a financially viable one and led to changes that might have saved AID from the necessity of waging a difficult struggle to save ERDEMIR from bankruptcy, the studies served to legitimize a project that the American and Turkish governments wished to implement.

The World Bank made its decisions just like the other decision-makers – on the basis of political criteria. Essentially ERDEMIR had arrived at a stage where its expansion could be justified only by ignoring the sunk costs. Thus the key decision was the one to consider only the incremental costs and benefits, a decision that was determined by President McNamara's policy goals towards Turkey. Once again the innumerable analyses of the project's desirability and feasibility validated a predetermined decision. And it behaved, like the other decision-makers, in another way – it focused upon the specific project rather than on any systematic comparison of potentially more desirable alternatives, even though it criticized the Turkish government for failing to do just that. It noted in its analysis of the Third Five Year Plan, for example, that '. . . the Plan does not contain a careful appraisal of projects to be included nor a consideration of alternative project specifications.'[14] Nor did the studies, so carefully prepared by its own experts and those of UEC, prove to be of any greater utility than those prepared by other actors for they too were replete with assumptions which were included to permit certain conclusions to be drawn or which were often rendered obsolete because of unanticipated economic and other developments.

The senders shared another common trait – they all failed to recognize that the future of Turkey's iron and steel industry depended on the degree to which the receiving organizations achieved control of the technologies that were transferred. Basically, all sought to ensure that the Turkish enterprises would learn how to operate, and perhaps maintain, the machinery effectively. As a result, they paid relatively little attention to the management dimension. Such areas as training and administration were relegated to a secondary level, despite their importance. Such neglect is difficult to understand but may be due to the belief systems of the decision-makers in each organization. Most of those who actually defined the projects and worked out their details were technical experts who believed that technologies are easily transferable, that an iron and steel plant in Turkey was the same as an iron and steel plant in the USA. Few recognized the role that the environment plays in shaping project implementation and operation or had any knowledge of the Turkish environment. As a result the focus was always upon the project itself, usually its design aspects, not with the issues that would determine, over the long term, the contribution that the project might make to national development. There was no recognition that project success must be defined in broader terms than merely learning how to operate and maintain machinery, that a much wider range of skills, including administrative, planning and research and development, were required. Because of this failure, the sending organizations failed to develop and implement strategies that would facilitate the ability of the receiving organization to absorb and master the technologies.

That the performance of the sending organizations can and should be criticized is not to suggest that the dependency theorists are correct. The state consistently played an active, independent role. The impetus, in each case, came from Turkish governments seeking to achieve national objectives. There is no evidence that the functioning of the international economic order or the interests of international capital were responsible for the policies that Ankara followed. Each project clearly originated within the domestic political system. Indeed, this situation differs from the norm in a significant way: not one of the projects was identified by an external agency eager to provide some sort of economic assistance to the country. Each accepted the Turkish state's definition of its interests, a definition shared by all its elites. They were all committed to the strategy of industrialization by import substitution and, believing that steel production was inherently good, that it would promote Turkey's national independence, tended to overlook the costs involved. And the other actors, for their own reasons, were willing to go along.

Nor does the evidence support the argument that foreign aid is inherently damaging or designed to exploit the recipient. Although foreign aid, on some occasions, has been used to obtain explicit political leverage, this was not the case here. Certainly each donor was motivated by self-interest and supported projects whose soundness can and has been questioned. But each also sought to build a successful project, though within the parameters that were established. The USA was extremely worried about ERDEMIR's impact upon the Turkish economy, upon ensuring that the consortium responsible for building the plant carry out its commitments honestly and fairly, and that the plant be profitable.[15] The World Bank also did its best to ensure that the expansions would promote the plant's well-being. And, though each project encountered serious difficulties, the donors strove to remedy defects that arose. After all, if donors provide aid as rewards or in order to influence the behavior of the recipient, a seriously flawed project is unlikely to further that objective.

The receiving organization

If new technologies are to be absorbed and mastered, qualified and skilled manpower at all levels is required but, as I have noted, minimal attention was devoted to training and retaining able personnel. This shortcoming was due partly to the policies of the sending organizations but even more to the managerial weaknesses that marked the receivers, weaknesses that severely constrained their capability at every stage of the project cycle. Sound management is essential while projects are being designed, while they are being implemented and when the project is operating, but good managerial techniques were evident primarily only when foreign experts were constructing the plants.

Able management depends on several factors. First, the individuals must possess an appropriate background in terms of experience, training and professionalism. Second, they must possess a set of values and attitudes that will lead them to behave in ways that will advance the economic well being of the organization. Unfortunately, only a few managers possessed the background and the values; many were deficient in one or the other. Thus they were unable to perform the necessary managerial tasks effectively and problems continually arose in regards to goal setting, motivation, communications, evaluations and providing leadership.

Even when qualified and dedicated persons were in key positions, however, the culture and structure that prevailed within the plants limited their effectiveness. Moreover, they were functioning in an administrative environment which further constrained their potential in two ways. The first is centralization. Since all decisions are made at the top of any hierarchy, they had to deal with high officials in Ankara, and local administrators who were sensitive to and aware of the problems and opportunities, were seldom able to persuade Ankara to adopt policies to deal with Ereğli's growth or to help it become a growth pole.[16] What planning did occur was removed from local conditions with little, if any, attempt to use local resources.

Second, one cannot ignore the question of administrative coordination, a perennial weak spot. Public enterprises and government agencies are not completely controlled by the state; they possess some ability to pursue their own agendas if public policy does not fit their interests. The attempt to control direct foreign investment illustrates this point well. Despite repeated efforts by several governments which all accorded the issue a high priority, no single organization was ever established to monitor the flow of direct foreign investments into Turkey. On the contrary, at least four entities exercised conflicting jurisdictions and no cooperation or coordination ever occurred.[17] Such an environment does not facilitate any technology transfer for it inevitably needs support from different agencies and organizations. A plant's infrastructure, for example, is dependent upon the cooperation of several agencies but this seldom occurred. The priorities and concerns of the railroad authority were different from those of the Ministry of Industry which in turn differed from those of the highway department. And even when agencies were supportive, arranging their activities so as to ensure that all the elements of a technological system be put in place in the right way and at the right time proved to be no simple matter. Inadequate coordination has also stifled the operation of the plants in many ways. Their effective functioning requires a constant, reliable supply of inputs but the railroad and other agencies paid little attention to the impact of decisions concerning price, allocations and schedules upon the plants. Such behavior is commonplace and has led one analyst to conclude that even if sound policies for technological transfer could be devised, they would be of little consequence because the bureaucracy lacks the means and flexibility to implement them effectively.[18]

The policy context

Sound policies, however, were seldom devised and the administrative and organizational problems which hindered the ability of the receiving organizations to operate effectively were aggravated by the nature of the policies that were implemented. The case of iron and steel was, unfortunately, quite typical for a recent study identified numerous examples of negative impacts by direct and indirect policies upon technology transfer projects.[19] In one case the government created a new firm, at great expense, that competed with another state enterprise that had already mastered the technology. In another, a company developed a particular technology but could not begin production because it would not be competitive with imports of that item that are allowed in duty-free in order to enhance the competitiveness of Turkish industry. Not surprisingly, the author found the substance of policy and its implementation to be the most serious obstacle to successful technology transfer.[20]

Likewise, the iron and steel industry was never the subject of explicit, coherent policy-making that would promote its development. The policy process was *ad hoc* and incremental; policy was seldom the result of careful planning. One must, of course, view the situation in comparative and historical perspective. Until the sixties planning efforts in practically every country were limited and seldom rigorous. National goals were seldom articulated in operational terms and the process of project selection and appraisal was not systematic. This was the environment in which ERDEMIR was conceived. Turkish development goals had not been specified and no development plans existed. It emerged because of the widely held feeling by many Turkish leaders that an iron and steel sector was a *sine qua non* for development. The introduction of systematic national planning after 1960 did not alter this situation greatly. ERDEMIR's expansion and ISDEMIR's construction were consonant with particular needs that were identified by planners but, even then, basic impetus came from elite perceptions of what national development entailed. And, once the decisions were made, limited attention was paid to developing the kinds of policies that would promote the establishment of a sound iron and steel sector.

The policies that were adopted failed to promote the well-being of the industry in several ways. To begin with, there was a limited concern with mastery. Because successive Turkish governments all erroneously defined the problem as how to acquire the capability to produce steel rather than as the development of an indigenous technological capability, their focus tended to be on measures designed to control and regulate. While it is quite understandable that policy-makers should not be sensitive to the importance of mastering the technologies when the first plant was built, by the sixties and seventies more learning should have taken place and they should have come to realize the significance of this capability and provide a supportive environment. This was simply not the case, particularly in the 1950–1980 period when government policies did not facilitate the acquisition of mastery and often impacted negatively upon the receiving organizations. No government ever implemented policies that would have led to the formation of a cadre of experienced iron and steel experts who could advise it, who could serve as the nucleus for achieving and diffusing technological knowledge. Karabük possessed the potential; its engineers had worked on many projects, its foremen were skilled and technologically sophisticated. Yet no attempt was made to preserve and enhance this valuable resource. As a result little learning took place; the same mistakes were repeated over and over.

Equally little attention was paid to research and development, essential activities if the iron and steel industry were to prosper. The country's research and development efforts remained quite limited and not proportionate to the country's needs, particularly since it relied heavily on the transfer of technology from abroad.[21] Turkish experts and planners recognized the damaging consequences of such neglect and called for the implementation of a coherent and integrated policy for many years, to little avail. This was certainly the situation as regards iron and steel. The first development plan in 1961 had emphasized the need for more and better research and development activities but this and subsequent attempts yielded meager results, despite the acknowledged need.[22] The most promising effort took place in the early seventies when a team at the Marmara Research Institute undertook a detailed and comprehensive analysis of the industry's condition in order to specify and prioritize the projects that should be carried out.[23] Unfortunately this work, which was discussed in Chapter 6, was never implemented or followed up, at least in part because of the intrusion of political considerations. Following a change in governments, a new director was appointed to head the Institute. Unfortunately he did not accord the same priority to the project as his predecessor and the team soon disintegrated.

The way in which iron and steel prices were set illustrates how the impact of poor policies was aggravated by the administrative problems discussed above.[24] Prices were adjusted yearly between 1973 and 1979 and semi-annually in 1979 and 1980, always upwards (for obvious financial reasons), even though world prices remained stable. Yet, this policy was implemented without any consideration of how it related to other policy areas. As a result there was no coordination with import policy even though the connection between the demand for, and the price of, domestic iron and steel was obviously affected by the availability of imports. Yet iron and steel imports were not always controlled by either customs regulations or tariffs so that even though it was known by mid 1974 that a domestic surplus was imminent, low cost imports were permitted and flooded the country, with damaging results. Two price levels existed in the market, speculative transactions were rampant, Karabük and ISDE-MIR were forced to cut production to levels significantly lower than originally planned, and TDÇI found itself saddled with large unsold stocks.[25]

In sum, it is obvious that the Turkish iron and steel industry was never the subject of the kinds of policies that would have permitted it to achieve mastery and to operate productively. The fundamental reason why this was the case is to be found in the nature of the development strategy and the political system which produced and applied it.

The development strategy

The policies that were implemented were shaped by the consensus that had emerged within the social core group concerning the development strategy that should be followed. Ataturk and all his successors sought to achieve and maintain national independence and economic self-sufficiency through an inward-looking strategy of industrialization in which the state would play a leading role. They were influenced by several factors including the distressing Ottoman experience with international capital, the example of the Soviet Union, the absence for some time of an entrepreneurial class, a fear of foreign investment (reinforced in the sixties by ideology), a concern with national security, and a belief that the country's natural resources could provide the basis for the development of basic industry. Nor should one overlook the conception of the state which the elites of the new Republic had inherited, a view of the state as transcendental.[26] One might expect that that this perspective, which legitimized governmental intervention at all levels of the economy, would be challenged by the private sector, but this proved not to be the case for it accepted, in return for significant economic benefits, policies that limited the market's role in resource allocation.[27] As a result the strategy remained sacrosanct, even when external actors expressed concern about its appropriateness in the forties and again in the seventies, and every government sought to expand the country's iron and steel capacity in any way possible. The rationale was always the same – to save foreign exchange; the real costs to the economy were never considered. Hence, the national profitability of each project was not calculated in any detail and no one made any attempt to consider alternative projects or to assess the opportunity and other costs. This narrow and short-sighted view of the problem that they wished to solve led policy-makers to focus always on the specific project, to disregard second- and third-order consequences and to ignore fundamental requirements for the successful development of the sector.

Two fundamental factors may be posited to explain why all Turkish leaders were so eager to develop the country's iron and steel industry. First, one cannot overlook the role of the military. Since the days of Ataturk, national security was an overriding goal and the needs of the military were always accorded a high priority. I have emphasized how the military were powerful advocates for a domestic iron and steel capacity since the early days of the Republic. And, even in the seventies ERDEMIR's expansion was changed to meet the navy's needs. Second, and more importantly, the military's views were shared by all the other state elites; they too defined national security and national well-being in terms of heavy industrialization. That view being widely held and extremely powerful remained unchanged over time both in terms of strategy and implementation.

What controversy there was centered on one point – the role of the private sector. ERDEMIR, which was deliberately designed to promote private enterprise, became a natural target of attacks by the left which regarded it as a channel for capitalist exploitation of the state. Its opponents did not, however, question the basic strategy; they merely wished the sector to be completely controlled by the state.

The role of the political system

This ideological consensus rendered the fundamental strategy impervious to short-term political fluctuations.[28] Every regime accorded an iron and steel project an important place on the political agenda and, once it had gained that position, it remained there, regardless of the particular government in power, since each was composed of people who shared the same view of how development could best be achieved. That iron and steel production would promote the national well-being was taken for granted.

This faith in heavy industrialization was accompanied by an equally strong dedication to what Hirschman called the 'hiding hand'. Turkish leaders all seemed to believe that it was desirable to launch a project under almost any circumstances. Projects, especially iron and steel ones, were the symbols of development, concrete evidence that Turkey was becoming a modern state. That poor projects were a burden on the state, that they might impede the nation's progress, was never adequately accepted. On the contrary, the consensus believed that any project was better than no project because, if it turned out to be defective, it could always be improved. One could always enlarge a small plant, eliminate imbalances, increase efficiency and improve quality. And, since production was oriented towards the domestic market, efficiency and quality were rarely accorded serious consideration. After all, as many have asked, 'How much quality does a country like Turkey need?' What was never recognized were the extremely high direct and indirect costs of the policies that such a mindset led to.

Turkish elites shared another set of perceptions. They all believed that technology transfer is a simple process. They did not understand the nature of technology, of technology transfer, of the need to master technology. Few power holders recognized that technology is a system, that it possesses organizational and cultural characteristics which must be anticipated and planned for. Not only can the entire technological system never be transferred but the new systems with which it interacts will also differ. More specifically, if a transfer is to yield desirable outcomes, it must be supported by an appropriate infrastructure and linkages to other organizations, but the infrastructure and the organizations in the new setting will inevitably differ from that which existed in the sending society. This too must be anticipated and planned for; a set of policies that will create the conditions for embedding the technology in the society in a truly productive manner is required. What seems to have been dimly perceived is that the creation of successful industry requires more than purchasing and learning to operate and maintain machinery, that complex systems are involved. Hence, the kinds of policies that would enhance the quality of the outcome were never considered, transportation and other subsystems were neglected, and no attention was paid to developing the skill levels and research and development activities that would lead to the creation of a dynamic sector. In time persons who understood technology did emerge within the State Planning Organization and other organizations but their role became significant only in the late seventies and especially after the 1980 revolution, with consequences that I will discuss below.

This general consensus established a framework within which other political variables, notably the specific character of the regime, did not influence policy except in one area – the concern with short-term political advantage. During the Ataturk era such considerations played a minor role; decisions were guided by analytic considerations, though limited technological knowledge led to disappointing results. During the pluralist system, on the other hand, questions of electoral advantage often influenced many aspects of the decisions that were made, most obviously in regards to staffing. This was true both during the 1950–60 period when Prime Minister Menderes dominated the polity and in the late seventies when weak coalition governments were the norm. When the military took over in 1980, the pattern of analytical decisions was reintroduced. These variations suggest that when a regime is characterized by weak governments, short-term political considerations affect all decisions but the existence of strong governments, whether military or civilian, does not necessarily lead to analytical outcomes. In these cases, individual belief systems come to the fore.

THE NATURE OF TECHNOLOGICAL DECISION-MAKING

These findings provide for a greater appreciation of the complexities of the decision-makimg process and of the utility of various models. From the perspective of decision-making theory, it is obvious that none of the dimensions, with the possible exception of the technological choices, were subject to rational analysis by any of the actors. Even then, the analysis occurred within parameters that were imposed as a result of non-rational decision processes.

Nor did all these efforts produce positive side effects, economic and intellectual, for other sectors or for the planning and decision process. Evaluation of outcomes was never undertaken systematically so that the same errors were, as I have noted, repeated within the sector. Why so little learning took place can be explained by the elite consensus discussed above and the conditions under which Turkish decision-makers strove to modernize, particularly the chronic resources constraints under which they had to operate. Accordingly, driven by an ongoing commitment to a strategy of heavy industrialization, they always 'satisficed' within a short-term perspective. Every government consistently acted incrementally and, since resources were always scarce, limited financial outlays as much as possible, even when outside actors such as AID applied pressure for additional investments that were considered important to a project's well-being. And decision-makers never took more than a short time-frame into account. In none of the projects did decision-makers, whether Turkish, American, British, Soviet or World Bank, consider any alternatives or pay any attention to trade-offs. They consistently operated under conditions of bounded rationality in which they made no effort to maximize their choices. Each of the actors consistently engaged in satisficing behavior. They usually sought to find a desirable rather than an optimal solution.

The power of cognitive elements is very apparent. The values and beliefs of the Turkish policy-makers overruled any consideration of optimality; any iron and steel plant was better than none. Ankara's desire for iron and steel dictated the type of project that would be selected. And once that decision had been made, as one moved along the phases of the project cycle, belief systems continued to influence choice. Moreover, the ways in which all the actors perceived technology and the transfer process further limited the results that could be achieved. All regarded technology as a given that could be transferred easily. An engineering mentality dominated each of the projects so that too little attention was paid to management in general and never to ways in which technological mastery could be achieved in particular. The focus was primarily upon the design, upon the pieces of equipment to be installed, upon building an operating plant. No one was particularly interested in impact issues, not even the economic costs and benefits, apart from, in some cases, concern about the extent to which loans would be repaid.

As a result Turkey's development was not promoted as effectively as it might have been. Though the 'hiding hand' did come to the rescue, it did so only to a limited extent, and at great expense. As I have emphasized, the original weaknesses were expensive and difficult to remedy and the attempts to do so usually created numerous other problems.

In this context, the thoroughness and quality of the myriad studies and analyses were ultimately irrelevant because the Turkish government badly wanted the particular projects for which the studies were being prepared and the sending organizations were willing to support them. In other words, the studies were mere formalities to be dealt with as expeditiously as possible; they were usually designed to please the external donor whose organizational norms required the studies to legitimize its decisions and whose financing was indispensable to the realization of the project. Project approval was not dependent upon the quality of studies but upon the outcome of bargaining between Ankara and the external donors, bargaining which was both cooperative and conflictual as each side sought to advance its own interests. Thus we are dealing with a situation where complex interactions among actors determine the fate of projects and the degree of mastery that will be achieved.

Political variables play a greater or lesser role depending upon the nature of the regime but the technology transfer process cannot be divorced from politics. The very act of defining problems and selecting projects is a political exercise. Obtaining external support for a project is also a political event, as is the decision by a donor to provide financing since by so doing he indicates his support for the particular regime. And, since several actors are always involved, each with their own objectives and resources, bargaining, not 'rationality', determines, to a considerable degree, all aspects of a project including its design.

The case of ERDEMIR illustrates both how the decision process worked and its consequences. Like the others, this project originated in the Turkish political elite's perceptions of how development could be achieved. But, since external funding was an essential prerequisite, donors soon became heavily involved. And, since each sought to achieve its own goals, disagreements quickly arose and the projects changed, sometimes dramatically (ERDEMIR's very organizational structure was imposed by the USA), as they passed through the project cycle. Even after the design had been settled, political considerations caused changes, as occurred when ERDEMIR insisted on substituting a sinter plant for a billet caster even though exhaustive studies had demonstrated the importance of the latter piece of equipment for the plant's profitability. Furthermore, once a project has been completed, its operation is also influenced to a large degree by political factors. It is for this reason that a manager needs political as well as technical skills; he has to obtain inputs ranging from raw materials to technical knowledge from organizations, domestic and foreign, over which he has little, if any, control and must therefore engage in bargaining and coalition building.

Hence the distinction between 'political' and 'technological' that has often been made cannot be maintained. The two are closely connected. It is unrealistic to expect that once a 'political' decision has been taken to initiate a project, technical experts can take over and determine outcomes in an 'objective' manner. The political context shapes the project from its inception and continues to do so even after it becomes operational, though the manner in which, and the degree to which, it does so depends upon the nature of the particular political system involved.

THE EMERGENCE OF A NEW PERSPECTIVE

Strategies and policies are not immutable; they can and do change as conditions and leaders change. This happened in Turkey and the nature and content of the policies that have been implemented in the past few years with regard to economic development in general and to iron and steel in particular are very different from those that existed before.

That it had taken so long for Turkey's policy-makers to make a change that had been made much earlier by many other countries, urged upon them by many Turkish and Western economists and by the World Bank and the IMF, was due to several factors, historical, psychological, political and empirical. It is no easy matter to abandon a strategy based on a widely shared belief system, especially one that grows out of historical experience and necessity, has been utilized for decades and produces acceptable results. Aided by foreign loans, a rapidly growing domestic market stimulated by a high rate of population increase and urbanization and remittances from abroad, Turkey did achieve middle income country status.[29]

In the late seventies, changing conditions in the international economy created a new reality. The sharp rise in oil prices confronted Turkey with the most severe crisis in its economic history. It had to finance a much larger import bill for which its major foreign exchange sources (workers' remittances and foreign loans), which had cushioned the first oil shock, no longer sufficed because Western Europe had entered a recessionary period and many migrants were unemployed. Now the Turkish economy's structural weaknesses came to the fore; inflation began to mount and the overvaluation of the currency led to a major shortage of foreign exchange.[30]

At first, Mr Ecevit, who had successfully formed a new government in 1978, turned to familiar instruments; he adopted a stabilization program designed to improve the balance of trade and halt the spiralling inflation. When the crisis continued he adopted somewhat more stringent measures (March 1979) but even these proved ineffective; though an agreement was reached with the IMF in July 1979, inflation continued to accelerate, the foreign exchange situation remained precarious, and imports had to be curtailed more drastically.[31]

The fall of the Ecevit government and its replacement by one headed by Suleyman Demirel, in late 1979, marked a turning point in Turkey's history for the new government jettisoned the strategy that had guided Turkey's development for so many years. Mr Demirel accepted a radical proposal that had been formulated by Mr Turgut Özal and announced a sweeping and far reaching reform program on 25 January 1980. Designed to alter fundamentally the country's economic structure by emphasizing market forces and moving away from planning and regulatory decrees, its goals were to promote exports and employment by enhancing international competitiveness, placing greater reliance on domestic savings and taxation in financing development, revitalizing the State Economic Enterprises, and improving the process of project planning and implementation. Specific measures include the elimination of all the administrative arrangements that had facilitated import substitution, the implementation of new procedures to facilitate exports, a sharp devaluation of the currency, and passage of a new foreign investment law.[32] Subsequently, other measures including tax reform, daily exchange rate adjustments, and the removal of interest rate ceilings were enacted.[33]

The theoretical significance of Prime Minister Demirel's decision deserves to be noted. On the basis of his past record one would not have expected such a decision because he had, after all, enthusiastically pursued inward-looking policies while in office from 1965 to 1971 and again in the seventies. It provides further evidence that political leaders can and do act in ways that cannot be anticipated on the basis of their belief systems and past behavior. Regardless of the attitudes and values of decision-makers, reality can and often does intrude. Whatever Prime Minister Demirel's wishes, the failure of his predecessor to deal with the crisis using traditional means created a situation that demanded a new strategy. A different leader might have chosen a different policy but the new environment created a situation where fundamental change was inevitable.

The impact of the new strategy was, at first, limited by the unstable domestic political scene. The economic crisis occurred at a time when the political system was being strained to the breaking point. Violence came to replace political discourse, and by the end of the decade assassinations and riots had become commonplace. Finally, in March 1980, the military intervened once again, this time with the intention of completely restructuring the political system so as to ensure political stability. It remained in power for three years, during which time it sponsored a new constitution and electoral system, moved harshly against all those whom it held responsible for the anarchy that had existed and implemented the liberalization policy cautiously. In 1983 elections were held and Mr Turgut Özal, the architect of the economic reforms, led his new party, the Motherland Party, to victory. Since then the liberalization program has been speeded up.[34]

These political developments impacted directly upon the economy. Within a short time Turkey's production structure changed dramatically – the share of agriculture in the GDP fell from 25.3 per cent in 1978 to 21.9 per cent in 1981 while that of manufacturing rose from 19.5 per cent to 21.8 per cent, the average level of manufacturing for middle income countries.[35] Economic conditions continued to improve. The GNP's growth rate climbed from 3.3 per cent in 1983 to 5.9 per cent in 1984, 5.1 per cent in 1985, and reached 7.9 per cent in 1986, when the industrial sector grew by 10.3 per cent. Exports which totalled TL 5.7 billion in 1983 climbed to TL 8.0 billion in 1986.[36] Whether such rates can be maintained and the degree to which further policy reforms are necessary and the costs of the new export-oriented strategy have been a matter of some debate.[37] I shall comment on issues of strategy below.

There is little doubt that the iron and steel sector benefitted greatly from these developments. The State Planning Organization, which is no longer politicized and enjoys more power than it has for many years, prepared a master plan which was accepted by the government of Prime Minister Özal. It takes, for the first time in the country's history, a systemic view of the sector's condition and needs. It emphasizes qualitative change, not quantitative growth, and it recognizes that technologies have to be mastered, that the effective utilization of any technology requires knowledge and understanding on the part of managers, skilled workers and even ordinary workers. The focus is upon training, upon making investments to eliminate bottlenecks, upon raising the quality of the product, increasing productivity, and providing good quality inputs in sufficient quantity. Improvements in the functioning of the existing plants is given priority. Only when they are operating satisfactorily is any attention to be paid to further expansion. Accordingly the plan called for postponing the SIDEMIR project, the continuing modernization of Karabük (with World Bank support), rounding off ERDEMIR's capacity at 2.2 million tons, and expanding ISDEMIR to 2 million tons. Further expansion will depend on how well the plants produce at that level and what the demand projections for their products will be.

The recommendation to postpone the SIDEMIR plant was not accepted easily. The SPO argued strongly against the project in the High Planning Council and, with the support of the Minister of Industry, persuaded the policy-makers to make a landmark decision. For the first time in Turkey's history a government opted against quantitative growth in the iron and steel sector!

The other parts of the master plan are being implemented steadily. The SPO has instituted training programs at all three plants, made investments to modernize planning, scheduling and control systems (especially at ISDEMIR), attempted to upgrade the quality of management by placing qualified persons in key positions and creating an environment in which they can function effectively, and moved to reduce the number of excess workers. The size of the labor force dropped from 35,000 to 32,000 between 1982 and 1986 and is expected to decline even more though, because of the high unemployment rate, the workforce is being reduced by attrition only.

These measures have yielded remarkable results. Capacity utilization has soared at ISDEMIR and production there has risen from 300,000 tons in 1980 to 1.6 million tons in 1985. Output at the three integrated plants totalled 4.8 million tons in 1985 and, if private sector production is included, Turkey expects to produce 7.5 million tons in 1987, making it the twentieth largest steel producer in the world.[38] Moreover, productivity has increased sharply, by 240 per cent since 1980.

The implications for Turkish development are, of course, very significant. For the first time in its history, Turkey's net steel trade balance is positive. Though it still imports various types of steels, Turkey is also now an exporting country, selling steel to Iran, Iraq, Algeria, Syria and even the USA, and, unlike the situation in earlier years when its steel exports were heavily subsidized, it is now obtaining a good price and earning enough to more than offset the cost of imports.[39] One reason for the increase in exports is the improvement in quality that has occurred. ERDEMIR used to produce flat sheets for automobiles, freezers and refrigerators that were so uneven that they were visibly thicker at one end than the other. Now, the situation is very different and the quality of the flat sheets produced at ERDEMIR is very good. Similar improvements in product quality are evident in the output of the other plants as well.

Such changes are the result of increased knowledge, of an increased level of technological mastery in the iron and steel industry. Turkish workers and managers are acquiring the basic knowledge for producing good quality basic steel products. The country can now meet almost all of its basic steel requirements locally and can even produce systems such as rolling mills for export. Moreover, because of the quality of management which characterizes the industry, Turkey has been able to take advantage of the low cost of billets in the world. It imported them, rolled them and exported them, thus capturing the value added for itself.

Clearly, a remarkable change has occurred – 1986 was the best year in the history of Turkish iron and steel. Can this situation continue? Has Turkey finally reached the point where decision-making is guided by an understanding of the nature of technology and the requirements for technological mastery? Although there are many hopeful signs, one must be careful not to overestimate the degree of change that has occurred, nor underestimate the possibility of a return to previous patterns. Much of the sector's improved performance is related to the situation in ISDEMIR where production was so low that merely bringing the level of its operation up to that of the other integrated iron and steel works was bound to produce a dramatic change in the sector's condition. Yet, as I have noted, a qualitative change is also observable because the level of technological capability has risen significantly. What remains to be seen, however, is whether the progress that has been achieved to date can be maintained and enhanced.

Several factors will determine the industry's future, some of which are beyond Turkey's control. The first of these involves the pattern of technological innovation within the industry. Technological change is occurring at a rapid rate thus confronting Turkey with a difficult situation: it has to struggle to close a gap that is increasing constantly. A new process in use in Europe, for example, coats a steel sheet on both sides in one day; in Turkey a week is required. To upgrade existing facilities in this area alone would require the allocation of $800 million. Yet if Turkey does not make such investments, it will find itself saddled with an obsolescent industry that cannot even serve its own domestic market for, as its economy develops, so the nature of the internal demand is shifting away from basic steel products to speciality steels. If consumers cannot obtain these inputs from local plants, they will be forced to turn to foreign suppliers. Here too the same issues arise: heavy investments and systematic policies are required to obtain and master the new technologies.

External developments will affect the industry in another way. Its future is inexorably linked to the outcome of the new development strategy, but Turkey's ability to export depends partly on its efforts, partly on conditions beyond its control. For exports to thrive, positive economic conditions in Western Europe and the Middle East (Turkey's primary markets) are essential but these are by no means assured. How the end of the Iran-Iraq war will affect Turkey's foreign trade, for example is unclear. Moreover, the forthcoming abolition of barriers within the EEC and the outcome of Turkey's application for membership in the Community will also play a significant role in shaping the country's future course. If it cannot, for whatever reason, continue to expand its exports, the possibility of a return to a protectionist stance cannot be ruled out.

Even if the external environment remains favorable, the Turkish iron and steel industry still faces serious obstacles. It will be no easy matter to achieve the level of technological mastery that is required if it is to become internationally competitive. At present costs of production remain higher than in Europe, running about $300 a ton in Turkey as compared to $250 a ton there. If this gap cannot be narrowed significantly, the sector will confront obvious problems, especially if Turkey's efforts to enter the Common Market prove successful since Europe's giant steel-makers have large amounts of unused capacity.[40]

One hopeful indicator that significant changes will be forthcoming is the recent statement by the General Director of TDÇI, Mr Ali Aktay, that iron and steel would be opened to foreign competition.[41] How the industry would fare without protection is unclear,[42] but such a decision would inevitably force it to concentrate on improvements in productivity and quality. Other measures, however, are required. It is necessary to engage in strategic planning and develop a set of policies that will, over a given time-frame, deal with the entire range of problems associated with the industry and to coordinate policy-making to ensure that all its problems are addressed. The goal would be to achieve an indigenous technological capability in the industry and to maintain it through an active program of research and development and active monitoring of technological developments abroad. Such a strategy cannot be implemented in an environment wherein short-term political considerations dictate policy, without regard to the consequences for technological mastery and for the well-being of the industry. I shall discuss the elements of such a strategy in more detail below.

The sector's performance will ultimately be determined by the way in which it is managed. Many of its deficiencies in this area are common to all State Economic Enterprises whose weak performance has been criticized for years. Their shortcomings, many of which I have already discussed in the context of the iron and steel industry, have recently been summarized as: (1) lack of profits and unsound structure of their capital; (2) delays in the implementation of projects and increasing costs of their investments; (3) inadequate coordination; (4) inefficient economic guidance and control, and (5) inflexible personnel systems.[43] Numerous reform measures have been proposed to transform them into financially viable and productive organizations, but only in 1983 and 1984 were significant actions taken.[44]

Although these are promising developments and the decision to postpone SIDEMIR and the other steps that have been taken do suggest that careful analyses are now being made and that economic criteria are playing a new role in decision-making, it is important to understand how and why that decision was taken. Two factors, one economic, the other political, played an important role in the decision and it is not clear that, in their absence, the outcome would have been very different. First, Turkey's demand for iron and steel has slowed down and the new demand projections are lower than those that were being made only a short time ago. Secondly, when discussions were being held over the content of the 24 January 1980 decrees, the World Bank and the IMF, whose assistance was desperately needed, objected strongly to a policy of locating industrial projects in underdeveloped regions. Given Turkey's economic condition, the government had to accede.

Whether it will continue to make sound decisions if new conditions emerge cannot be foretold but certain measures that have been adopted recently do raise concerns. The first of these is the decision to build a rolling mill in Sivas. When campaigning there at the time of the 1983 general elections, Prime Minister Turgut Özal promised that the iron and steel plant would be built. Subsequently he realized the costs of carrying through this promise and tried to avoid having to do so. The parliamentarians from Sivas, however, insisted that he keep his word. In an attempt to resolve the dilemma constructively, the State Planning Organization suggested that a pipe mill be constructed there; there is a great need for sewage and water pipe in Turkish cities and, indeed, throughout the Middle East. This solution was not acceptable to the Sivas MPs, perhaps because no strong attempt was made to persuade them of the wisdom of the project, perhaps because of a romantic attachment to iron and steel. Finally, a compromise was reached on a rolling mill. This project takes advantage of the pattern of rail transportation whereby trains which previously returned from Iskenderun empty after having carried the iron ore from the fields near Sivas to ISDEMIR would now come loaded with billets for rolling. Although the solution is a reasonable one, it remains to be seen whether the rolling mill is the only part of the projected iron and steel works that will actually be erected or whether, when domestic demand increases and the aid of the World Bank and the IMF are no longer so sorely needed, it will be followed by other components, until an entire plant has been constructed in Sivas. Some observers fear that, since a relatively strong government, like Mr Özal's, and one committed to a rational policy of export-oriented growth, could not prevent the construction of the rolling mill, future leaders will face even greater pressures.

A second indicator of renewed politicization is provided by the decision, prior to the 1986 interim elections, not to increase the price of steel by $20 to the level being charged by the private sector, even though ISDEMIR may lose money as a result. The possibilities for speculation and profiteering from this situation do not require elaboration.

A third troublesome indicator is the pattern of recent managerial appointments. In the past few years, administrators were selected on ability criteria; at present the tendency to appoint persons on the basis of loyalty to the minister is reappearing. ISDEMIR in particular has been affected by such appointments; a highly qualified General Director recently resigned in disgust as did several other key managers. As a result, the quality of administration is no longer as high as it was a year or two ago. ERDEMIR, because of its special status, remains buffered, at least for the present.

Under these circumstances, one cannot predict the future course of the Turkish iron and steel sector. Until the late seventies and early eighties its future looked bleak indeed. Now there is some reason to anticipate that it can contribute in a truly significant way to the country's development. Yet recent decisions suggest that the difficulties inherent in achieving and maintaining technological mastery may again be compounded by the intrusion of short-term electoral calculations.

CONCLUSIONS

Whether such developments will occur or whether analytic processes will retain their dominance in policy-making towards the industry will be determined by the nature of future political systems and the values and quality of their leadership. This study has amply demonstrated the extent to which technological decision-making is as much a political as a technical process.

In that process the state plays a key role, a finding that is relevant to the ongoing debate between proponents and opponents of the dependency paradigm. The Turkish state was a powerful, indeed dominant, actor in all the transfers. It was never a passive instrument of international capital. The state consistently followed its own agenda as the social core group tried to advance the national interest under more or less difficult circumstances, always seeking support for its policy of heavy industrialization, regardless of the views of external actors. Accomplishments and shortcomings can be attributed to the ideological orientation which drove policy and to the character of particular regimes, more specifically to the political configurations that prevailed at specific times: weak governments tended to politicize projects more than strong ones. Although the case does not fit the traditional dependency paradigm, it also suggests that one cannot, as many developmental theorists have done, assume that the international economic system plays only a minor role. On the contrary, the autonomy of the state is limited in at least two ways. First, the external environment and changes within it greatly influence the opportunities which are available to the state and the constraints under which it operates. For example, Turkey's strategic position, and its alignment with the West in a bi-polar world, enabled it to obtain financing from the USA and the USSR for projects to which it accorded a high priority. Second, any international technology transfer project requires linkages between the government and other actors, internal and external. Their nature and the manner in which the various actors interact largely determine whether a particular project will be implemented, the shape that the project will take, the degree to which it will fail or succeed, and the amount of technological learning that will take place. The significance of the international environment extends even beyond the immediate well-being of a project, for its future is inextricably linked to the state's role in the international system, to its foreign policies and to the policies of other major actors, state and non-state. Thus the external environment and the domestic political system interact to produce a specific technology transfer outcome in ways that do not conform to what might be anticipated on the basis of at least the more simplistic dependency and developmentalist approaches.

These findings are also relevant to the literature dealing with decision-making models. I have emphasized the importance of belief systems, how they sustained a particular strategy for many decades. Nevertheless, it appears to be conceptually misleading to focus only on those variables and to minimize the role of the actual situation with which decision-makers have to deal. The decisions that are reached are influenced by the mental maps of the policy-makers but the reality of a given situation may differ from those maps and become a factor in its own right. Mental maps can become obsolete for decision-makers may not monitor the environment in a sensitive enough manner to pick up the necessary cues that would permit them to adjust their images to changing realities. But even when the signals are quite obvious, established belief systems may be so powerful as to discount or even to ignore them completely. As a result, perceptions tend to diverge from the reality of the environment. This had obviously happened to Turkish leaders as far as the economy was concerned. Sometimes change in the environment occurs abruptly as with the oil shocks of the late seventies. In either case leaders must adjust to the new situation for it has a force of its own; if they fail to do so, their policies will be ineffective, their position endangered, and the stabilty of the regime threatened. One cannot predict, however, what the specific policy will be. Various options are available and many factors affect the choice but one can posit that, in critical circumstances, when all other alternatives appear unlikely to resolve the situation, one course of action will impose itself. Moreover, the extraordinary continuity of policy suggests that decisions are seldom isolated single cases; they are, and must be, analyzed as part of a historical process. It is not possible to understand how and why actors behaved in the manner that they did if one does not pay attention to the stream of previous policies and decisions. Sharp breaks with the past seldom occur: incrementalism tends to be the rule.

The rational actor model does not apply to any of the decision processes. None of the actors reached their decisions in a rational comprehensive manner and none of the choices regarding the various dimensions conforms completely to the model. At best one could say that some of the technical details were approached synoptically. Most of the other aspects were treated incrementally and reactively; limited actions were taken only when negative potentials or adverse consequences were quite obvious. Essentially each actor settled for an acceptable solution which emerged as a result of bargaining. The bureaucratic politics model describes this process well. Despite its apparent lack of utility in the area of international conflict, especially war and peace decisions,[45] the model does fit this case. Each actor's policy preferences were determined by the organizational affiliations. All Turkish government officials behaved in the same way as did the World Bank and the AID representatives. Each also made compromises on those elements to which it accorded the lowest priority in order to achieve its higher goals. The outcome was determined by the skill, power and resources of the various players. Despite the basic technological nature of all the projects each actor, whether in the private or in the public sector, was primarily concerned with such traditional political issues as power, influence and access to resources. Further research designed to test the relevance of the bureaucratic politics model to other international technology transfer cases would be helpful as would studies that examined its applicability to other issue areas.

The tendency to reach decisions in ways that do not conform to the rational model does not mean that it can or should be ignored, or that it does not play a role. Although a synoptic view of decision-making is inferior, descriptively, to the bureaucratic politics model wherein each actor satisfices, it must remain as the ideal towards which to strive, as the goal to be approached as closely as human creativity permits. Despite its unreasonable requirements and other limitations, rationality remains the only criterion that can be used to evaluate decisions and policies; no alternative is available. Moreover, if political leaders fail to seek optimal solutions, the resulting choices will be of poorer quality than would otherwise be the case. Scarce resources will be wasted, national aspirations sacrificed, the expectations of the populace frustrated. Still, even in the best of circumstances, even in a political system with technocratic values, rationality can never be more than an ideal because of the nature of the policy process.

At the project level, rationality is an essential goal even though the methodologies are clearly fallible. Further improvements in statistical and analytical techniques can be anticipated which will make greater precision possible and enhance the quality of decision-making.[46] Such advances, however, can improve the situation only if they are applied appropriately. If the existing methodologies were utilized comprehensively and widely, the rate of project success would also improve but, as we have seen, many human factors prevent this from happening. At the most elementary level one has to confront the problems of poorly trained personnel. This can, and is being, increasingly taken care of through better educational programs which emphasize both the technical aspects as well as a broad understanding of the technology transfer process. The development and utilization of such expertise will reduce planning errors and unanticipated events but, even if well trained professionals apply the best methodologies rigorously, the unexpected may still occur. No decision-maker can ever have complete information; decisions can be made only on the basis of known risks, but surprises are inevitable. Still, if one prepares for such eventualities, difficulties can be minimized and costs reduced. Two steps may be helpful in this regard. First, financial reserves should be set aside as 'insurance' to deal with unexpected costs. Second, all planning should be carried out with the expectation that unpleasant surprises will happen; all the assumptions that underlie the studies should be conservative ones.

Rationality can be systematically approached, however, only if the analysts function as true professionals, if they are willing to produce results that may not please decision-makers and if the policy-makers are committed to the use of analytical approaches. Unfortunately, as we have seen, these two conditions are seldom present; the projects that decision-makers wish to sponsor are often justified, others rejected. Thus we return to the centrality of political variables. For the fundamental reason that so many technology transfer projects yield sub-optimal results does not lie with the qualifications of the analysts or planners or with the methodologies that they use but in the political context in which they work.

Only some political systems are willing to accept the discipline of analytical processes when making technological decisions. Many leaders still do not understand the heavy costs that are incurred if one does not strive to optimize the process of technology transfer, the fundamental issues that are inherent in planning and implementing successful projects, the need to develop an indigenous technological capability, or possess the skill, will and resources to implement an appropriate strategy effectively. More than wise and able leadership is required, however, for leaders make the choices they do because they operate in particular situations. I suggested in Chapter 1 that regimes could be characterized on the basis of two variables, whether the social core group is integrated or divided and whether the state was pluralistic or authoritarian. These variables do influence the policies that are implemented and their outcomes but this study suggests that it is necessary to recognize explicitly the centrality of the state and its relationship to society. States do follow autonomous strategies that cannot be explained on the basis of either domestic pressures or external constraints, particularly if the state possesses a certain level of capacity, its social core group is integrated and supportive of the strategy, and the leadership possesses the ability to mobilize resources and to engage the key elements in the relevant arena. With such a conceptualization it appears possible to explain why both democratic and non-democratic states (India and South Korea, for example) have successfully achieved high levels of technological mastery in various sectors and why Turkey has so far achieved only limited success.

Even if an appropriate political context does exist, it is no simple matter to achieve technological mastery. The state has to play a guiding role; it must stimulate technological advancement in carefully selected sectors in order to achieve mastery of particular technologies. To do so it must allocate resources, articulate the goals, identify the time-frame, design and implement appropriate policies and establish linkage and integrative mechanisms. It must develop the capability to bargain effectively with external donors and foreign suppliers and be prepared not only to participate actively in all the initial investments needed to acquire the technologies, to build the necessary infrastructure and to establish control over them but also to institute a continuing process of monitoring international technological developments, of evaluation and of technological learning. To design and implement such a strategy is no easy matter, even if the political environment is favorable. Many areas, levels and actors are involved. Some areas are sector specific, others affect the entire economy; some must be carried out by the industry, some by the other private actors, including foreign partners. Thus leadership and able management at several levels is required, at the center, in the sectors, and in the projects. A supportive technological environment in which innovative organizations can function effectively must be developed.

The greater the role of the state, the greater the tendency to centralize administration and to limit participation. Yet effective technological development requires the commitment of individuals in numerous organizations and sectors. Decentralization and opportunities for participation can help promote the kinds of behaviours that are required for technological development. One specific issue (which is relevant for Turkey as well as many other countries) involves the degree to which, and manner in which, parastatals should be controlled for there appears to be a negative relationship between productive operations and centralized political control. Accordingly, many analysts have argued that if state enterprises are to become effective contributors to national development, they must be run like private firms, free from government interference. Only under these conditions can they plan and implement the kind of long-term strategy that is essential if they are to contribute fully to national development. Their managers should be held accountable for the results that they achieve. The experience of the three Turkish iron and steel firms strengthens this viewpoint, but the question of how to achieve efficiency in a state enterprise, while maintaining an appropriate level of accountability to the political elite, remains a theoretical and practical challenge.

The goal must be to reach the highest level on the scale of technological mastery that I outlined in Chapter 1, 'autonomy', the ability to meet specific needs by developing new technologies and combining them with existing ones in novel ways. Turkey, for example, possesses extensive lignite deposits and would benefit greatly if it could develop and integrate technology that would use this raw material to produce metallurgical coke economically. To become 'autonomous' requires that activities such as the following be implemented – training and educational programs, an information system on patents, licenses, equipment and services, an active research and development effort, and the creation of a local network of suppliers of equipment and services. The particular capabilities that have to be developed within the sector include consulting and assessment, managerial and administrative, operation and maintenance, adaptation and innovation, bargaining and negotiations with foreign suppliers, and the disaggregation of technological packages. International agencies and foreign donors can, and should, play an important role in the development of these capabilities.

Moreover, one can envisage the establishment of a central design and evaluation unit that would enhance the quality of technology transfers and facilitate the achievement of mastery. This approach is not without potential dangers; it must not become a cumbersome bureaucracy or an inquisitorial tribunal, its members should avoid any potential conflict of interest, and it should be structured so as to gain as much legitimacy as possible in the given political context. The group should be composed of professionals with different skills, backgrounds and perspectives and should be involved in major projects from their inception, including the negotiations with foreign actors. Its experts should evaluate every aspect of a project – the alternative preliminary designs, the financing arrangements, the impacts and the plans for personnel preparation – in order to determine whether the project is well designed and likely to lead to mastery. Specific criteria should be built into every project and, once it begins operation, its performance should be evaluated regularly. Some countries may have to rely on foreign consultants for such analyses but the development of a domestic capability should be a priority. Whatever its organization (and several models are available), the group must obviously have access to the centers of power and be able to participate fully in the decision-making process if it is to be truly effective.

Such activities can be implemented in the context of practically any development strategy, though positive results are easier to achieve if the market is allowed a significant degree of freedom. The import substitution strategy has been severely criticized for many valid reasons, not least of which, as occurred in Turkey, is the tendency to restrain competitive forces and to continue the strategy long after it has outlived its usefulness. Yet some form of industrialization by import substitution is probably inevitable in the early stages of growth, while technological learning takes place and the capability to compete with foreign firms is built up. The essential point is that such learning be actively promoted, otherwise only a limited amount of technological mastery will occur, with adverse consequences for future growth. And, even if an export orientation is pursued, it is important to note that no country that has mastered technology has followed an export promotion policy without, simultaneously, protecting selected sectors and activities for a specific period. Furthermore, questions of social justice can be addressed satisfactorily even when market forces and exports are emphasized.

The fundamental issue is how to move towards a system with the characteristics that enable it to implement the kinds of structures and policies discussed above for it is clear that the political realm determines all aspects of project success or failure. As I have stressed, projects fail for two fundamental reasons: defects at the design and implementation stage and an inability to master the technologies. Many actors and factors are involved in each. The litany of reasons is a long one; it includes, among others, defective studies, weak administrative and managerial practices, incompetent consultants, planners and decision-makers, unexpected events, inadequate resource allocations, and the priorities, objectives and resources of sending and receiving organizations and discrepancies between them. But all these are themselves caused primarily by the nature and functioning of the receiving country's political system whose decisions, policies and capabilities enhance the likelihood that such factors will be present and influential.

Success or failure in technology transfer projects, then, is basically determined by the way in which the domestic political system operates, the pattern of its relations with external actors and the attitudes and skills of its elites. If the conditions for success are created, then sound projects will be disigned and implemented and technological learning will flourish and a high percentage of projects will be successful; if not, then most projects will fail. Since history is not exactly replete with examples of such leaders and systems, it is unlikely that the world of tomorrow will be very different from the world of today. Despite the pleas for greater rationality in project selection and implementation and the emphasis upon improving techniques and procedures, projects will continue to fail because human and organizational forces constitute powerful obstacles to the realization of a technocratic utopia. Utopia must remain a literary dream that stirs men's imaginations. Still, the lessons are clear: political and institutional arrangements must be devised that create a policy process wherein decisions are made intelligently and wisely, where parochial concerns are balanced with longer term considerations in a way that does not vandalize technological or economic rationality. Only states that can do so will be able to cope with the demands of the future, for development has always been, and inevitably will continue to be, forged not in the blast furnace or the laboratory, but in the political system.

Notes

PREFACE

1. In 1986, The Case Clearing House of Great Britain and Northern Ireland, Cranfield Institute of Technology, also published the study.

CHAPTER 1   TECHNOLOGICAL DECISION-MAKING AND NATIONAL DEVELOPMENT

1. A detailed analysis of the available studies indicates that thousands of projects throughout the world have encountered problems of some sort; 3,500 had cost overruns. Peter W. G. Morris and George H. Hough, *The Anatomy of Major Projects: A Study of the Reality of Project Management* (New York: John Wiley, 1987), pp. 7 ff.
2. See, for example, O. Grine, 'Transfer of technology in the Arab steel industry', in A. B. Zahlan (ed.), *Technology Transfer and Change in the Arab World* (New York: Pergamon, 1978), pp. 451–70. See also W. O. Johnson, *The Steel Industry of India* (Cambridge, Mass.: Harvard University Press, 1968); P. Desai, *The Bokaro Steel Plant* (NY: American Elsevier, 1972); R. H. Chilicote, *Spain's Iron and Steel Industry* (Austin, Tex.: University of Texas Press, 1968); W. Baer, *The Development of the Brazilian Steel Industry* (Nashville, Tenn.: Vanderbilt University Press, 1969).
3. On the strengths and weaknesses of this methodology, see Harry Eckstein, 'Case study and theory in political science', in F. I. Greenstein and N. Polsby (eds). *Handbook of Political Science*, vol. 7 (Reading, Mass.: Addison Wesley, 1975) pp. 79–137. See also J. Feldman, *Concorde and Dissent* (Princeton: Princeton University Press, 1985), pp. 165–70.
4. A. O. Hirschman, *Development Projects Observed* (Washington, DC: The Brookings Institute, 1967), p. 1.
5. Ibid., p. 14.
6. Paul R. Schulman, *Large- Scale Policy Making* (New York: Elsevier, 1980).
7. Gerald M. Steinberg, 'Comparing technological risks in large scale national projects', *Policy Sciences,* Vol. 18, 1985, pp. 79–93.
8. Peter Hall, *Great Planning Disasters* (Berkeley, Calif.: University of California Press, 1980), p. 3.

9. Ibid., pp. 4–11; for a study which analyses the significance of this type of uncertainty in advanced industrialized countries see Yoshi-hiro Kogane (ed.), *Changing Value Patterns And Their Impact On Economic Structure* (Tokyo: University of Tokyo Press, 1982).
10. Ibid., pp. xxv–xxvi.
11. Ibid., p. xxvi.
12. Kathleen J. Murphy, *Macroproject Development In The Third World* (Boulder, Colo.: Westview Press, 1983), p. 19.
13. Ibid., pp. 8–10, 47–53.
14. Ibid., pp. 19–20.
15. Another expert, however, concludes that iron and steel plants are highly complex technological systems, both to construct and to operate (Tugrul Atamer, 'Choix des partenaires et modalités de transfert international de technologie', Thèse pour le doctorat de 3ème cycle, Université des Sciences Sociales de Grenoble, 1980, p. 142).
16. Murphy, op. cit., pp. 80–1.
17. Ibid., pp. 21 ff.; the quote is from p. 24.
18. Morris and Hough, op. cit., p. 7; the model is to be found on p. 268.
19. E. J. Feldman, 'Patterns of failure in government megaprojects: economics, politics, and participation in industrial democracies', in Samuel P. Huntington and Joseph S. Nye Jr, *Global Dilemmas* (Boston, Mass.: The Center for International Affairs and University Press of America, 1985), *passim*; the quote is from p. 151.
20. Hirschman, op. cit., p. 42.
21. Although there is no precise and accepted definition of 'technology' practically every expert in this field accepts a broad definition such as 'any kind of practical know-how' or 'any set of standardized operations that yields predetermined results' and would include, in addition to machines and tools of all kinds, methods, routines and procedures as well as patterns of organization and administration. I treat this and some of the following issues in my *Technology and International Affairs* (New York: Praeger, 1981). The definitions are taken from Bernard Gendron, *Technology and The Human Condition* (New York: St. Martin's Press, 1977), pp. 22–3; and David M. Freeman, *Technology and Society* (Chicago: Markham 1974), pp. 5–9.
22. See N. Bruce Hannay and R. E. McGinn, 'The anatomy of modern technology: prolegomenon to an improved public policy for the social management of technology', *Daedalus*, Winter 1980, pp. 25–53; Harold Linstone, *Multiple Perspectives For Decision Making* (New York: North Holland, 1984); T. Atamer, op. cit.
23. Atamer, op. cit., pp. 12 ff.
24 These elements are discussed by H. V. Perlmutter and T. Sagafi-Necad, *International Technology Transfer* (New York: Pergamon, 1981); see also UNCTAD, *Guidelines for the Study of the Transfer of Technology* (New York: United Nations, 1972), p. 15.
25. For a model of this process see S. N. Bar Zakay, 'A technology transfer model', *Technological Forecasting and Social Change*, 1971, pp. 321–77; Dennis Goulet, *The Cruel Choice* (Washington, DC:

IDRC, 1977) analyses the critical role of values in shaping outcomes.

26.   Atamer, op. cit., pp. 121 ff.
27.   Carl Dahlman and Larry Westphal, 'The meaning of technological
        mastery in relation to transfer of technology', in Howard Pack (ed.),
        Technology Transfer: New Issues, New Analyses (Philadelphia, Pa.:
        The Annals of the American Academy of Political and Social
        Science, 1983), p. 14; see also Robert Stobaugh and L. Wells Jr,
        Technology Crossing Borders (Boston, Mass.: Harvard Business
        School Press, 1984).
28.   Dahlman and Westphal op. cit., pp. 15–16.
29.   Ibid., p. 15.
30.   G. Ranis and G. Saxonhouse, 'International and domestic determi-
        nants of technology choice in the less developed countries', in B. G.
        Lucas and S. Freedman (eds), *Technology Choice and Change in
        Developing Countries: Internal and External Constraints* (Dublin:
        Tycooly International, 1983), pp. 7–27.
31.   Atamer, op. cit., pp. 334, 314–15.
32.   My concern with placing this case in a larger theoretical framework
        requires that I make an effort to be conceptually precise and
        consistent. Accordingly it is appropriate to specify the key concepts
        that I shall be using. To begin with, I view the state as that set of
        institutions (and the persons who man them) which integrates the
        diverse elements of society and defines the structure of power within
        a given territory. For stylistic reasons, I shall sometimes use the term
        'country' to refer to a specific state. I shall use the term 'social core
        group' to refer to those who occupy elite positions within the state
        institutions. The government comprises the formal policy-making
        positions and the persons who occupy them. I shall refer to these
        officials as 'government leaders'. When discussing the network of
        activities, transactions and flows related to the 'authoritative alloca-
        tion of values' (to use David Easton's well-known formulation), I
        shall use the term 'political system'. I shall differentiate among
        political systems on the basis of 'regime type' (democratic, authori-
        tarian, military, etc.). For a useful introduction to the contemporary
        debate over the state and its role, see G. Almond, 'The return of the
        state', and E. Nordlinger, T. J. Lowi and S. Fabbrini, 'The return of
        the state: critiques', *American Political Science Review*, Vol. 82, No.
        3, September 1988, pp. 853–900.
33.   *Technology and Steel Industry Competitiveness* (Washington, DC:
        Office of Technology Assessment, n.d.), pp. 22–23; hereafter
        referred to as OTA.
34   F. Stewart, 'Facilitating indigenous technical change in Third World
        countries' in Martin Fransman and Kenneth King, *Technological
        Capabilities in the Third World* (London: Macmillan, 1984), pp.
        81–94.
35.   Dahlman and Westphal, op. cit., p. 18.
36.   Linsu Kim, 'Stages of development of industrial technology in a
        developing country: a model', *Research Policy*, 1980.

37.   Atamer, op. cit., pp. 126 ff.
38.   R. Dore, 'Technological self-reliance: sturdy ideal or self serving rhetoric', in Fransman and King, op. cit., pp. 65–80.
39.   Fransman and King, op. cit, p. 10.
40   F. S. Erber, 'Science and technology policy: a view from the periphery', in Szyliowicz, op. cit., pp. 173–200, eloquently advances this position.
41.   For a useful introduction to this literature see R. Chilcote, *Theories of Comparative Politics* (Boulder, Colo.: Westview Press, 1981), pp. 296–312.
42.   K. Z. Poznansky, 'Technology transfer: west-south perspective', *World Politics,* October 1984, pp. 134–52.
43.   See N. Caiden and A. Wildavski, *Planning and Budgeting in Poor Countries* (New York: John Wiley, 1974).
44.   Francisco Sagasti, *Science and Technology for Development: Main Comparative Report on the STPI Project* (Ottawa, Canada: International Development Research Center, 1978).
45.   David Williams, 'Choice of technology and parastatal firms', in Stobaugh and Wells, op. cit., pp. 128–50.
46.   *Technology Transfer to the Middle East* (Washington, DC: Office of Technology Assessment, n.d.), pp. 71 ff. 425 ff.
47.   F. Sagasti, *Technology, Planning and Self Reliant Development* (New York: Praeger, 1979), pp. 19 ff.
48.   Ibid., p. 20.
49.   For a useful summary of the state of our knowledge, with particular reference to the literature dealing with Latin America, see John D. Martz, *Politics and Petroleum in Ecuador* (New Brunswick, NJ: Transaction Books, 1987), pp. 7 ff.; see also B. G. Peters, J. C. Doughtie and M. K. McCulloch, 'Types of democratic systems and types of public policies', *Comparative Politics*, April 1977, pp. 327–55, who demonstrate that the nature of policy outputs is related to the form of the policy process.
50.   For an elaboration of this concept see S. Keller, *Beyond The Ruling Class* (NY: Random House, 1963).
51.   P. G. Roeder, *Two Tiers of Soviet Policy Making,* paper presented to the International Studies Annual Convention, Washington, DC, 1987, p. 21.
52.   Richard Zeckhauser and Elmer Schaefer, 'Public policy and normative economic theory', in R. A. Bauer and K. J. Gergen (eds), *The Study of Policy Formation* (New York: Free Press, 1968), pp. 27–101.
53.   Herbert A. Simon, *Administrative Behavior* (New York: Free Press, 1957) pp. xxiii–xxvii.
54.   James G. March and H. Simon, *Organizations* (New York: John Wiley, 1958); Richard M. Cyert and James G. March, *A Behavioral Theory of the Firm* (Englewood Cliffs, NJ: Prentice Hall, 1963).
55.   Charles E. Lindblom, 'The science of muddling through', *Public Administration Review,* 19 (1959), pp. 79–88. See also his *The Intelligence of Democracy* (New York: Free Press, 1965) and *The*

Policy Making Process (Englewood Cliffs, NJ: Prentice Hall, 1968).
56.   A. Etzioni, 'Mixed scanning: a "third" approach to decision making', *Public Administration Review*, 19678, pp. 385–92, and 'Mixed scanning revisited', *Public Administration Review*, 1986, pp. 8–14; J. Gershuny advocates an 'iterative mixed scanning strategy' in his 'policy making rationality', *Policy Sciences*, 1978, pp. 295–316.
57.   G. Allison,*Essence of Decision* (Boston Mass.: Little Brown, 1971), p. 2.
58.   G. Allison and M. Halperin, 'Bureaucratic politics: a paradigm and some policy implications', *World Politics*, Spring 1972, pp. 40–80.
59.   Desmond J. Ball, 'The blind men and the elephant: a critique of bureaucratic politics theory', *Australian Outlook*, April 1974, pp. 71–92; S. D. Krasner, 'Are bureaucracies important? (Or Allison Wonderland)', *Foreign Policy*, Summer 1972, pp. 159–79; James A. Nathan and James K. Oliver, 'Bureaucratic politics: academic windfalls and intellectual pitfalls', *Journal of Political and Military Sociology*, Spring 1978, pp. 81–91; R. Art, 'Bureaucratic politics and American foreign policy: a critique', *Policy Sciences*, No. 4, 1973, pp. 467–90.
60.   M. Brecher, *Decisions in Israel's Foreign Policy* (London: Oxford University Press, 1974); J. Steinbrunner, *The Cybernetic Theory of Decision;* (Princeton, NJ: Princeton University Press, 1974).
61.   Janice G. Stein and Raymond Tanter, *Rational Decision-Making: Israel's Security Choices, 1967* (Columbus: Ohio State University Press, 1980).
62.   David Braybrooke and Charles E. Lindblom, *A Strategy of Decision* (New York: Free Press, 1963), p. 78.
63.   Richard Barke, *Science, Technology and Public Policy* (Washington, DC: Congressional Quarterly, 1986), pp. 10–11.
64.   Robert F. Baker, R. M. Michaels and E. S. Preston, *Public Policy Development: Linking the Technical and Political Processes* (New York: John Wiley, 1975), p. 256.
65.   Linstone, op. cit., Chapter 4.
66.   These categories overlap somewhat with Linstone's dimensions (design and impact are 'technical', management incorporates the organizational and personal), but they represent only elements to be studied, not 'lenses' of analysis as well. The framework was originally elaborated and applied in R. Rycroft and J. Szyliowicz, *Decision Making In A Technological Environment: The Case of The Aswan High Dam* (Boston, Mass.: Intercollegiate Case Clearing House, 1980), and subsequently in 'The case of the Aswan Dam', *World Politics*, October 1980, pp. 36–61.
67.   'Why projects fail', lecture by Arthur Hazlewood, Queen Elizabeth House, Oxford University, 15 February, 1985.
68.   J. D. Bryce, *Industrial Development* (New York: McGraw-Hill, 1960), p. 106.
69.   See, for example, F. Stewart, *Technology and Underdevelopment* (London: Macmillan, 1978), D. Morawetz, 'Employment implica-

tions of industrialization in developing countries: a survey', *Economic Journal*, 1974, pp. 491–542, J. Enos, 'The choice of technique vs the choice of beneficiary: what the Third World chooses', in F. Stewart and J. James, *The Economics of New Technology in Developing Countries* (Boulder, Colo.: Westview Press, 1982), pp. 69–82.

70. D. Forsyth, N. McBain and R. Solomon, 'Technical rigidity and appropriate technology in developing countries', in Stewart and James, op. cit., p. 65.
71. Stobaugh and Wells, op. cit., pp. 3 ff.
72. Bryce, op. cit., p. 122.
73. Ibid., p. 129.
74. Ibid., p. 122.
75. Idem.
76. Ibid., p. 118.
77. Ibid., p. 130.
78. Ibid., p. 132.
79. Ibid., p. 33.
80. I.M.D. Little and J. A. Mirrlees, *Manual of Industrial Project Analysis in Developing Countries, Volume II, Social Cost–Benefit Analysis* (Paris: OECD, 1969); P.S. Dasgupta, S. A. Marglin and A. K. Sen, *Guidelines for Project Evaluation* (New York: United Nations, 1972); L. Squire and H. G. van der Tak, *Economic Analysis of Projects* (Washington, DC: World Bank Research Publication, 1975); Ministry of Overseas Development, *A Guide to the Economic Appraisal of Projects in Developing Countries* (London: HMSO, 1977); *Evaluation Handbook* (Washington, DC: USAID, 1972).
81. O. Murelius, *An Institutional Approach to Project Analysis in Developing Countries* (Paris: Development Centre, OECD, 1981).
82. H. Schwartz and R. Berney, *Social and Economic Dimensions of Project Evaluation* (Washington, DC: InterAmerican Development Bank, 1977), p. 6.
83. For a balanced and systematic exploration of the role of cost utility and related techniques in policy decisions, and an overview of these techniques, see Michael Carley, *Rational Techniques in Policy Analysis* (London: Heinemann Educational, 1980).
84. Murelius, op. cit., pp. 111–12.
85. Ibid., pp. 1, 9.
86. See Peter Self, *Econocrats and the Policy Process* (London: Macmillan, 1975).
87. Murelius, op. cit., p. 12.
88. See, for example, Murelius, op. cit., p. 9. For a discussion of the approaches and techniques that AID and the World Bank use in their project evaluations, see H. M. Selim, *Development Assistance Policies and the Performance of Aid Agencies* (London: Macmillan, 1983), pp. 52–53, 350–357.
89. For a detailed analysis of how managerial deficiencies have adversely affected a number of projects in Greece, see S. M. Theopa-

nides, 'Project planning and implementation in Greece', in W. D. Cook and T. E. Kuhn, *Planning Processes in Developing Countries: Techniques and Achievements* (New York: North Holland, 1982), pp. 70–3.

90.   See Murelius, op. cit., p. 6.

91.   Cited in D. A. Rondinelli, *Planning Development Projects* (Strouds-burg, Pa.: Dowden, Hutchinson & Ross, 1977), p. 3.

92.   The World Bank breaks the project cycle down into six phases: identification, preparation, appraisal, negotiations, implementation and evaluation. The UN identifies eight (conception, formulation, analysis and evaluation, approval, implementation, reporting and feedback, transition to normal administration, evaluation) and one scholar expands these to twelve (identification, formulation, preparation and approval, activation and organization, implementation and operation, supervising, monitoring and control, completion and termination, transition to normal administration, evaluation, follow-up analysis and action). See Murelius, op. cit., p. 4.; Rondinelli, Op. cit., pp. 6 ff; UNPAD, 'Development planning as a framework for project administration', in Rondinelli, op. cit., pp. 30 ff.

93.   On the role of political symbolism as a driving force, see G. Steinberg, 'Large-scale national projects as political symbols: the case of Israel', *Comparative Politics* (forthcoming).

94.   Murelius, op. cit., p. 10. For a detailed discussion of this stage, see D. Rondinelli, 'Project identification in economic development', in Rondinelli, op. cit., pp. 69–94. Hereafter referred to as 'Project identification'.

95.   These are derived from the discussion in 'Project Identification', pp. 86 ff.

96.   Bryce, op. cit., p. 37.

97.   Murelius, op. cit., p. 18.

98.   Y. J. Ahmad, 'Project identification, analysis and preparation in developing countries: a discursive commentary', in Rondinelli, op. cit., p. 161.

99.   Murphy, op. cit., pp. 23–4.

100.   UNPAD, op. cit., p. 40.

101.   'Project identification', p. 91.

102.   UNPAD, op. cit., p. 39.

103.   M. S. Grindle (ed.), *Politics and Policy Implementation in the Third World* (Princeton, NJ: Princeton University Press, 1980).

104.   UNPAD, op. cit., p. 43.

CHAPTER 2   IRON AND STEEL AND DEVELOPMENT IN TURKEY

1.   Hollis Chenery, *Structural Change in Development Policy* (Oxford: Oxford University Press, 1979), pp.26 ff.

2.   For a recent analysis of the advantages of export promotion over the import substitution strategy, see J. N. Bhagwati, 'Rethinking trade strategy', in J. P. Lewis and V. Kallab (eds.), *Development Strate-*

gies Reconsidered (New Brunswick, NJ: Transaction Books, 1986) pp. 91–104.

3. OECD, *The Impact of the Newly Industrializing Countries on Production and Trade in Manufacture* (Paris: OECD, 1979), pp. 18–19.

4. Cited in J. D. Bryce, *Industrial Development* (New York: McGraw-Hill, 1960), p. 3.

5. W. P. Blass, 'Steel mills for developing economies', *Social and Economic Studies,* June 1962, p. 157.

6. A. O. Hirschman, *The Strategy of Economic Development* (New Haven, Conn.: Yale University Press, 1970), pp. 105–106; O. Grine, 'Transfer of technology in the Arab steel industry', in A. B. Zahlan (ed.), *Technology Transfer and Change in the Arab World* (New York: Pergamon, 1978), p. 453.

7. Hirschman, op. cit., p. 204.

8. Unido, *Draft World-Wide Study of the Iron and Steel Industry, 1975–2000* (UNIDO/CIS 25/15 December, 1976), p. 111.

9. 'Steel yard blues', *NACLA Report on the Americas,* Vol. 12, No. 1, Jan–Feb. 1979, p. 18.

10. T. R. Howell, W. A. Noellert, J. G. Kreier and A. W. Wolff, *Steel and the State* (Boulder, Colo.: Westview Press, 1988), pp. 16 ff.

11. The spread of these technologies is analyzed by George F. Ray, *The Diffusion of Mature Technologies* (Cambridge, UK: Cambridge University Press, 1984), the differences in the speed with which the two countries adopted new technologies in Leonard H. Lynn, *How Japan Innovates: A Comparison with the U.S. in the Case of Oxygen Steelmaking* (Boulder, Colo.: Westview Press, 1982). Lynn concludes that the Japanese innovated more rapidly than the USA because their companies had access to superior knowledge which came from the extensive and sophisticated mechanisms that they utilized to scan technological progress abroad and had the ability to use that knowledge to solve their problems.

12. R. Christopher, 'Don't blame the Japanese', *New York Times Magazine,* October 18, 1981.

13. Howell *et al.,* op. cit., Table 16, p. 10. pp. 26 ff.

14. By concentrating on the last stages of the process these plants bypass the expensive 'front end' components (coke ovens and blast furnaces) of the integrated plants and are, therefore, cheaper to build and operate. And, because they usually serve a regional market, they enjoy low transportation costs.

15. D. Barnett and R. Crandall, *Up From the Ashes,* (Washington, DC: Brookings Institution, 1986).

16. Unido, *Industry in a Changing World* (New York: Unido, 1983), p. 274, hereafter referred to as UNIDO 'Industry'.

17. I. Çelebi, *Türkiye'de Demir Çelik Sanayiīnin Yapīsī ve Sorunlarī* (Ankara: Devlet Planlama Teşkilatī, 1979), Tables 25, 26, pp. 74, 75.

18. *The Burgeoning LDC Steel Industry: More Problems for Major Steel Producers* (Washington, DC: National Foreign Assessment Center,

CIA, July 1979), p. 4; hereafter referred to as *LDC Steel Industry;
Annual Report, 1985* (Ankara: Ereğli Demir ve Çelik Fabrikalari,
TAŞ, 1986), p. 15; Hereafter referred to as '1985 Annual Report'.

19.   Unido, 'Industry', pp. 275–6.

20.   For a discussion of how policy-makers reacted to these changes see
S. Woolcock, 'The international politics of trade and production in
the steel industry', in J. Pinder (ed.), *National Industrial Strategies
and the World Economy* (London: Croom Helm, 1982).

21.   For a skeptical view of the Third World's steel potential see
B. Chateau and B. Lapillone, *Energy Demand: Facts and Trends*
(New York: Springer Verlag, 1982), pp. 166–7.

22.   For the socio-political history, I have drawn upon my 'Elites and
modernization in Turkey', in F. Tachau, *Political Elites and Political
Development* (New York: John Wiley, 1975), pp. 22–66.

23.   On economic policy under Ataturk, see Z. Y. Hershlag, *Turkey:
The Challenge of Growth* (Leiden: E. J. Brill, 1968l), p. 61–127. On
these early efforts at planning see also E. Günce, 'Early planning
experiences in Turkey', in S. Ilkin and E. Inanç, *Planning in Turkey*
(Ankara: Middle East Technical University, 1967), pp. 1–27.

24.   These details are from S. S. Aydemir, *Ikinci Adam* (Istanbul: Remzi
Kitabevi, 1968), cited in I. Çelebi, op. cit., pp. 48–9. See also
Cumhuriyetin 50 Yilinda Türkiye Demir ve Çelik Işletmeleri (An-
kara: TDÇI; *Türkiye'de Modern Bir Demir Çelik Sanayii Kurmak
Için Yapilan Ilk Çalismalar* (Karabük Genel Müdürlüğü, n.d.),
Mimeo, hereafter referred to as Karabük; and Hershlag, op. cit.,
pp. 103 ff.

25.   Çelebi, op. cit., p. 50.

26.   TDÇI, p. 10.

27.   Çelebi, op. cit., p. 54.

28.   Ibid., p. 51.

29.   Personal Interview with Mr George Thomas, Chairman, John Miles
Company Ltd, Croydon, UK, 13 June 1985.

30.   Hershlag, op. cit. p. 104.

31.   TDÇI, p. 17.

32.   Idem.

33.   For a good introduction to the issues involved in planning an iron
and steel plant, see E. K. Sandbach, 'The iron and steel industry in a
developing economy', *Iron and Steel,* March 1964, pp. 109–21. The
quote is from p. 111.

34.   TDÇI, p. 11.

35.   Idem.

36.   Bertil Walstedt, *State Manufacturing Enterprises in Mixed Economies: The Turkish Case* (Baltimore, Md.: Johns Hopkins University
Press, 1980), p. 74.

37.   *The Making of Steel* (Washington, DC: American Iron and Steel
Institute, n.d.) provides a clear, illustrated introduction to the
industry; for a good, short discussion of the technologies, see
Emission Control Costs in the Iron and Steel Industry (Paris: OECD,
1977), pp. 14–25; *Technology and Steel Industry Competitiveness*

(Washington, DC: Office of Technology Assessment, 1979) provides a detailed analysis of technological change in the industry.

38. In the early sixties at least 1.6 tons of ore, 0.65 tons of coke, 0.2 tons of limestone and 0.05 tons of iron and steel scrap and 4 tons of air were required to produce one ton of pig iron: W. Baer, *The Development of the Brazilian Steel Industry* (Nashville, Tenn.: Vanderbilt University Press, 1969) p. 11.

39. T. G. A. Muntz, *Turkey* (New York: Philosophical Library 1950), p. 62; M. W. Thornburg, G. Spry and G. Soule, *Turkey: An Economic Appraisal* (New York: Twentieth Century Fund, 1949), p. 100.

40. On the development of this technology see Ray, op. cit., pp. 5–20.

41. I. S. Barutçugil, *Türkiye'de Demir Çelik Endüstrisi* (Istanbul: Bursa Universitesi Iktisadi ve Sosyal Bilimler Fakultesi, 1978), p. 96.

42. A sympathetic analyst considers this to be 'the most valid charge levelled against it': Morris Singer, *The Economic Advance of Turkey, 1938–1960* (Ankara: Turkish Economic Society, 1977), p. 33.

43. IBRD, *The Economy of Turkey* (Baltimore, Md.: Johns Hopkins University Press, 1951), p. 117.

44. Interview with Mr George Thomas, John Miles Company Ltd, 13 June 1985.

45. IBRD, op. cit., pp. 114–15, 117; Singer, op. cit., p. 277.

46. IBRD, op. cit., p. 115.

47. Thornburg, *et al.*, op. cit., p. 109.

48. For a judicious evaluation of economic policy and results in this period, see Hershlag, op. cit., Chapter 14.

49. Ozay Mehmet, 'Turkey in crisis: some contradictions in the Kemalist development strategy', *International Journal of Middle East Studies*, Vol. 15, 1983, pp. 47–66.

50. Osman Okyar, *Public International Development Financing in Turkey* (New York: Columbia University School of Law Research Projects on Public International Development Financing, Report No. 3, 1962), pp. 4 ff.

51. These studies were published as Thornburg, *et al.*, op. cit., and IBRD, op. cit.

52. Thornburg *et al.*, op. cit., pp 10–12; 227–30.

53. Günce, op. cit., p. 23.

54. Anne O. Krueger, *Foreign Trade Regimes and Economic Development: Turkey* (New York: Columbia University Press for the National Bureau of Economic Research, 1974), pp. 6. ff.

55. Singer, op. cit., p. 404.

56. Ibid., p. 474. On the 1953–58 period see Krueger, op. cit., Chapter 2.

57. Although thought was given to the adoption of the new oxygen steel furnace technology, it was rejected as too risky.

58. Singer, op. cit., pp. 277, 311.

59. Singer argues that Karabük was not producing at capacity during these years because imports accounted for a high percentage of steel

consumption in the late fifties and that Menderes was therefore 'seeking to promote output growth and capital formation without engaging in an adequate appraisal of markets and without planning sufficiently for the required complementary activities and inputs.' His data, however, shows that Karabük was producing about 150,000 tons a year, about its capacity in these years. Moreover, these imports may well have been in the form of flat products which Karabük did not produce. Ibid., pp. 277–8. The issue of planning for the new plant which was designed to complement Karabük will be addressed in detail in Chapter 3.

60. T. Tayanç, *Sanayileşme Süresinde 50 Yil* (Istanbul: Millyet Yayïnlarï, 1973), p. 151.

61. Okyar, op. cit., p. 16.

62. Ibid., p. 61 ff.

63. Department of State, AID, *Turkey: Ereğli Iron and Steel Works, Capital Assistance Paper AID/DLC/P567* (Washington, DC, 14 May 1967), p. 21; hereafter referred to as *P567*.

64. Devlet Planlama Teşkilatï, *First Five Year Development Plan* (Ankara: State Planning Organization, 1963), p. 268. Hereafter referred to as First Plan.

65. Ibid., p. 274.

66. T. Candir and A. Candir, 'Türkiye Demir-Çelik Talep' Tahminleri (Ankara: Devlet Planlama Teşkilatï, 1966), mimeo, p. 130.

67. Devlet Planlama Teşkilatï, *Second Five Year Development Plan*, (Ankara: State Planning Organization, 1967) pp. 510–17.

68. Devlet Planlama Teşkilatï, *Third Five Year Development Plan*, (Ankara: State Planning Organization, 1972) pp. 462 ff.

69. Devlet Planlama Teşkilatï, *Fourth Five Year Development Plan*, (Ankara: State Planning Organization, 1978) pp. 584.

70. On developments in this period and the structure of the polity, see C. H. Dodd, *Democracy and Development in Turkey* (Hull, UK: Eothen Press, 1979).

71. IBRD, op. cit., p. 255.

72. Devlet Planlama Teşkilatï, *Fourth Five Year Development Plan*, pp. 583ff; TDÇI p. 138.

73. 1979 Annual Report (Ankara: Ereğli Demir ve Çelik Fabrikalarï TAŞ, 1980), p. 10.

74. Barutçugil, op. cit., Table 13; 1979 Annual Report, p. 11.

75. Idem. Çelebi, op. cit., Table 32, p. 90, calculates the GNP increase at 470 per cent.

76. Barutçugil, op. cit., Tables 14, 16, 17, 18, 19.

77. Barutçugil, op. cit., Table 14, p. 30; Demir-Çelik Özel Ihtïsas Komisyonu Raporu, Son Taslak (Ankara: Devlet Planlama Teşkilatï, 1983), Table 1, p. 3. Hereafter referred to as Rapor.

78. Barutçugil, op. cit., Tables 17, 21, 22, pp. 32, 37.

79. World Bank, *Turkey: Policies and Prospects for Growth* (Washington, DC: World Bank, 1980), pp. 1 ff.

80. Idem.

81. Ibid., p. 108.

82. J. D. Lewis and S. Unata, *Turkey: Economic Performance and Medium Term Prospects, 1978–1990* (Washington, DC: World Bank Staff Working Paper, 1982), pp. 12 ff.
83. Ibid., p. 2; the quote is from p. 12.
84. Merih Celasun, *Sources of Industrial Growth and Structural Change: The Case of Turkey* (Washington, DC: World Bank Staff Working Paper. 614, 1983), p. 18.
85. Krueger, op, cit., pp. 255 ff.
86. Walstedt, op. cit., p. 106, calculates that, between 1972, and 1976, the value added ratio on fixed investments stood at 3.4, the employment ratio (in TL 1,000) at 245. In Appendix C, pp. 305—8, he discusses Krueger's conclusions and the criticisms contained in Medrih Celasun's review of her book which appeared in *Journal of Development Economics,* Vol. 3, 1976, pp. 203–5.
87. Celasun, op. cit., p. 110.

CHAPTER 3 THE DECISION TO BUILD ERDEMIR

1. For the historical background of this project, I have drawn upon numerous unpublished documents in the AID and Koppers archives as well as on personal interviews with numerous AID and Koppers officials. I have noted mainly the formal studies that were prepared in the course of the project cycle.
2. *Development of Private Industry Through Public Aid* (Washington, DC: ICA Office of Industrial Resources, 1958), prepared for ICA by J. K. Adler, Stanford Research Institute, September 1958 (mimeo). The quote is from p. 36.
3. Osman Okyar, *Public International Development Financing in Turkey* (New York: Columbia University School of Law, Research Project on Public International Development Financing, Report No. 3, November 1962), p. 25.
4. Department of State, AID, *Turkey: Ereğli Steel Mill, Proposal and Recommendations of the Managing Director, Development Loan Fund AID/DLC/P262* (Washington, DC, 8 November, 1960) mimeo, p. 9. Hereafter referred to as P262.
5. Ibid., p. 18.
6. Department of State, AID, *Turkey: Ereğli Iron and Steel Works, Capital Assistance Paper AID/DLC/P567* (Washington, DC, 14 May 1967), p. 21; hereafter referred to as *P567*.
7. P262, p. 8.
8. P567, p. 6.
9. For the history of Ereğli and the evolution of its social structure, see F. Mansur, *Ereğli, Ağır Sanayiden Önce Bir Sahil Kasabasï* (Ankara: Devlet Planlama Teşkilatï, 1964). See also M. D. Rivkin, *Area Development for National Growth* (New York: Praeger, 1965).
10. P262, Annex 1, pp. 2–5.
11. Ibid., Annex 1, p. 5.
12. Ibid., p. 25.

13. Ibid., Annex 1, p. 30.
14. Ibid., Annex 1, p. 9.
15. Ibid., p. 5; Annex 1, p. 35.
16. Ibid., p. 17.
17. Ibid., p. 4.
18. Ibid., Annex 1, p. 32; the following discussion is also taken from this section.
19. Ibid., p. 29.
20. Since the cost of the plant had climbed to $245 million, the costs were actually about $620 per ton of product and $500 per ton of ingot capacity.
21. Idem. Critics of the project subsequently produced very different data. See below, p. 110 ff.
22. Ibid., p. 37.
23. Ibid., p. 28.
24. Ibid., pp. 24–5.
25. Ibid., pp. 22–4.
26. Ibid., pp. 1–4.
27. Ibid., pp. 11–12.
28. The material in this section is based on interviews with Koppers personnel who were personally involved with the construction of the plant.
29. *Report of the Iron Ore Study Committee* (Ankara: Ereğli Iron and Steel Works, 19 June 1961); *Action Memo* from R. B. Wagner *et al.* to W. S. Gaud, 21 January 1964, mimeo, Table II. Hereafter referred to as *Action Memo*.
30. *Action Memo*, p. 5.
31. Ibid., p. 6.
32. Ibid., Annex 1.
33. *P567*, p. 2.

CHAPTER 4   SALVAGING THE PROJECT

1. Department of State, AID, Turkey: *Ereğli Iron and Steel Works, Capital Assistance Paper AID/DLC/P567* (Washington, DC, 14 May 1967), p. 19; hereafter referred to as *P567*.
2. Idem.
3. Ibid., p. 18.
4. Ibid., Annex H.
5. Ibid., p. 20.
6. Ibid., p. 22.
7. Ibid., p. 23.
8. *Development Program for 1965–1970,* Prepared for Ereğli Demir ve Çelik Fabrikalari Türk Anonim Şirketi (Pittsburgh, Pa., Koppers Company, October, 1965), mimeo; hereafter referred to as *Development Program*.
9. Ibid., Section A, p. 2.
10. Ibid., pp. 1–2.

11. Ibid., Section B, p. 2.
12. George Harris, *Troubled Alliance: Turkish–American Problems in Historical Perspective, 1945–1971* (Washington, DC: American Enterprise Institute, 1972), p. 100.
13. I. Küçükömer, 'Ereğli Demir Çelik Kurumu ve Egemenliğimiz', *Yön*, No. 4, 1964; see also 'Ereğli Demir Çelik Rezaleti', *Yön*, No. 20, 1962.
14. A. N. Ganioğlu, 'Yabancı Sermaye ve Ereğli Demir Çelik Tesisleri', *Sosyal Adalet*, Vol. 2, 1964, p, 23.
15. A. N. Ganioğlu, 'Ereğli Demir Çelikte Yerseçimi ve Kuruluş Maliyeti', *Sosyal Adalet*, Vol. 2, 1965, p. 34.
16. Idem.
17. Kapitalizmin Harikasï, *Yön*, 28 October 1966.
18. N. Şeni, *Emperyalist Sistem'de Kontrol Sanayii ve Ereğli Demir Çelik* (Ankara: Birikim Yayinlarï Yerli Araştirmalar Dizisi, 1978).
19. John White, *The Politics of Foreign Aid* (St. Martin's Press, 1974), p. 21; B. E. Moon, 'Consensus or compliance: foreign policy change and external dependence, *International Organization*, Vol. 39, pp. 297–329, argues that donors are not motivated by pure humanitarianism but that they respond to development needs in order to reinforce the recipient's existing behavior which is favorable to the donor.
20. Department of State, AID, *Turkey: Ereğli Steel Mill, Capital Assistance Paper, AID/DLC/P506* (Washington, DC, 1 February 1967), mimeo, p. 1; hereafter referred to as *P506*.
21. Ibid., p. 2.
22. Ibid., p. 4.
23. Ibid., p. 26.
24. Ibid., p. 29.
25. Ibid., pp. 30–1.
26. Idem.
27. Ibid., Annex M.
28. Idem, fn. 32.
29. Ibid., p. 44.
30. Ibid., pp. 49–50; Annex S.
31. Ibid., p. 37.
32. Ibid., p. 38.
33. Ibid., p. 39.
34. Ibid., p. 47.
35. Ibid., Annex M, P. 3.
36. Ibid., p. 53.
37. Ibid., p. 48. The loans were for thirty years at 2.5 per cent per annum but included a ten-year grace period with interest of 1 per cent a year. The Turkish government's twenty-year subloan to the company would be at 6 per cent a year with a grace period of five years. It would also provide ERDEMIR a local currency loan of TL 55.8 million ($6.2 million) on similar terms.
38. Department of State, AID, *Turkey: Ereğli Iron and Steel Works, Capital Assistance Paper AID/DLC/P735* (Washington, DC, 14 June

                1968), p. 2; hereafter referred to as *P735*.
39.   Ibid., p. 6.
40.   Ibid., p. 12.
41.   *Erdemir Sinter Plant: Final Report* (Koppers Corporation, 1973),
         mimeo, p. 1.

CHAPTER 5   THE EXPANSION OF ERDEMIR

1.   World Bank, *Appraisal of the ERDEMIR Steel Plant Expansion
         Project, Turkey* (Washington, DC: IBRD, Industrial Projects
         Department 15 October 1971), mimeo, p. 3; hereafter referred to as
         IBRD *Appraisal*.
2.   Department of State, AID, *Turkey: Ereğli Steel Mill Expansion –
         Stage I, Capital Assistance Paper AID/DLC/P985* (Washington, DC,
         18 June 1971), mimeo, p. 3; hereafter referred to as *P985*.
3.   Idem.
4.   *Feasibility Study for Ereğli Iron and Steel Works, Inc., Facilities
         Expansion Program* (Pittsburgh, Pa.: USS Engineeers and Consul-
         tants, September 1970), p. 4; hereafter referred to as UEC *Feasibility
         Study*.
5.   UEC *Feasibility Study, passim*.
6.   World Bank, *Report and Recommendation of the Executive Directors
         on a Proposed Loan to the Republic of Turkey for the ERDEMIR
         Steel Plant Expansion Project* (Washington, DC: IBRD, 1 March
         1972), mimeo, hereafter referred to as *Recommendation*.
7.   For a discussion of this plan in the context of the World Bank see
         Bertil Walstedt, *State Manufacturing Enterprises in Mixed Econo-
         mies: The Turkish Case* (Baltimore, Md.: Johns Hopkins University
         Press, 1980), p. 86.
8.   IBRD *Appraisal*, pp. 1–2; *P985*, p. 5.
9.   IBRD *Appraisal*, p. 5.
10.   *P985*, p. 14.
11.   IBRD *Appraisal*, p. 5.
12.   *P985*, p. 3.
13.   *P985*, p. 6.
14.   The details are provided in Table 22, IBRD *Appraisal*.
15.   Ibid., p. 9.
16.   *Recommendation*, p. 10.
17.   IBRD *Appraisal*, p. 8.
18.   Department of State, AID, *Turkey: Ereğli Steel Mill Expansion –
         Stage I, AID/DLC/P985/2* (Washington, DC, 4 April 1972), mimeo,
         p. 7; hereafter referred to as *P985/2*.
19.   Ibid., Annex 1.
20.   IBRD *Appraisal*, p. 12.
21.   Ibid., p. 11.
22.   Ibid., Annex 4.
23.   Ibid., p. 17.
24.   Ibid., Annex 6, p. 2.

25. Ibid., Annex 6, p. 3.
26. Idem.
27. Ibid., pp. 21, 24.
28. Ibid., p. 18.
29. *P985/2*, p. 20.
30. Walstedt, op, cit., p. 160, n. 20.
31. Ibid., p. 124, n. 38.
32. *Recommendation*, p. 8.
33. *Ereğli Iron and Steel Works, Inc., Facilities Expansion Program, Expansion Case – State I June 1973 Projection* (Pittsburgh, Pa.: USS Engineers and Consultants, 29 June 1973), mimeo, Section 2, p. 5; hereafter referred to as *June 1973 Projection*.
34. Ibid., p. 11.
35. *Country Programming Background Papers for Turkey* (Ankara: UNDP, October 1972), mimeo, pp. 241–2.
36. IBRD Appraisal, pp. 4–5, 10.
37. Idem, Annex 3, p. 72.
38. Ibid., p. 10.
39. *P985/2*, pp. 12–13.
40. *Ecology Study of the Ereğli Iron and Steel Mill* (Pittsburgh, Pa: USS Engineers and Consultants, 1974), mimeo, p. 7.
41. The Bank's shortcomings in the environmental area came under increasing criticism in the late seventies and early eighties, especially after several of its projects turned out to be ecological disasters and contributed little to sustainable national development. See John Walsh, 'World Bank pressed on environmental reforms', *Science*, 14 November 1986, p. 813. The Bank reacted by implementing, in 1987, a significant policy change that assigned a new priority to environmental issues. The staff was increased by 350 per cent and its power within the organization enhanced. Although these changes were generally welcomed, many of the Bank's critics expressed concern about the prevailing attitudes and the extent to which these changes would lead to basic changes in the way that the Bank dealt with environmental issues: C. Holden, 'World Bank launches new environment policy', *Science*, 15 May 1987, p. 769.
42. *Project Management Evaluation* (Pittsburgh, Pa.: USS Engineers and Consultants, 1974), mimeo, p. 7.
43. *Feasibility Study for Ereğli Demir ve Çelik Fabrikalari, TAŞ (ERDEMIR), Stage II Expansion* (Pittsburgh, Pa.: USS Engineers and Consultants, 25 March 1976), mimeo, p. 1.
44. Ibid., Section II, pp. 1–2; *Revised Feasibility Study Expansion Program Stage II for Ereğli Demir ve Çelik Fabrikalari, TAŞ* (Pittsburgh, Pa.: USS Engineers and Consultants, 17 December 1976), mimeo, Section II, p. 3.
45. Idem.
46. *Ereğli Annual Report, 1985*, p. 21.
47. I. Çelebi, *Türkiyede Demir Çelik Sanayiinin Yapisi ve Sorunlari* (Ankara: Devlet Planlama Teşkilati, May 1979), p. 130.
48. Walstedt, op. cit., pp. 48–9.

49. Ibid., p. 50.
50. Compiled from ERDEMIR annual reports.
51. A. N. Shabon and I. U. Zeytinoğlu, *The Political, Economic and Labor Climate in Turkey* (Philadelphia, Pa.: University of Pennsylvania Industrial Research Unit, 1985), pp. 186 ff.
52. *1977 Annual Report,* p. 41; *1978 Annual Report,* p. 37; *1979 Annual Report,* p. 31.
53. *1979 Annual Report* (Ereğli Demir ve Çelik Fabrikalarī, TAŞ, 1980), p. 16.
54. Ibid., p. 17.

CHAPTER 6 ISDEMIR, SIDEMIR, KARABÜK: PROJECTS AND COMPARATIVE PERSPECTIVES

1. The details in this section, unless otherwise noted are from Türkiye Demir ve Çelik Işletmeleri Genel Müdürlüğü, *Cumhuriyetin 50 Yīlīn'da Türkiye Demir ve Çelik Işletmeleri* (Ankara: TDÇI), pp. 135–50; hereafter referred to as TDÇI.
2. I. Çelebi, *Türkiye'de Demir Çelik Sanyiīnīn Yapīsī ve Sorunlari* (Ankara: Devlet Planlama Teşkilatī, 1979), p.73. Actually the cost may have been even higher because the John Miles Company, in their original feasibility study carried out in 1967, estimated the cost of the first phase at TL 2.5 billion and of the entire plant at TL 3.5 billion.
3. I. S. Barutçugil, *Türkiyede Demir Çelik Endüstrisi* (Istanbul: Bursa Universitesi Iktisadi ve Sosyal Bilimler Fakultesi, 1978), p. 101.
4. The SPO's estimates, as embodied in the Second Five Year Plan, were 3.7 and 7 million tons respectively.
5. John Miles Company Ltd, *Studies for the Third Turkish Steel Works* (Croydon, England, 1967, 6 vols), Vol. 1, Market Review and Recommended Market Capacity', p. 13.
6. Ibid., Vol. 2, 'Iron Ore and Raw Material Survey', passim.
7. Çelebi, op, cit., p. 73; TDÇI, p. 136.
8. TDÇI, p. 150.
9. Erdoğan Dağdelen, *Isdemir Muessessesi Ile Ilgili Toplu Bilgiler* (Iskenderun Demir Çelik, 1981), mimeo, pp. 3, 5, 6.
10. TDÇI, p. 150.
11. S. Atamer, 'Choix des partenaires et modalités de transfert international de technologie', Thèse doctorate de 3ème cycle, Université des Sciences Sociales de Grenoble, 1980, p. 315.
12. B. L. Fernandez, *Training of Personnel for the Turkish Iron and Steel Company* (Ankara: Unido Project DP/TUR/76/038, January 1983), p. 37.
13. Dağdelen, op. cit., p. 1.
14. Ibid., p. 8.
15. Ibid., p. 37.
16. Çelebi, op. cit., pp 70–1.
17. Rapor, p. 52.

18. Leningrad State Institute for Designing Iron and Steel Works, *Iskenderun Iron and Steel Works in Turkey, Feasibility Report, 1979,* mimeo.
19. Ibid., p. v.
20. Ibid., p. 171.
21. Devlet Planlama Teşkilatï, *Fourth Five Year Development Plan (1979–1983)* (Ankara: State Planning Organization, 1978), p. 585.
22. For sophisticated analyses of regional voting patterns see E. Özbudun, *Social Change and Political Participation in Turkey* (Princeton, NJ: Princeton University Press, 1976) and Ilhan Tekeli and Raşit Gökçeli, *1973 ve 1975 Seçimleri* (Istanbul: Milliyet Yayïnlarï, 1977).
23. John Miles Company Ltd, *Feasibility Study for TDÇI on the Establishment of Iron Steel Plant at Sivas for the Production of 2 Million Tons,* February 1977.
24. Idem.
25. *Feasibility Report for SIDEMIR Iron and Steel Works prepared for TDÇI by Kaiser Engineering and Ayyildiz Engineering,* February 1979, 2 vols.
26. Ibid., section 4.1, p. 14.
27. Ibid., section 6, p. 3.
28. See also *Demir Çelik Özel Ihtisas Komisyonu Raporu, Son Taslak* (Ankara: Devlet Planlama Teşkilatï, 1983), hereafter 'Rapor', p. 59.
29. *Türkiye'de Modern Bir Demir Çelik Sanayii Kurmak Için Yapilan Ilk Çalişmalar* (Karabük Genel Müdürlüğü, n.d.), mimeo, pp. 22–4.
30. Unless otherwise noted, the following sections draw upon William Kirwan, *Final report: Consulting Services for Turkish Iron and Steel Company, Karabük Works* (Unido Contract T/81/105/MK, January 1983), mimeo.
31. Ibid., section 10, p. 5.
32. Rapor, p. 49.
33. Kirwan, op. cit., p. 26.
34. Ibid., section 10, p. 3.
35. Rapor, p. 49.
36. Kirwan, op. cit., section 10, pp. 3–4.
37. Ibid., section 4, p. 4.
38. Ibid., p. 6.
39. Kirwan, op. cit., section 10, 'General Management'.
40. Ibid., section 9, p. 15.
41. Idem.
42. Ibid., p. 1.
43. Ibid., section 10, p. 6.
44. Ibid., section 10, pp. 10–12.
45. Çelebi, op. cit., p. 62.
46. M. Oral *et al., Araştïrma Geliştirme Projeleri Demir Çelik Entegre Tesislei* (Gebze, Kocaeli: Marmara Bilimsel ve Endüstryel Araştïrma Enstitusu, May 1977).
47. S. Tan, *Demir-Çelik Sanayiïnde Verimlilik* (Ankara: Milli Prodüktivite Merkezi, 1983), Table 119, p. 108.
48. Tan, op. cit., p. 151.

49.   Rapor, pp. 104 ff.
50.   Rapor, p. 5.
51.   *Iskenderun Demir Çelik, Master Plan* (Pittsburgh, Pa: USS Engineers and Consultants, Inc.) p. 12.
52.   Rapor, p. 29.

CHAPTER 7   PROJECTS AND POLITICS

1.   O. Baykal, I. Gülmez and G. Incir, *Demir Çelik Endüstrisinde Dağitim* (Ankara: Milli Prodüktivite Merkezi, 1981), pp. 13–14. Between 1972 and 1978 prices rose by 1,111 per cent as compared to 56 per cent for the world price; idem. According to T. Atamer, 'Choix des partenaires et modalités de transfert international de technologie, Thèse doctorat de 3ème cycle, Université des Sciences Sociales de Grenoble, 1980, p. 314, Turkish consumers were paying double the world price for iron and steel.

2.   Peter W. G. Morris and George H. Hough, *The Anatomy of Major Projects* (New York: John Wiley, 1987), Table 1.1, pp. 8–11.

3.   Particularly significant are the studies by I. Çelebi, *Türkiye'de Demir-Çelik Sanayiïnin Yapïsï ve Sorunlarï* (Ankara: Devlet Plan-lama Teşkilatï, 1979), S. Tan, *Demir-Çelik Sanayiïnde Verimlilik* (Ankara: Milli Prodüktivite Merkezi, 1983), and Devlet Planlama Teşkilatï, *Demir-Çelik Özel Ihtisas Komisyonu Raporu, Son Taslak* (Ankara: DPT, 1983).

4.   *Ereğli Demi ve Çelik Fabrikalarï, TAŞ, Master Plan* (Pittsburgh, Pa.: USS Engineers and Consultants, 1976), Annex 8b, p. 7; hereafter referred to as *Master Plan*.

5.   *Master Plan*, section 9, pp. 1–2.

6.   See sources cited in Note 3.

7.   World Bank, *Turkey: Prospects and Problems of an Expanding Economy* (Washington, DC: IBRD, 1975) p. 255.

8.   Bertil Walstedt, *State Manufacturing Enterprises in Mixed Econo-mies: The Turkish Case* (Baltimore, Md.: Johns Hopkins University Press, 1980), p., 44.

9.   O. Guvemci, *Yatïrïm Projelerinin* (Istanbul: Çağlayan Kitabevi, 1979), p. 17.

10.   M. D. Rivkin, *Area Development for National Growth* (New York: Praeger, 1965), p. 177.

11.   Ibid., p. 186.

12.   See Note 3.

13.   *Rapor*, pp. 6 ff.

14.   World Bank, op. cit., p. 230.

15.   AID possesses extensive documentation on the ERDEMIR project including the specifications for each unit of the plant, the bids that were submitted for each, copies of all consultants reports, monthly financial statements, quarterly progress reports during construction, monthly procurement reports, and general plant standards and loan authorizations. This voluminous material takes up many filing cabi-

nets and indicates the care with which the figures were checked, specific issues considered, and questions raised, for many of them contained underlinings and marginalia in the form of question marks, exclamation points, additions of figures and other calculations. Attention to detail, while praiseworthy, merely indicates a pattern of organizational behavior. It does not illuminate the quality of the decision to build a small, highly leveraged plant.

16. Ibid., p. 177.
17. Asïm Erdilek, *Direct Foreign Investment in Turkish Manufacturing* (Tubingen: J. C. B. Mohr, Kieler Studien, 169, 1982), p. 15.
18. Atamer, op, cit., pp. 314–16.
19. Atamer, op. cit., *passim*.
20. Idem.
21. Ergun Türkcan, *Teknolojinin Ekonomi Politiği* (Ankara, Ankara Iktisadi ve Ticari Ilimler Akademisi, 1981), pp. 219–40.
22. See, for example, Report, p. 14.
23. M. Oral *et al.*, *Araştïrma Geliştirme Projeleri Demir Çelik Entegre Tesisleri* (Gebze, Kocaeli: Marmara Bilimsel ve Endüstryel Araştïrma Enstitusu, May 1977).
24. Baykal, Gülmez and Incir, op. cit., pp. 13 ff.
25. Ibid., pp. 18 ff; see also *Demir Çelik Kakkinda Not* (Ankara: Devlet Planlama Teşkilatï) April 1975.
26. For a thoughtful essay which analyzes the significance of this view for Turkish political development, see M. Heper, *The State Tradition in Turkey* (Hull, UK: Eothen Press, 1985).
27. Erdilek, op. cit., pp. 228–9.
28. A similar situation seems to have characterized agriculture. As one scholar has noted, '. . . there have been dominant economic motives behind support policies. At the root is the goal of developing agriculture . . . . Short term electoral considerations, emphasized by many researchers, were actually subservient to the realization of this long term policy.' K. Samel, 'Agricultural support policies in Turkey, 1950–1980: an overview', in Alan Richards (ed.), *Food, States and Peasants* (Boulder, Colo.: Westview Press, 1986), p. 118.
29. Merih Celasun, *Sources of Industrial Growth and Structural Change: The Case of Turkey* (Washington, DC: World Bank Staff Working Paper No. 614, 1983), pp. 111 ff., also discusses why Turkish policy-makers remained so dedicated to their development strategy.
30. J. D. Lewis and S. Unata, *Turkey: Economic Performance and Medium Term Prospects, 1978–1990* (Washington, DC: World Bank Staff Working Paper No. 602 1983), p. 1.
31. Lewis and Unata, op. cit., p. 17.
32. World Bank, *Turkey: Policies and Prospects for Growth* (Washington, DC: World Bank, 1980), pp. 164 ff.
33. Lewis and Unata, op. cit., p. 17.
34. Erdilek, op. cit., pp. 173–4.
35. Lewis and Unata, op. cit., pp. 20 ff.
36. 'Turkey's growth rate highest among OECD countries', *Newspot*, 19 December 1986, p. 3.

37. See, for example, Asĭm Erdilek, 'Turkey's new open-door policy of direct foreign investment: a critical analysis of problems and prospects', and Ziya Oniş, 'Stabilisation and growth in a semi-industrial economy: an evaluation of the recent Turkish experiment, 1977–1984', *METU Studies in Development*, Vol. 13, No 1 and 2, 1986, pp. 7–28, 171–92, and the contents of *Deux décennies d'industrialisation en Turquie, 1960–1980* (Paris: Cahiers du Groupe d'Études sur la Turquie Contemporaine, Fondation de la Maison des Sciences de l'Homme), No. 2, Winter, 1985–1986.

38. 'Turkey's iron and steel production increasing', *Newspot*, 16 May 1986, pp. 1, 7.

39. Exports to the USA rose from 44,000 tons in 1984 to 407,00 tons in 1987. In that year iron and steel products accounted for 11 per cent of Turkey's total exports. Howell *et al.*, op. cit., p. 366.

40. A recent simulation, based on 1973 data, of how the economy would fare if Turkey entered the EEC, revealed that the iron and steel industry ranked 56th out of 66 sectors on an index that measured comparative advantage. The sectors that stood below the 35th were non-competitive. Tercan Baysan, 'Some economic aspects of Turkey's accession to the EC: resource shifts, comparative advantage, and static gains', *Journal of Common Market Studies*, Vol. XXIII, No. 1, September 1984, p. 27.

41. 'Turkey's iron and steel industry', *Newspot*, 17 April 1987, p. 4.

42. For a pessimistic assessment see, Howell *et al.*, op. cit., p. 338.

43. Cevat Karataş, 'Public Economic Enterprises in Turkey – Reform Proposals, Pricing and Investment Policies', METU Studies in Development, vol. 13, Nos 1 and 2, 1986, p. 139.

44. Ibid., *passim*.

45. Robert Jervis, *Perception and Misperception in International Politics* (Princeton: Princeton University Press, 1976), pp. 24–8.

46. Particularly promising is the work now being done on the development of mathematical models designed to analyze operational problems and assess investment strategies at the sectoral and industry level rather than as individual projects. D. A. Kendrick, A. Meerous and J. Alatorre, *The Planning of Investment Programs in the Steel Industry* (Baltimore, Md.: John Hopkins University Press for the World Bank, 1984).

Bibliography

BOOKS

AHMAD, Y. J., 'Project Identification, Analysis and Preparation in Developing Countries: A Discursive Commentary', in *Planning Development Projects*, ed. D. A. Rondinelli, pp. 161–8, Dowden, Hutchinson & Ross, Stroudsburg, Pa., 1977.

ALLISON, GRAHAM, *Essence of Decision*, Little, Brown, Boston, 1971.

AYDEMIR, S.S., *Ikinci Adam*, Remzi Kitapevi, Istanbul, 1968.

BAER, W., *The Development of the Brazilian Steel Industry*, Vanderbilt University Press, Nashville, Tenn., 1969

BAKER, ROBERT F., R. M. MICHAELS and E. S. PRESTON, *Public Policy Development: Linking the Technical and Political Processes*, John Wiley, New York, 1975.

BARKE, RICHARD, *Science, Technology and Public Policy*, Congressional Quarterly, Washington, DC, 1986.

BARNETT, D. and R. CRANDALL, *Up From The Ashes*, Brookings Institution, Washington, DC, 1986.

BARUTÇUGIL, I.S., *Türkiyede Demir Çelik Endüstrisi*, Bursa Universitesi Iktisadi ve Sosyal Bilimler Fakultesi, Istanbul, 1978.

BAYKAL, OLCAY, ILYAS GÜLMEZ and GÜLTEN INCIR, *Demir-Çelik Endüstrisinde Dağitim*, 254, Milli Prodüktivite Merkezi, Ankara, 1981.

BHAGWATI, J. N., 'Rethinking Trade Strategy', in *Development Strategies Reconsidered*, ed. J. P. Lewis and V. Kallab, pp. 91–104, Transaction Books, New Brunswick, NJ, 1986.

BRAYBROOKE, DAVID and CHARLES LINDBLOM, *A Strategy of Decision*, Free Press, New York, 1963.

BRECHER, M., *Decisions in Israel's Foreign Policy*, Oxford University Press, Oxford, 1976.

BRYCE, J. D., *Industrial Development*, McGraw-Hill, New York, 1960.

Cahiers du Group d'Étrudes sur la Turquie Contemporaine, in *Deux décennies d'Industrialisation en Turquie, 1960–1980*, Vol. 2, Fondation de la Maison des Sciences de l'Homme, Paris, 1985–6.

CAIDEN, N. and A. WILDAVSKI, *Planning and Budgeting in Poor Countries*, John Wiley, New York, 1974.

CARLEY, MICHAEL, *Rational Techniques in Policy Analysis*, Heinemann Educational Books, London, 1980.

CHATEAU, B. and B. LAPILLONE, *Energy Demand: Facts and Trends*, Springer-Verlag, Vienna and New York, 1982.

251

CHENERY, HOLLIS, *Structural Change in Development Policy*, Oxford University Press, Oxford, 1979.

CHILCOTE, R., *Theories of Comparative Politics*, Westview Press, Boulder, Colo., 1981.

CHILCOTE, R., *Spain's Iron and Steel Industry*, University of Texas Press, Austin, Tex. 1968.

COLE, WILLIAM, *Steel and Economic Growth in Mexico*, University of Texas Press, Austin, Tex., 1967.

CYERT, RICHARD M. and JAMES G. MARCH, *A Behavioral Theory of the Firm*, Prentice Hall, Englewood Cliffs, NJ, 1963.

DASGUPTA, P. S., S. A. MARGLIN and A. K. SEN, *Guidelines for Project Evaluation*, United Nations, New York, 1972.

DESAI, P., *The Bokaro Steel Plant*, American Elsevier, New York, 1972.

DODD, C. H.,*Democracy and Development in Turkey*, Eothen Press, Hull, UK, 1979.

DORE, RONALD, 'Technological Self-Reliance: Sturdy Ideal or Self Serving Rhetoric', in *Technological Capability in the Third World*, ed. Martin Fransman and Kenneth King, pp. 65–80, Macmillan, London, 1984.

ECKSTEIN, HARRY, 'Case Study and Theory in Political Science', in *Handbook of Political Science*, ed. F. I. Greenstein and N. Polsby, Vol. 7, pp. 79–137, Addison Wesley, Reading, Mass., 1975.

ENOS, J., 'The Choice of Technique vs The Choice of Beneficiary: What the Third World Chooses', in *The Economics of New Technology in Developing Countries*, ed. F. Stewart and J. James, pp. 69–82, Westview Press, Boulder, Colo., 1982.

ERBER, F. S., 'Science and Technology Policy: A View From the Periphery', in *Technology and International Affairs*, ed. Joseph S. Szyliowicz, Praeger, New York, 1981.

ERDILEK, ASÎM, *Direct Foreign Investment*, Kieler Studien, 169, J. C. B. Mohr, Tubinugen, 1982.

FELDMAN, E. J., 'Patterns of failure in government megaprojects: economics, politics, and participation in industrial democracies', in *Global Dilemmas*, eds. Samuel P. Huntington and Joseph S. Nye Jr, pp. 138–58. University Press of America, Washington, DC 1985.

FORSYTH, D, N. McBAIN and R. SOLOMON, 'Technical Rigidity and Appropriate Technology in Developing Countries', in *The Economics of New Technology in Developing Countries*, ed. F. Stewart and J. James, Westview Press, Boulder, Colo., 1982.

FRANSMAN, MARTIN and KENNETH KING, *Technological Capability in the Third World*, Macmillan, London, 1984.

FREEMAN, DAVID M., *Technology and Society*, Markham, Chicago, 1974.

GARDNER, CLARK M., *The Development of China's Steel Industry and Soviet Technical Aid*, Cornell University Press, Ithaca, NY, 1973.

GENDRON, BERNARD, *Technology and The Human Condition*, St. Martin's Press, New York, 1977.

GOULET, DENNIS, *The Cruel Choice*, IDRC, Washington DC, 1977.

GREENE, DAVID, *Steel and Economic Development: Capital–Output Ratios in Three Latin American Plants*, Michigan State University, East Lansing, Mich., 1967.

GRINDLE, M. S. (ed.), *Politics and Policy Implementation in the Third World*, Princeton University Press, Princeton, NJ, 1980.

GRINE, O., 'Transfer of Technology in the Arab Steel Industry", in *Technology Transfer and Change in the Arab World*, ed. A. B. Zahlan, Pergamon, New York, 1978.

GÜNCE, E., 'Early Planning Experiences in Turkey,' in *Planning in Turkey*, ed. S. Ilkin and E. Inanç, Middle East Technical University, Ankara, 1967.

GUVEMCI, O., *Yatïrïm Projelerinin*, Çağlayan Kitabevi, Istanbul, 1979.

HALL, PETER, *Great Planning Disasters*, University of California Press, Berkeley, Calif., 1980.

HARRIS, GEORGE, *Troubled Alliance: Turkish–American Problems in Historical Perspective, 1945–1971*, American Enterprise Institute, Washington, DC, 1972.

HEPER, METIN, *The State Tradition in Turkey*, Eothen Press, Beverley, UK, 1985.

HERSHLAG, Z.Y., *Turkey: The Challenge of Growth*, E. J. Brill, Leiden, 1968.

HIRSCHMAN, A.O., *Development Projects Observed*, Brookings Institute, Washington, DC, 1967.

HIRSCHMAN, A.O., *The Strategy of Economic Development*, Yale University Press, New Haven, Conn., 1970.

HOGAN, WILLIAM, *World Steel in the 1980s: a Case of Survival*, Lexington Books, Lexington, Mass., 1983.

HOWELL, T. R., W. A. NOELLERT, J. G. KREIER, and A. W. WOLFF, *Steel and the State*, Westview Press, Boulder, Colo., 1988.

IBRD, *The Economy of Turkey*, Johns Hopkins University Press, Baltimore, Md., 1951.

JERVIS, ROBERT, *Perception and Misperception in International Politics*, Princeton University Press, Princeton, NJ, 1976.

JOHNSON, W.O., *The Steel Industry of India*, Harvard University Press, Cambridge, Mass., 1966.

KELLER, SUZANNE, *Beyond The Ruling Class*, Random House, New York, 1963.

KING, KENNETH, 'Science, Technology and Education in the Development of Indigenous Technological Capability', in *Technological Capability in the Third World*, ed. Kenneth King, pp. 65–80., Macmillan, London, 1984.

KOGANE, YOSHIRO, ed., *Changing Value Patterns and Their Impact on Economic Structure*, University of Tokyo Press, Tokyo, 1982.

KRUEGER, ANNE O., *Foreign Trade Regimes and Economic Development: Turkey*, Columbia University Press for the National Bureau of Economic Research, New York, 1974.

LIEDHOLM, CARL, *The Indian Iron and Steel Industry: An Analysis of Comparative Advantage*, Michigan State University, East Lansing, Mich.,

1972.
LINDBLOM, CHARLES E., *The Intelligence of Democracy*, Free Press, New York, 1965.
LINSTONE, HAROLD, *Multiple Perspectives for Decision Making*, Elsevier, New York, 1984.
LITTLE, I. M. D. and J. A. MIRRLEES, *Manual of Industrial Project Analysis in Developing Countries, Vol. II, Social-Cost Benefit Analysis*, OECD, Paris, 1969.
LYNN, LEONARD H., *How Japan Innovates: A Comparison With The U.S. in the Case of Oxygen Steelmaking*, Westview Press, Boulder, Colo., 1982.
MANSUR, F., *Ereğli, Ağır Sanayiden Önce Bir Sahil Kasabası*, Devlet Planlama Teşkilatı, Ankara, 1964.
MARCH, JAMES G. and HERBERT A. SIMON, *Organizations*, John Wiley, New York, 1958.
MARTZ, JOHN D., *Politics and Petroleum in Ecuador*, Transaction Books, New Brunswick, NJ, 1987.
Milli Prodüktivite Merkezi, *Demir-Çelik Semineri*, 264, Ankara, 1982.
Ministry of Overseas Development, *A Guide to the Economic Appraisal of Projects in Developing Countries*, HMSO, London, 1977.
MORRIS, PETER W. G. and GEORGE H. HOUGH, *The Anatomy of Major Projects: A Study of the Reality of Project Management*, John Wiley, New York, 1987.
MUNTZ, T. G. A., *Turkey*, Philosophical Library, New York, 1950.
MURELIUS, OLOF, *An Institutional Approach to Project Analysis in Developing Countries*, Development Centre, OECD, Paris, 1981.
MURPHY, KATHLEEN J., *Macroproject Development In the Third World*, Westview Press, Boulder, Colo. 1983.
OECD, *Emission Control Costs in the Iron and Steel Industry*, Paris, 1977.
OECD, *The Impact of the Newly Industrializing Countries on Production and Trade in Manufacture*, OECD, Paris, 1979.
OFFICE OF TECHNOLOGY ASSESSMENT, *Technology and Steel Industry Competitiveness*, Washington, DC, 1980.
OFFICE OF TECHNOLOGY ASSESSMENT, *Technology Transfer to the Middle East*, Washington, DC, 1983.
ÖZBUDUN, ERGUN, *Social Change and Political Participation in Turkey*, Princeton University Press, Princeton, NJ, 1976.
PERLMUTTER, H.V. and T. S. SAGAFI-NECAD, *International Technolgoy Transfer*, Pergamon, New York, 1981.
RANIS, G, and G. SAXONHOUSE, 'International and Domestic Determinants of Technology Choice in the Less Developed Countries', in *Technology Choice and Change in Developing Countries*, ed. B. G. Lucas and S. Freedman, pp. 7–27, Tycooly International, Dublin, 1983.
RAY, GEORGE F., *The diffusion of Mature Technologies*, Cambridge University Press, Cambridge, 1984.
RIVKIN, M. D., *Area Development for National Growth*, Praeger, New York, 1965.
RONDINELLI, D. A., 'Project Identification in Economic Development', in *Planning Development Projects*, ed. D. A. Rondinelli, pp. 69–94.,

Dowden, Hutchinson & Ross, Stroudsburg, Pa., 1977.

SAGASTI, FRANCISCO R., *Science and Technology for Development: Main Comparative Report on the STPI Project,* International Development Research Center, Ottawa, 1978.

SAGASTI, FRANCISCO R., *Technology, Planning and Self Reliant Development,* New York, Praeger, 1979.

SAMEL, K., 'Agricultural Support Policies in Turkey, 1950–1980: An Overview', in *Food, States and Peasants,* ed. Alan Richards, Westview Press, Boulder, Colo., 1986.

SCHULMAN, PAUL R., *Large-Scale Policy Making,* Elsevier, New York, 1980.

SCHWARTZ, H. and R. BERNEY, *Social and Economic Dimensions of Project Evaluation,* Inter-American Development Bank, Washington, DC, 1977.

SELF, PETER, *Econocrats and the Policy Process,* Macmillan, London, 1975.

SELIM, H. M., *Development Assistance Policies and the Performance of Aid Agencies,* Macmillan, London, 1983.

ŞENI, N., *Emperyalist Sistem'de Kontrol Sanayii ve Ereğli Demir Çelik,* Birikim Yayinları Yerli Araştirmalar Dizisi, Ankara, 1978.

SHABON, A. N. and I. U. ZEYTINOĞLU, *The Political, Economic, and Labor Climate in Turkey,* University of Pennsylvania Industrial Research Unit, Philadelphia, Pa., 1985.

SIDHU, S. S., *The Steel Industry in India: Problems and Perspectives,* Vikas, Delhi, 1983.

SIMON, HERBERT A., *Administrative Behavior,* Free Press, New York, 1957.

SINGER, MORRIS, *The Economic Advance of Turkey, 1938–1960,* Turkish Economic Society, Ankara, 1977.

SQUIRE, L. and H. G. VAN DER TAK, *Economic Analysis of Projects,* World Bank Research Publication, Washington, DC, 1975.

STEIN, JANICE and RAYMOND TANTER, *Rational Decision Making: Israel's Security Choices, 1967,* Ohio State University Press, Columbus, Ohio, 1980.

STEINBRUNNER, JOHN, *The Cybernetic Theory of Decision,* Princeton University Press, Princeton, NJ, 1976.

STEWART, FRANCES, *Technology and Underdevelopment,* Macmillan, London, 1978.

STEWART, FRANCES, 'Facilitating Indigenous Technical Change in Third World Countries', in *Technological Capability in the Third World,* ed. Kenneth King, pp. 81–94, Macmillan, London, 1984.

STOBAUGH, ROBERT and LOUIS T. WELLS JR, *Technology Crossing Frontiers,* Harvard University Business School, Cambridge, Mass., 1984.

SZYLIOWICZ, JOSEPH S., 'Elites and Modernization in Turkey', in *Political Elites and Political Development,* ed, F. Tachau, John Wiley, New York, 1975.

SZYLIOWICZ, JOSEPH S., *Technology and International Affairs,* Praeger, New York, 1981.

TAN, SERDAR, *Demir-Çelik Sanyiinde Verimlilik (1982),* 271, Milli

Prodüktivite Merkezi, Ankara, 1983.

TAYANÇ, T., *Sanayileşme Süresinde 50 Yil,* Millyet Yayĩnlarĩ, Istanbul, 1973.

TEKELI, ILHAN and RAŞIT GÖKÇELI, *1973 ve 1975 Seçimleri,* Milliyet Yayĩnlarĩ, Istanbul, 1977.

THEOPANIDES, S. M., 'Project Planning and Implementation in Greece', in *Planning Processes in Developing Countries: Techniques and Achievements,* ed. W. D. Cook and T. E. Kuhn, pp. 50–87, North Holland, New York, 1982.

THORNBURG, M. W., G. SPRY, and G. SOULE, *Turkey: An Economic Appraisal,* Twentieth Century Fund, New York, 1949.

TÜRKCAN, ERGUN, *Teknolojinin Ekonomi Politiği,* Ankara Iktisadi ve Ticari Ilimler Akademisi, Ankara, 1981.

TÜRKIYE DEMIR VE CELIK İŞLETMELERI GENEL MÜDÜRLÜĞÜ, *Cumhuriyetin 50 Yĩlĩn'da Türkiye Demir ve Çelik İşletmeleri,* Ankara, 1974.

UNIDO, *Draft World-Wide Study of the Iron and Steel Industry 1975–2000.* Unido/CIS 25/15 December, 1976.

UNIDO, *Industry in a Changing World.* New York, 1983.

UNPAD, 'Development Planning as a Framework for Project Administration', in *Planning and Budgeting in Poor Countries,* ed. D. A. Rondinelli, Dowden, Hutchinson & Ross, Stroudsburg, Pa., 1977.

USAID, *Evaluation Handbook* Washington, DC, 1972.

WALSTEDT, BERTIL, *State Manufacturing Enterprises in Mixed Economies: The Turkish Case,* Johns Hopkins University Press, Baltimore, Md., 1980.

WHITE, JOHN, *The Politics of Foreign Aid,* St. Martin's Press, New York, 1974.

WOOLCOCK, S., 'The International Politics of Trade and Production in the Steel Industry', in *National Industrial Strategies and the World Economy,* ed. J. Pinder, Croom Helm, London, 1979.

ZECKHAUSER, RICHARD and ELMER SCHAEFER, 'Public Policy and Normative Economic Theory', in *The Study of Policy Formulation,* ed. R. A. Bauer and K. J. Gergen, Free Press, New York, 1957.

PERIODICAL ARTICLES

ALLISON, G. and M. HALPERIN, 'Bureaucratic Politics: A Paradigm and Some Policy Implications', *World Politics,* pp. 40–80, Spring 1972.

ALMOND, G., 'The Return of the State', and E. Nordlinger, T. Lowi, and S. Fabbrini, 'Critiques', *American Political Science Review,* pp. 853–900, September 1988.

ART, R., 'Bureaucratic Politics and American Foreign Policy. A Critique', *Policy Sciences,* pp. 467–90, 1973.

BALL, DESMOND J., 'The Blind Men and the Elephant: A Critique of Bureaucratic Politics Theory', *Australian Outlook* pp. 71–92, April 1974.

BAYSAN, TERCAN, 'Some Economic Aspects of Turkey's Accession to the EC', *Journal of Common Market Studies,* Vol. 23, No. 1, September 1984.

BLASS, W. P., 'Steel Mills for Developing Economies,', *Social and Economic Studies,* June 1962.

CHRISTOPHER, R., 'Don't Blame the Japanese', in *New York Times Magazine,* 18 October 1981.

C. J. DAHLMAN, and L. E. WESTPHAL, 'The Meaning of Technological Mastery in Relation to Transfer of Technology', *Annals of the American Academy of Political and Social Science,* pp 12–26, 1983.

DENIZ, MEHMET and EMRE GÜLTEKIN, 'Günümüz Türkiyesinde Demir-Çelik Sorunu Üzerine', *Ülke,* Vo. 10, pp. 191–221, 1980.

ERDILEK, ASİM, 'Turkey's New Open-Door Policy of Direct Foreign Investment: A Critical Analysis of Problems and Prospects', *METU Studies in Development,* Vol. 12, Nos 1 and 2, pp, 7–28. 1986.

"EREĞLI DEMIR ÇELIK REZALETI," *Yön,* No. 20. 1962.

ETZIONI, A., 'Mixed Scanning: A "Third" Approach to Decision Making', *Public Administration Review,* pp. 385–92, 1967.

ETZIONI, A., 'Mixed Scanning Revisited', *Public Administration Review,* pp. 8–14, 1986.

GANIOĞLU, A. N., 'Yabancï Sermaye ve Ereğli Demir Çelik Tesisleri', *Sosyal Adalet,* Vol. 2, 1964.

GANIOĞLU, A. N., 'Ereğli Demir Çelikte Yerseçimki ve Kuruluş Maliyeti', *Sosyal Adalet,* Vol. 2, 1965.

GERSHUNY, J., 'Policy Making Rationality', *Policy Sciences,* pp. 295–316, 1987.

HANNAY, N. BRUCE and R. E. McGINN, 'The Anatomy of Modern Technology: Prolegomenon to An Improved Public Policy for the Social Management of Technology', *Daedalus,* pp. 25–53, Winter 1980.

HOLDEN, C., 'World Bank Launches New Environment Policy', *Science,* p. 769, 15 May 1987.

'KAPITALIZMIN HARIKASI', *Yön,* 28 October, 1966.

KARATAŞ, ÇEVAT 'Public Economic Enterprises in Turkey – Reform Proposals, Pricing and Investment Policies', *METU Studies in Developments,* Vol 13, Nos 1 and 2, 1986, pp. 135–69.

KIM, Linsu, 'Stages of Development of Industrial Technology in a Developing Country: A Model', *Research Policy,* pp. 250–77, 1980.

KRASNER, S. D., 'Are Bureaucracies Important? (or Allison Wonderland)', *Foreign Policy,* pp. 159–79, Summer 1972.

KÜÇUKÖMER, I., 'Ereğli Demir Çelik Kurumu ve Egemenliğimiz', *Yön,* No. 4, 1964.

LINDBLOM, CHARLES E., 'The science of muddling through', *Public Administration Review,* pp. 79–88. 1959 .

MEHMET, OZAY, 'Turkey In Crisis: Some Contradictions in the Kemalist Development Strategy', *International Journal of Middle East Studies,* Vol. 15, pp. 47–66, 1983.

MOON, B. E., 'Consensus or Compliance: Foreign Policy Change and External Dependence', *International Organization,* Vol. 39, pp. 297–329a.

MORAWETZ, D., 'Employment Implications of Industrialization in Developing Countries: A Survey', *Economic Journal,* pp. 491–542, 1974.

NATHAN, J. A. and J. K. OLIVER, 'Bureaucratic Politics: Academic Windfalls and Intellectual Pitfalls', *Journal of Political and Military*

Sociology, pp. 81–91, Spring 1978.

ONIŞ, ZIYA, 'Stablilization and Growth in a Semi-Industrial Economy: An Evaluation of the Recent Turkish Experiment, 1977–1986', *METU Studies in Development,* Vol. 13, Nos 1 and 2, pp. 171–92, 1986.

PETERS, B. G and McCULLOCH, M. K., 'Types of Democratice Systems and Types of Public Policies', *Comparative Politics,* pp. 327–55, April 1977.

POZNANSKY, K. Z., 'Technology Transfer: West–South Perspective', *World Politics,* pp. 134–52, October 1984.

RYCROFT, R. and J. SZYLIOWICZ, 'The Case of the Aswan Dam', *World Politics,* pp. 36–61, October 1980.

SANDBACH, E.K., 'The Iron and Steel Industry in a Developing Economy', *Iron and Steel,* pp. 109–21, March 1964.

'Steel Yard Blues', *NACLA Report on the Americas,* Vol. 12, No. 1, Jan-Feb 1979.

STEINBERG, G., 'Comparing Technological Risks in Large Scale National Projects', *Policy Sciences,* Vol. 18, pp. 79–93, 1985.

STEINBERG, G., 'Large-Scale National Projects as Political Symbols: The Case of Israel', *Comparative Politics,* pp, 331–46, April 1987.

WALSH, JOHN, 'World Bank Pressed on Environmental Reforms', *Science,* p. 813, 14 November 1986.

ZAKAY, S. N. BAR, 'A Technology Transfer Model', *Technological Forecasting and Social Change,* pp. 321–37, 1971.

PRIMARY AND OTHER SOURCES

Action Memo from R. B. WAGNER et al. to W. S. Gaud. 21 January 1964. (mimeo).

ADLER, J. K., *Development of Private Industry Through Public Aid,* ICA (Office of Industrial Resources), Washington, DC, 1958. (mimeo).

AMERICAN IRON AND STEEL INSTITUTE, *The Making of Steel,* Washington, DC, n.d.

ATAMER, S., 'Choix des partenaires et modalités de transfert international de technologie', Thèse doctorat de 3e cycle, Université des Sciences Sociales de Grenoble, 1980.

AYKIN, NURAY, 'Demir-Çelik Sanayii Yerleşim-Dağitim Modeli', Milli Prodüktivite Merkezi, 259, Ankara, 1981.

CALSAT, J. H. 'Ereğli, Zonguldak, Karabük Sanayi Bölgeleri: Bölgenin Düzenlenmesi ve Imarī Için Yapilack Çalişmalara Ait Ön Rapor', Devlet Planlama Teşkilatī, Ankara, n.d.

CANDIR, ATTILA, 'Demir-Çelik ve Metalurji Sanaat Sempozyumu Tebliğ Yayinlarī', Milli Prodüktivite Merkezi, Ankara, 1968.

CANDIR, TÜLIN and ATTILA CANDIR, 'Türkiye Demir–Çelik Talep Tahminleri', Devlet Planlama Teşkilatī, Ankara, 1966.

CELASUN, MERIH, *Sources of Industrial Growth and Structural Change: The Case of Turkey,* World Bank Staff Working Paper No. 614, Washington, DC, 1983.

CELEBI, I., *Türkiye'de Demir-Çelik Sanayiinin Yapīsī ve Sorunlarī*, Devlet Planlama Teşkilatī, Ankara, 1979.

DAĞDELEN, ERDOĞAN, *Isdemir Muessesesi Ile Ilgili Toplu Bilgiler*, Iskenderun Demir Çelik, 1981, mimeo.

DAHLMAN, CARL, A Microeconomic Approach to Technological Change: The Evolution of the USIMINAS Steel Firm in Brazil. Unpublished PhD Dissertation, Yale University, 1979.

DEPARTMENT OF STATE, AID, *Turkey: Ereğli Steel Mill, Capital Assistance Paper, AID/DLC/P506*, Washington, DC, February 1, 1967.

DEPARTMENT OF STATE, AID *Turkey: Ereğli Steel Mill, Proposal and Recommendations of the Managing Director, Development Loan Fund, AID/DLC/P262*, Washington, D.C., November 8, 1960. (mimeo).

DEPARTMENT OF STATE, AID, *Turkey: Ereğli Iron and Steel Works, Capital Assistance Paper AID/DLC/P567*, Washington, DC, 14 May, 1967.

DEPARTMENT OF STATE, AID, *Turkey: Ereğli Iron and Steel Works, Capital Assistance Paper AID/DLC/P735*, Washington, DC, 14 June, 1968.

DEPARTMENT OF STATE, AID, *Turkey: Ereğli Steel Mill Expansion-Stage I, Capital Assistance Paper AID/DLC/P985*, Washington, DC, June 18, 1971.

DEPARTMENT OF STATE, AID, *Turkey: Ereğli Steel Mill Expansion-Stage I, AID/DLC/P985/2*, Washington, DC, 14 May, 1972.

Devlet Planlama Teşkilatī, 'Demir-Çelik Hakkinda Not', Ankara, April 1975.

Devlet Planlama Teşkilatī, *First Five Year Development Plan (1963–1967)*, Ankara, 1963.

Devlet Planlama Teşkilatī, *Second Five Year Development Plan (1968–1972)*, Ankara, 1967.

Devlet Planlama Teşkilatī, *Third Five Year Development Plan (1973–1977)*, Ankara, 1972.

Devlet Planlama Teşkilatī, *Fourth Five Year Plan (1979–1983)*, Ankara, 1978.

Devlet Planlama Teşkilatī, *Türkiye'de Demir Çelik Sanayiinin Yapīsī ve Sorunlarī*, Ankara, 1979.

Devlet Planlama Teşkilatī, *Demir-Çelik Özel Ihtisas Komisyonu Raporu, Son Taslak*, Ankara, 1983.

Devlet Planlama Teşkilatī, *Fifth Five Year Plan (1985–1989)*, Ankara, 1985.

Devlet Planlama Teşkilatī, *Türkiyede Demir Çelik Sanayiīnīn Yapīsī ve Sorunlarī*, Ankara, May 1979.

Devlet Planlama Teşkilatī, 'Türkive Izabeciler ve Haddeciler Agustos 1971, Tarihli 'Demir-Çelik Sektoru Hakkīndaki Teknik ve Ekonomik Rapor Muhtiras' Hakkinda Gorüş,', Ankara, 1971.

Ereğli Demir ve Çelik Fabrikalarī T.A.Ş, (ERDEMIR), *Annual Report (1968–1985)*, Ankara.

Ereğli Demir ve Çelik Fabrikalarī, TAS, 'Faaliyet Raporu, Haziran 1983', Genel Müdürlük Bürosu Müdürlüğü, 20 July 1983.

Ereğli Iron and Steel Works, *Report of the Iron Ore Study Committee*, Ankara, 19 June, 1961.

FERNANDEZ, B. L., *Training of Personnel for the Turkish Iron and Steel Company*, Project: DP/TUR/76/038, Unido, Ankara, Jan 1983. (mimeo).

GÜRAY, TURGUT, 'Türkiyenin Demir-Çelik Yassï Mamul Talebi ve Ereğli Demir-Çelik Fabrikalarï Tevsii', Ereğli Demir ve Çelik Fabrikalarï, TAŞ, July 1983.

HAZLEWOOD, ARTHUR., *Why Projects Fail*. Lecture at Queen Elizabeth House, Oxford University, 15 February 1985.

JOHN MILES COMPANY LTD., *Feasibility Study for TDÇI on the Establishment of Iron Steel Plant at Sivas for the Production of 2 Million Tons*, February 1977.

JOHN MILES COMPANY LTD., *Studies for the 3rd Turkish Steel Works*, 1967. 6 vols.

KAISER ENGINEERING and AYYÏLDÏZ ENGINEERING, *Feasibility Report for SIDEMIR Iron and Steel Works prepared for TDCI*, February 1979. 2 vols.

KARABÜK DEMIR ÇELIK TESISLERI, *Karabü Tarihçesi*, 1985, mimeo.

KARABÜK GENEL MÜDÜRLÜĞÜ, Türkiye'de modern bir demir çelik sanayii kurmak için yapilan ilk çalişmalar, n.d. (mimeo).

KIRWAN, WILLIAM, *Final Report: Consulting Services for Turkish Iron and Steel Company, Karabuk Works*, Contract, T/81/105/MK, January 1983. (mimeo).

KOPPERS COMPANY, INC., *Development Program for 1965–1970; Prepared for Ereğli Demir ve Çelik Fabrikalarï Türk Anonim Şirketi*, Pittsburgh, Pa., October, 1965. (mimeo).

KOPPERS CORPORATION, *Erdemir Sinter Plant: Final report*, 1973. (mimeo).

KUTLAY, M., 'Türkiye Demir-Çelik Endüstrisindeki Gelişmeler ve Demir Cevheri Madenciliğimizde Optimizasyon Problemi,' Eğe Üniversitesi, Izmir, June 1975.

LENINGRAD STATE INSTITUTE FOR DESIGNING IRON AND STEEL WORKS, *Iskenderun Iron and Steel Works in Turkey, Feasibility Report*. 1979. (mimeo).

LEWIS, J. D. and S. UNATA, *Turkey: Economic Performance and Medium Term Prospects, 1978–1990*, World Bank Staff Working Paper No 602, World Bank, Washington, DC, 1983.

LEWIS, JEFFREY D. and SHUJIRO UNATA, *Turkey: Recent Economic Performance and Medium Term Prospects, 1978–1990*, World Bank Staff Working Paper, Washington DC, 1982.

MILLI PRODÜKTIVITE MERKEZI, 'Demir-Çelik ve Metalurji Endustrisi Semineri', Ekonomi ve Istatistik Şubesi, Ankara, 1969.

NATIONAL FOREIGN ASSESSMENT CENTER, CIA, *The Burgeoning LDC Steel Industry: More Problems for Major Steel Producers*, Washington, DC, July 1979.

NEWSPOT, 'Turkey's Growth Rate Highest Among OEC Countries', Countries', 19 December 19856, p3.

NEWSPOT, 'Turkey's Iron and Steel Industry', 17 April, 1987, p. 4.

NEWSPOT, 'Turkey's Iron and Steel Production Increasing', 16 May, 1986, pp. 1,7.

OKYAR, OSMAN, *Public International Development Financing in Turkey*, Columbia University School of Law Research Project on Public International Development Financing, Report No. 3, New York, November 1962.

ORAL, M., *et al.*, *Araştīrma Geliştirme Projeleri Demir Çelik Entegre Tesisleri*, Marmara Bilimsvel ve Endüstryel Araştīrma Enstitusu, Gebze, Kocaeli, May 1977.

ROEDER, J., *Two Tiers of Soviet Policy Making*. Paper presented at International Studies Annual Convention, Washington, DC, 1987.

Personal Interviews with:. Mr George Thomas, Chairman, John Miles Company Ltd; Mr William Kahl, Mr Jim Van Ackeren, Mr Fletcher Byrom and Mr Lawrence Smith, The Koppers Company, inc.; Mr William P. O'Neil and Mr Beril Walstedt, The World Bank; Mr J. R. Rankin, USS Engineers and Consultants, Inc., and Mr Rodney Young (formerly AID).

RYCROFT, ROBERT and JOSEPH S. SZYLIOWICZ, *Decision Making in a Technological Environment: The Case of the Aswan Dam*, Intercollegiate Clearing House, Boston, Md, 1982.

SZYLIOWICZ, JOSEPH S., *Planning, Managing and Implementing Technological Projects: The Case of the Ereğli Iron and Steel Works*, Intercollegiate Clearing House, Boston, Md, 1982.

TAN, SERDAR, *Demir-Çelik Sanayiinde Verimlilik*, Milli Prodüktivite Merkezi, ANkara, 1983.

TANKUT, Y., Y. INKAYA AND G. ERONAT, 'Karadeniz Ereğlisi Kenti Yapizal Arastirmalar', Orta Doğu Teknik Üniversitesi, Şehir Planlama Bölümü, 1969. (mimeo).

TDÇI GENEL MÜDÜRLÜĞÜ,K *Cumhuriyetin 50 Yīlīnda Türkiye Demir ve Çelik Işletmeleri*, Ankara, 1974.

TÜMER, NIHAL and ALP ESEN ERCAN, 'Bütünleşik Demir-Çelik Tesislerinde Yerleştirme Planlamasī,' Karabük Demir Çelik Tesisleri, 1977.

UNCTAD, *Guidelines for the Study of the Transfer of Technology*, United Nations, New York, 1972.

UNDP, *Country Programming Background Papers for Turkey*, Ankara, October, 1972. (mimeo).

USS ENGINEERS and CONSULTANTS, *Ecology Study of the Ereğli Iron and Steel Mill*, Pittsburgh, Pa., 1974. (mimeo).

USS ENGINEERS and CONSULTANTS, Inc., *Feasibility Study for Ereğli Iron and Steel Works, Inc., Facilities expansion Program*, Pittsburgh, Pa., September 1970.

USS ENGINEERS and CONSULTANTS, INC., *Ereğli Iron and Steel Works, Inc., Facilities Expansion Program, Expansion Case-Stage I June 1973 Projection*, Pittsburgh, Pa, June 29, 1973.

USS ENGINEERS and CONSULTANTS, INC., *Ereğli Demir ve Çelik Fabrikalarī, TAŞ, Master Plan*, Pittsburgh, Pa., 1976.

USS ENGINEERS and CONSULTANTS, INC., *Project Management Evaluation*, Pittsburgh, Pa, 1974.

USS ENGINEERS and CONSULTANTS, INC., *Iskenderun Demir Çelik*

Master Plan, Pittsburgh, Pa, 1976.

USS ENGINEERS and CONSULTANTS, INC., *Revised Feasibility Study Expansion Program Stage II for Ereğli Demir ve Çelik Fabrikalarï, TAŞ*, Pittsburgh, Pa, December 17, 1976.

USS ENGINEERS and CONSULTANTS, INC., *Feasibility Study for Ereğli Demir ve Çelik Fabrikalarï, TAŞ, (ERDEMIR), Stage II Expansion*, Pittsburgh, Pa, March 25, 1976.

WORLD BANK, *Appraisal of the Erdemir Steel Plant Expansion Project, Turkey*, Industrial Projects Department, Washington, DC, October 15, 1971. (mimeo).

WORLD BANK, *Report and Recommendation of the Executive Directors on a Proposed Loan to the Republic of Turkey for the ERDEMIR Steel Plant Expansion Project*, Washington, DC, March 1, 1972. (mimeo).

WORLD BANK, *Turkey: Prospects and Problems of an Expanding Economy*, Washington, DC, 1975.

WORLD BANK, *Turkey: Policies and Prospects for Growth*, Washington, DC, 1980.

YILPAR, KAYNAK, '1971 Demir Çelik Sektörü Program: Ön Calişmalarï', Devlet Planlama Teşkilatï, Ankara, 1971.

Index

administration *see* Management
Adalet Partisi (AP) *see* Justice Party
Agency for International Development
  (AID) 77, 79, 80, 83, 107–9, 114–15,
  250n15
ARMCO 114, 116, 117, 118, 121, 122
Ataturk, Mustapha Kemal 2, 19, 48,
  49, 51, 62, 63, 74, 103, 189, 208, 209,
  211
Australia 25

Bessemer process *see* iron and steel,
  technologies
Brassert, H. A., Co. 51, 54, 55
Brazil 25

Chase Manhattan Bank 78
Cumhuriyet Halk Partisi (CHP) *see*
  Republican People's Party (RPP)
coal *see also* Raw materials 50, 52, 53,
  67, 72, 79, 84, 87, 88, 92, 107, 109,
  119, 132, 140, 143, 150, 158, 159, 160,
  161, 164, 167, 169, 172, 181, 182, 183,
  192
coke 50, 51, 53–4, 61, 63, 67, 68, 87,
  88, 117, 123, 157, 162, 173, 174, 181,
  182, 183, 187, 227

decision-making *see also* ideology;
  politics; projects; values
  and technology 21–4, 222–9
  in Turkish agriculture 251n28
  in Turkish steel industry
    191ff 211–14
  models of 20–2, 24, 155, 212, 223–4
  politics and 7, 18, 22, 28, 34, 35,
    152, 201ff, 211ff, 222ff
Demirel, Suleyman 67, 68, 69, 114,
  129, 130, 151, 215
Democrat Party (DP) 62, 63, 114
Denmark 41
dependency theory 14–16, 112, 203,
  222, 223 and ERDEMIR 110ff
development *see also* Turkey,
  economic development
  industrialization and 39–40

iron and steel, role in 41–3
  strategies of 17–18, 39–41, 208–9,
  214
Development Loan Fund (DLF) 77–9,
  81, 82, 83, 87, 91, 92, 95, 98, 99, 100,
  101, 104
development plans *see also* Turkey,
  economic development 16, 47, 61,
  66, 67, 68, 70
DISK *see* Trade Unions

Eckaus, Professor R. S. 114
Eisenhower, Dwight D. 77
electric furnace *see* iron and steel,
  technologies
electricity *see* energy
elites *see also* social core group 1, 5,
  16, 42, 43, 52, 62, 203, 208, 209, 210
energy 45, 46, 48, 55, 72, 150, 155,
  172, 181, 182, 183, 184
environment *see also* pollution 6, 7, 8,
  10, 16, 28, 36, 43, 114, 115, 122, 124,
  219, 222, 223, 226
ERDEMIR
  original plant
    beginnings 64–5
    construction 96ff
    cost benefit evaluations 95–6
    decision-making and 103–5, 213
    design issues 84–90
      raw materials 87–8
      location 84–5
      size 86
      technologies 88–90
    financing 76, 80–1, 99–103
    management 96, 106
    performance 106–8, 114–15, 120–1
    studies for 85–6, 107–8
  interim expansion 117–24, 126
    cost benefit evaluations 119–20
    decision-making and 122, 124–5
    design issues 108–9, 115–19, 122–3
    financing 121
    management issues 120–1
    performance 123–4, 125, 126–7
    political environment 109–14

Erdemir (*continued*)
  Stage I and II expansions
    cost benefit evaluations   126–8,
      132–6, 144
    decision-making and   67, 127,
      129–32, 147–8, 154
    design studies   126–8, 136, 137,
      140–4
    environmental issues   132–6
    implementation   145–7, 150
    management issues   144, 148–9,
      151–3
    performance   125, 126, 150, 153–4
    political environment   150–3
    raw materials   140
  performance of plant
    in 1970s   180ff
    in 1980s   217–18
  future expansion   193
Ereğli   53, 144, 154, 192, 194, 198
Ereğli Demir Celik Fabrikalari,
  Inc.   *see* ERDEMIR
EXIM (Export Import) Bank   82, 130,
  132, 145
feasibility studies *see also* Karabuk,
  ERDEMIR, ISDEMIR, SIDEMIR
  design issues; impact issues;
  management issues;   24ff, 194–8, 225
foreign aid   61, 62, 63, 65, 77, 80,
  110ff, 195, 204, 243n19
foreign exchange   42, 51, 57, 63, 71,
  73, 76, 77, 91, 95, 103, 109, 111, 112,
  120, 126, 130, 132, 142, 150, 161, 170,
  171, 173, 186

Granigg, Dr   49
Great Britain   44, 50, 58
HAK-IS   *see* Trade Unions
'hiding hand'   4, 154, 208, 209, 210,
  212

ideology *see also* values   1, 41, 60, 104,
  110, 114, 202, 208, 209, 222
International Bank for Reconstruction
  and Development (IBRD)   *see*
  World Bank
Inonu, Ismet   62, 63
iron ore   25, 49, 52, 53, 54, 67, 70, 72,
  87, 88, 98–9, 105, 109, 117, 118, 121,
  122, 123, 126, 140, 141, 143, 150, 158,
  159, 160, 161, 164, 167, 168, 169, 171,
  172, 181, 182, 195, 196
iron and steel industry   *see also*
  Turkey, iron and steel industry

characteristics   6, 24–5, 231n15
  global structure   44–8
  in USA   44–5
  minimills   44–5, 237n14
  technologies   25, 53–7, 88–90
ISDEMIR
  beginnings   68, 156–7
  cost benefit evaluations   161–2,
    247n2
  construction   162, 165
  design issues
    raw materials   164
    site selection   158–9
    size   159–61
    technologies   164
  expansion   70, 165
  future   165–6
  management issues   162, 163–4, 165,
    221
  politics and   163–4, 221
  performance
    in 1970s   165, 180ff
    in 1980s   217, 218
  pollution   165

Japan   10, 18, 19, 44, 111, 142, 148,
  237n11
Justice Party (JP)   67, 69, 114, 129,
  130, 151

Karabuk
  cost benefit evaluations   57, 161–2
  design issues
    location   52–3, 59
    size   51
    technologies   53–7, 60
  expansions   61, 63–4, 67–8, 171–2
  management issues   58–9, 176–9
  origins   49–51
  performance   172–9, 180ff, 239n59
  politics and   50–1, 64
Kirrikale   50
Koppers Co. Inc.   76, 78, 79, 80, 82,
  85–93, 96, 99, 101, 102, 106–9,
  116–18, 120, 121–3, 127, 134, 145,
  146, 147, 155

labor force   *see* skills; trade unions;
  ERDEMIR, Karabuk, ISDEMIR
  management issues
leadership *see also* elites, social core
  group   18–19, 129, 204, 222, 225, 226
limestone   53, 88, 109, 123

Linz-Donawitz (L-D) process *see* iron and steel industry, technologies

McNamara, Robert 143, 202
management *see also* ERDEMIR, Karabuk, ISDEMIR management issues 198–201, 220, 221
Marshall Plan 39, 61
Menderes, Adnan 63, 65, 66, 76–7, 80–1
MISK *see* trade unions

National Salvation Party (NSP) 69, 151, 153, 163
Nehru, J. 41
New Zealand 41
Norway 41

open hearth process *see* iron and steel industry, technologies
Organization for Economic Cooperation and Development (OECD) 28
Organization for European Economic Cooperation (OEEC) *see also* OEDC 95

Peru 25
planning *see* development, planning for; State Planning Organization; Turkey, planning
politicization 64, 147, 184, 200, 201, 216, 221, 222
politics *see also* Turkey, government and politics
    political regimes,
        definition of 11n32
        types of 19–20, 68
    political systems 5, 7, 36, 151, 201, 208, 214, 216, 222, 223, 224, 229
    and decision-making 20–2, 222ff
    and public policy 19
    and technological mastery 19
    and technology transfer 225–7
    definition of 11n32
    in Turkey 19–20
pollution 53, 57, 133–6, 165, 169, 197–8
ports 191–2
projects
    analyses 26ff, 104–5
    decision-making and 22ff
    defined 3–4
    dimensions 24ff
    failure, reasons for 4ff, 229

importance 2, 6
management 34–8
planning 30–4
proliferation 6
sources of 30, 32–3
stages of 30–8, 30n92

railroads 52, 84, 85, 88, 164, 166, 167, 171, 172, 192, 195, 205, 221
rationality *see* decision-making
raw materials *see also* coal; iron ore; limestone; ERDEMIR; Karabuk; ISDEMIR; SIDEMIR
regional development 192–3
Republican People's Party (RPP) 49, 62, 63, 69, 70, 76–7, 114, 151, 153
research and development 13, 14, 16, 17, 18, 26, 28, 67, 181, 203, 207, 219, 227
roads 84, 97, 102, 192

satisficing *see* decision-making
Saudi Arabia 18, 19
sea transportation 25
SIDEMIR
    cost benefit evaluations 170
    design issues
        site selection 166–7
        raw materials 169
        size of 168–9
    financing 170
    origins 68, 166, 168
    politics and 167–8
    pollution 169–70
skills *see also* technicians; workers 4, 18, 36, 38, 120, 146, 164, 165, 176, 189, 196, 199, 203, 207
social core group *see also* elites 222, 226, 232n32
South Korea 18, 19
Soviet Union (USSR) 44, 58, 155, 185, 208, 222
State *see also* elites
    and economic development 45, 49, 60, 61, 130, 131, 190
    and technology 1, 2, 11, 12, 16ff
    conceptions of 61–2, 208, 210
    interests of 60
    role in technology transfer 8, 203, 222–3, 226ff
state economic enterprises 64, 77–8, 91, 144, 150, 163, 165, 179, 186, 205, 206, 215, 220, 227
State Planning Office 66, 116, 130,

State Planning Office (*Cont'd*)
149, 156, 171, 178, 211, 216, 217
State Power Authority   117
state coal works *see also* coal   164
Switzerland   41

TDCI   *see* Turkish Iron and Steel
Directorate
Taiwan   18
technicians *see also* skills; workers   162,
173
technological mastery   *see also*
technology transfer; technology
planning
achievement of   2, 10
definition   13–14
planning and   16–19
politics and   18–19, 227–8
significance of   11–13, 24, 60, 191
the State and   225–9
in Turkish iron and steel
industry   38, 60, 64, 105, 125, 126,
154, 155, 164, 173, 175, 176, 189,
199, 206–7, 208, 212, 213, 218, 219,
220, 223
technological processes   *see*
ERDEMIR, Karabuk, ISDEMIR,
SIDEMIR design issues
technological projects   *see* projects
technology   *see* technological mastery;
technology planning; technology
transfer
belief in   1–2
defined   8, 231n21
Technology planning   *see also* projects;
Turkey, economic planning
difficulties of   17–19
implicit vs explicit policies   17
in Turkey   206ff
politics and   18–19
technology transfer
importance   2
nature of   8–11; figs 1.1, 1.2, 1.3,
1.4, 1.5; 222–3
receiving organizations   9–10, 11–14,
204–6
'greenfield transfer'   9–10
external factors, role of   10–11, 223
sending organizations   11, 201–4
politics and   201ff
external actors and   189, 201ff
the State and   222, 226ff
to Turkey   6, 9, 190, 201ff
Thornburg, M. W.   61
Tinbergen, Professor J.   82

trade unions   152–3
Transportation   *see also* roads;
railroads; ports; sea transportation
adequacy of Turkish system   164, 192
Turkey
economic development
under Ataturk   48–9
in 1940s   60–1
in 1950s   62–3, 65, 81
in 1960s   66, 73
in 1970s   68–70, 73
in 1980s and after   214–16, 251n40
effectiveness of development
strategy   73–5, 208–9
politics and   209–11
economic planning
early efforts   49, 60, 61
introduction of national
planning   66, 82
1st Five Year Plan   66, 67, 207
2nd Five Year Plan   67, 130, 156
3rd Five Year Plan   68, 70, 166,
171, 194, 202
4th Five Year Plan   70, 166, 194
in 1980s   216–17
government and politics   *see also*
Democrat party; Justice Party;
National Salvation Party;
Republican People's Party; Turkish
Labor Party
under Ataturk   48–9
1946 elections   62
1950 elections   62
1954 elections   63
1960 revolution   66
in 1960s   110, 114
1971 military intervention   69
in 1970s   69–70
1980 revolution   216
Turkish iron and steel industry   *see
also* Karabuk; ERDEMIR;
ISDEMIR; technological mastery;
technology transfer
beginnings   49–51
contribution to national
development   189–90
demand projections   66–7
facilities   Table 2.4 p.71
future of industry   218ff, 251n28
production/consumption   Table 2.5
p.72
role in economy   71ff
state of industry
in late 1970s   179ff, 251n39
in mid-1980s   214–22

Turkish Iron and Steel Directorate (TDCI) 50, 169, 186, 187, 208, 219
Turkish Labor Party 110

United Nations Industrial Development Organization (UNIDO) 11, 32, 45, 179
United States Agency for International Development (USAID) *see* AID
United States Steel Corporation (*see* United States Steel Engineers and Consultants, Inc)
United States Steel Engineers and Consultants, Inc. (UEC) 127–30, 134, 136–7, 143, 146–7, 148–9, 155

USSR; *see* Soviet Union

Values 5, 9, 16, 18, 19, 25, 28, 39, 48, 179, 188, 196, 197, 204, 209–11, 212, 223, 224

Workers 17, 18, 27, 58, 97, 100, 120, 141, 144, 152, 161, 162, 163, 186, 200, 214, 216, 217, 218
World Bank 4, 11, 29, 65, 67, 82, 83, 127, 129ff, 147–8, 154, 155, 195, 197, 200, 202, 204, 212, 214, 217, 221, 236n92 246n21

Zorlu, F. R. 65, 77

DUE DATE

JUL 2 8 1997			
			Printed in USA